Henri de Lubac and the Drama of Human Existence

Henri de Lubac

and the Drama of Human Existence

Jordan Hillebert

UNIVERSITY OF NOTRE DAME PRESS
NOTRE DAME, INDIANA

Notre Dame, Indiana 46556
undpress.nd.edu

Published in the United States of America

Library of Congress Control Number: 2020946987

ISBN: 978-0-268-10857-1 (Hardback)

ISBN: 978-0-268-10860-1 (WebPDF)

ISBN: 978-0-268-10859-5 (Epub)

In grateful and loving memory of

John B. Webster

CONTENTS

ACKNOWLEDGMENTS

I had no intention of writing a book on de Lubac's "hermeneutics of human existence" or of venturing too deeply into the stormy waters of twentieth-century debates on nature and grace. This book began as a doctoral thesis (first at the University of Aberdeen and then at St. Andrews University) that was meant to adjudicate between de Lubac and his (primarily Protestant) detractors on the sacramentality of the church, a means, I suppose, of sorting through the ecclesial tensions in my own "Catholic and Reformed" intuitions on my journey to becoming a postulant for holy orders in the Anglican Church. Early into my research, however, I found myself continually bumping up against statements in de Lubac's writings that seemed to sit uncomfortably within prevailing interpretations of his famous *Surnaturel* thesis. A few marginal notes soon multiplied, swiftly taking on a life of their own, and eventually led to an entirely different book from the one I originally set out to write. I was guided and encouraged throughout these investigations by the generous and insightful supervision of my doctoral supervisor, the late John Webster. Studying with John was an immense privilege. His patience and clarity as a thinker, his charity as a reader, and the joyful seriousness with which he approached the "delightful activity" of Christian dogmatics made him an invaluable mentor. John exemplified the intellectual and spiritual virtues of the theologian-as-disciple. The words of Tilliette, reflecting on his time spent studying with de Lubac at Fourvière, apply just as aptly to John: "He himself was never concerned about having 'disciples'—'One is your Master'—but rather about inspiring them to be diligent theologians. Their studies were supposed to give form to their existence and train them to be witnesses to Christ."[1] It is to

John that I owe the greatest intellectual debt of gratitude in the writing of this book, and so it is to John especially that the following pages are dedicated.

This book began in Aberdeen, was written largely in St. Andrews, and was finally completed in Cardiff. Along the way it benefited from innumerable friendships, scholars, churches, and pubs. Tim Baylor and Tyler Wittman were (and remain) a constant source of theological insight and lively conversation. Countless afternoons spent playing croquet together and discussing Thomas Aquinas may have delayed the completion of this work, but they also deeply informed the theological intuitions and commitments contained herein. I am sincerely grateful for their wisdom and their friendship. I am grateful also for my doctoral examiners, Fergus Kerr and Karen Kilby, for their probing questions and warm support for the original thesis. Karen's continued enthusiasm for the project has been a source of great encouragement throughout the revision and preparation of this manuscript for publication. My thanks to Francesca Murphy for warmly recommending this work to University of Notre Dame Press, to the UNDP readers for their very helpful suggestions, and to Stephen Little for his editorial support and encouragement.

My thanks also to Adonis Vidu for first introducing me to the writings of Henri de Lubac and for encouraging me to pursue doctoral studies, to Mark Clavier for welcoming me to Wales and for modeling so well the vocation of a scholar-priest, to the congregation of Christ Church Roath Park for supporting me and my family throughout my curacy, and to the staff and students at St. Padarn's for collaborating to create such an edifying context for theological study and conversation. Finally, the writing of this book owes much to the love and encouragement of family— my parents and sister, my mother- and father-in-law, and my surrogate family in the United Kingdom, the Baylors, Lowerys, and Burdetts. As ever, words fall short of expressing the depth of my gratitude for Krisi— for her love, her wisdom, her generosity, and her tireless support.

Jordan Hillebert
Cardiff, Feast of St. Cuthbert, 2020

ABBREVIATIONS OF WORKS BY HENRI DE LUBAC

(See bibliography for complete bibliographic details)

AMT *Augustinianism and Modern Theology*

ASC *At the Service of the Church: Henri de Lubac Reflects on the Circumstances That Occasioned His Writings*

BC *A Brief Catechesis on Nature and Grace*

C *Catholicism: Christ and the Common Destiny of Man*

CF *The Christian Faith: An Essay on the Structure of the Apostles' Creed*

CM *Corpus Mysticum: The Eucharist and the Church in the Middle Ages*

CPM *The Church: Paradox and Mystery*

DAH *The Drama of Atheist Humanism*

DG *The Discovery of God*

HS *History and Spirit: The Understanding of Scripture according to Origen*

MC *The Motherhood of the Church*

ME *Medieval Exegesis*

MP *More Paradoxes*

MS *The Mystery of the Supernatural*

PF	*Paradoxes of Faith*
PS	*La Postérité spirituelle de Joachim de Flore*
RD	*La Révélation divine*
S	*Surnaturel: Études historiques*
SC	*The Splendor of the Church*
TF	*Theological Fragments*
TH	*Theology in History*
VCN	*Vatican Council Notebooks*

Introduction

A Hermeneutics of Human Existence

The publication of Henri de Lubac's *Surnaturel* (1946) was a pivotal event in twentieth-century Roman Catholic thought, precipitating one of the century's most heated and wide-ranging theological debates and culminating in a new (or rather a *renewed*) historical, methodological, and theological consensus. On the surface, the controversy engendered by *Surnaturel* centered on rival interpretations of Thomas Aquinas. At the time, most Thomist commentators discovered in Aquinas an account of humanity's *twofold* finality—one purely natural, the other supernatural. De Lubac's reading of Aquinas advanced, to the contrary, a *single*, supernatural finality: humanity's graced enjoyment of the beatific vision of God. Even as a strictly exegetical dispute, this discrepancy over the proper interpretation of Aquinas would have been enough to place de Lubac at the center of controversy. St. Thomas is, after all, the *Common* Doctor: "His teaching above that of others, the canonical writings alone excepted, enjoys such a precision of language, an order of matters, a truth of conclusions, that those who hold to it are never found swerving from the path of truth, and he who dare assail it will always be suspected of error."[1] This assertion by Innocent VI was taken up with equal resolve in Leo XIII's 1879 encyclical *Aeterni Patris*, exhorting all clergy and Catholic educators "to restore the golden wisdom of St. Thomas, and to spread it far and wide for the defense and beauty of the Catholic faith, for the good of society, and for the advantage of all the sciences."[2] In offering a seemingly novel interpretation of Aquinas on a matter as consequential as humanity's telos, de Lubac risked muddying those crystalline waters drawn from the fount of the Angelic Doctor, "or at least from those rivulets which, derived from the very fount, have thus far flowed, *according to the established agreement of learned men*, pure and clear."[3] For de Lubac, however, as indeed for his critics, what was ultimately at stake in the *études historiques* undertaken in *Surnaturel* went well beyond a decision concerning the proper interpretation of Aquinas. What concerned de Lubac was the contemporary urgency of a distinctly Christian interpretation of human existence, a theological account of the imprint of a transcendent finality upon human being and human history more generally. Like so many of de Lubac's writings, *Surnaturel* thus makes a case for a particular "hermeneutics of human existence," the implications of which, according to de Lubac, determine both the church's response to modern unbelief and her own confident articulation of the gospel's claim on human beings.

The purpose of this book is twofold: first, to offer a critical exposition of de Lubac's hermeneutics of human existence, demonstrating the pervasiveness and the significance of this interpretive enterprise throughout de Lubac's writings and the precise role prescribed by de Lubac for such a hermeneutics in the church's contemporary apologetic endeavors; second, to defend a particular reading of de Lubac's theology on this point in contradistinction to what is quickly becoming one of the—if not *the*—most influential interpretations of his work. In recent years, de Lubac's decades-long confrontation with theological extrinsicism has been enlisted to great effect by proponents of a radical theological *intrinsicism.* That is, de Lubac's refusal of a purely immanent teleology has been taken as a tacit acknowledgment that human nature always already participates in the supernatural that fulfills it. Such a construal of the relation between human nature and the supernatural mounts a provocative theological rejoinder to the bourgeoning hegemony of "secularized" nature in modern philosophical and political (not to mention theological) discourse, but it does so, I argue, at the expense of the transfigurative novelty of the economy of divine grace. The supernatural perfection of human being is no longer seen as coming "from without" (*exothen*) but is rather envisaged as the culmination of a movement intrinsic to the (always already graced) dynamism of human existence. To the contrary, herein I argue for a more "paradoxical" reading of de Lubac's theological hermeneutics of human existence, one that seeks to avoid both the Scylla of extrinsicism and the Charybdis of intrinsicism. According to this reading, the intrinsic relation between human being and humanity's supernatural finality is best considered, not in terms of an inchoate participation of the former in the latter, but rather according to the "supernatural insufficiency of human nature," by what de Lubac designates as "a longing born of lack." Human being is teleologically ordered to an end that infinitely surpasses the powers of nature to attain. Humanity's essential restlessness is the ontological sign of this disproportion between human nature and humanity's vocation. As I will argue throughout, this insufficiency of human nature and the inquietude it engenders leads de Lubac to insist on the necessary compenetration of theology and apologetics—on, that is, the immanently compelling character of the church's dogma. The "proof" of Christian revelation is not something external to it. Revelation's truthfulness is guaranteed by its own content, by what Erich Przywara describes as "the internal coherence of the vision of the world proposed by faith."[4] A hermeneutics of human existence operating under the impulse of this compenetration of theology and apologetics will thus seek to demonstrate the extent to which human existence is ultimately unintelligible in abstraction from the revelation of humanity's supernatural vocation. The efforts of "pure reason" to secure the meaning of human existence terminate at the acknowledgment of reason's own insufficiency. Only the revelation of God reveals us to ourselves.

THE GENESIS OF A THEOLOGICAL PROJECT

Henri Marie-Joseph Sonier de Lubac, SJ (1896–1991) arrived on the Lyon peninsula in September 1929 at the age of thirty-four. Because of the early retirement of Fr. Albert Valensin, de Lubac was somewhat hastily appointed to the chair of fundamental theology in the Faculty of Theology at the Université Catholique de Lyon. With little preparation, and with even fewer resources at his disposal,[5] de Lubac delivered his inaugural lecture the following month on the subject of "apologetics and theology." The lecture was largely well received by those in attendance (a group of about fifteen candidates for the licentiate or doctoral degrees) and was published the following year as "Apologétique et Théologie" ("Apologetics and Theology") in the *Nouvelle revue théologique* by the Jesuits of Louvain. Years later, however, de Lubac was reluctant to include this article in collections of his work, because it seemed to him to have something "too scholarly or too academic" about it, "something too abstract, too distanced from human reality, from its conflicts, its tragedy."[6] This judgment, shared by at least one of de Lubac's pupils,[7] may be true enough with respect to the *style* of de Lubac's inaugural lecture. The relatively abstract and technical prose of "Apologetics and Theology" bears little literary resemblance to the majority of the Lubacian corpus. However, it would be a mistake to view this article in abstraction from the "human reality" within which it emerged and the "conflicts" and "tragedy" to which it responded. Like nearly all of de Lubac's writings, "Apologetics and Theology" is an occasional piece, arising not simply from the demands of a lectureship in fundamental theology, but also from his readings and experiences as a student of theology in the 1920s and, more generally, the theological and political landscape of French Catholicism in the early twentieth century. Like *Surnaturel*, "Apologetics and Theology" mounts a provocative challenge to both the "immanentism" of secular modernity and the "extrinsicism" of the then regnant forms of Roman Catholic theology. That is, in "Apologetics and Theology," de Lubac attempts to subvert what he believes to be the common methodological and metaphysical commitments underwriting both contemporary atheism and Roman Catholic neo-Scholasticism.

As its title suggests, de Lubac's lecture offers an investigation of the relationship between the tasks of theology and Christian apologetics. "Apologetics and Theology" begins with a critical assessment of contemporary forms of apologetics, apologetics forged largely in reaction to the rationalism of the Enlightenment project and the fideism and/or traditionalism to which many in the Roman Catholic Church (particularly in France) sought refuge.[8] According to de Lubac, "It is a fact that there exists an apologetics that is small-minded, purely defensive, too opportunistic or completely superficial—not from temporary necessity, but from principle—and, thus, its value is meager."[9] De Lubac is careful to avoid implicating any contemporary exponents of this "small-minded" apologetics—a fact that, however politically expedient, risks positing something of a straw man in his argument—but he clearly has in mind the excesses of a whole school of neo-Scholastic apologetics emerging particularly in the wake of Vatican I (1869–70) and the Anti-Modernist Oath of 1910. According to this school of thought, the task of apologetics is concerned primarily, if not exclusively, with establishing the *fact* of revelation "scientifically."[10] The supernatural *content* of revelation is thus relegated to the domain of theology, while the task of apologetics is restricted to the rational demonstration of the credibility of the Christian religion.

According to Vatican I, the submission of the intellect to the truth of revelation is contingent on the internal assistance of the Holy Spirit and the supernatural virtue of faith. However, "in order that the submission of our faith should be in accord with reason," God also willed that there should be "outward indications of his revelation" suited to the understanding of believers and nonbelievers alike. First and foremost among such external evidences are miracles and fulfilled prophecies.[11] "The Oath against the Errors of Modernism" promulgated by Pius X expands on this pronouncement on the demonstrability of the authority of revelation. The clergy who attached their signatures to this oath confessed: "I admit and recognize the external arguments of revelation, that is, divine facts, and especially miracles and prophecies, as very certain signs of the divine origin of the Christian religion; and I hold that these same arguments have been especially accommodated to the intelligence of all ages and men, even of these times."[12] Without impugning the Vatican documents—indeed, de Lubac appeals explicitly to Vatican I in *support* of his argument[13]—de Lubac expresses concern about the form of apologetics that arose in their wake. Or rather, de Lubac calls into question an entire construal of the nature and task of theology, a system of theologizing that actually preceded the Vatican documents by more than two centuries and, according to de Lubac, deleteriously influenced the way that these documents were received by nineteenth- and twentieth-century Catholic apologists:

> The error consists in conceiving of dogma as a kind of "thing in itself," as a block of revealed truth with no relationship whatsoever to natural man, as a transcendent object whose demonstration . . . has been determined by the arbitrary nature of a "divine decree." According to these theologians, when the apologist wishes to pass from reason to faith, he has only to establish a completely extrinsic connection between the two, just as one builds a footbridge to connect separate banks. He has only to observe, with the support of certain signs, that "God has spoken" in history. And, just as it has never been his business to ask what man might be expecting, he is not to concern himself with what God has said.[14]

Already in his inaugural lecture, therefore, de Lubac adopts a line of critique that would come to permeate his theological writings for the next fifty years. In an effort to protect the gratuity of the supernatural and the integrity of nature, certain theologians had posited a strictly extrinsic relation between these two orders. This "separated theology," de Lubac argues, "makes dogma into a kind of 'superstructure,' believing that, if dogma is to remain 'supernatural,' it must be 'superficial.' . . . Such a theology has acted as though the same God were not the author of both nature and grace, and of nature in view of grace!"[15] The apologetics engendered by such a "small-minded theology" thus remains "indefinitely at the threshold of the temple—that temple within whose walls dogma nourishes deep thought."[16] Such an apologetics presumes to demonstrate the *truth* of revelation without properly attending to its *content.*

In place of such extrinsic accounts of the relationship between theology and apologetics, de Lubac's lecture gestures in the direction of an alternative construal of these two disciplines based on what he insists to be a more "traditional" account of the relation between nature and grace.[17] Rather than considering apologetics and theology in abstraction from one another—as two largely autonomous enterprises corresponding to the heteronomous realms of nature and grace—de Lubac insists on their compenetration. For according to de Lubac, "*a theology that does not constantly maintain apologetical considerations becomes deficient and distorted*, while, on the other hand, *all apologetics that wishes to be fully effective must end up in theology.*"[18] In order to retain its "forcefulness of thought" and its "spiritual value," theology must concern itself with the demands of evangelism, the rendering intelligible of the vivifying truth of the gospel in ever-changing contexts and circumstances. Theology must therefore attend to the concerns and the aspirations of each new generation in order to provide an adequate response.[19] Apologetics, meanwhile, if it hopes to be effectual, must venture beyond the "threshold of the temple," beyond, that is, the strictures of "pure reason." For though reason itself is wholly incapable of arriving at the supernatural truth of revelation, the latter alone is capable of satisfying the dynamism of human reason. For de Lubac, therefore, "there is no better way . . . for *giving an explanation* of our Faith . . . than to work with all our strength for its *understanding*. We must, by the *fides quaerens intellectum* [faith seeking understanding], step forward to meet the *intellectus quaerens fidem* [understanding seeking faith]."[20] As we will see in what follows, the *intellectus quaerens fidem* names precisely the intimate relation between nature and the supernatural at the heart of de Lubac's theology of human existence. Nature is teleologically ordered to the supernatural. Reason finds its fulfillment only in the revelation of God. As such, the credibility of the Christian faith resides, not primarily in external proofs, but rather in the intelligibility of the faith itself and in the understanding of all things (including the movement of reason) in the light of this truth.[21] According to de Lubac, it is therefore doctrine "that attracts and conquers intelligence."[22]

De Lubac concludes his inaugural lecture by insisting that this conquering of the intelligence by doctrine, this compenetration of theology and apologetics, is the proper task of fundamental theology.[23] It is the task, in other words, to which de Lubac understood himself to have been appointed as the chair of fundamental theology at the Université Catholique de Lyon.

THE THEOLOGICAL TASK CONFRONTING THE CHURCH TODAY

More than thirty years after his inaugural lecture in Lyon, by which time de Lubac had himself "retired" from his chair in the Faculty of

Theology,[24] de Lubac returned to the question of fundamental theology, to the apologetic function of Christian doctrine and the properly theological task of the church's apologetics. The impetus for these reflections was the invitation to deliver a lecture at a symposium in 1966 on "The Theological Task Confronting the Church Today" at Saint Xavier College (now Saint Xavier University) in Chicago.[25] This lecture, entitled "Nature and Grace," was subsequently developed and significantly expanded in de Lubac's *Athéisme et sens de l'homme* in 1968.[26] There are a number of striking similarities between these writings and de Lubac's earlier lecture "Apologetics and Theology." In both the 1966 lecture and the 1968 publication, de Lubac retains his earlier polemic against a "separated theology," against a purely extrinsic construal of the relation between nature and the supernatural in which the latter appears "as an artificial superstructure."[27] De Lubac likewise continues to insist on the importance of theology's attentiveness to the aspirations and concerns of the particular context in which it finds itself. Finally, de Lubac remains emphatic that it is the supernatural content of Christian doctrine that provides the ultimate *apologia* for the truth of the Christian religion.

In the later writings, however, the abstract generalizations of de Lubac's inaugural lecture take on a certain concreteness, and a radical shift in the theological and political landscape of twentieth-century Roman Catholicism permits a noticeable change of key in de Lubac's rhetoric. Whereas the 1929 lecture was largely defensive—the protest of a newly appointed lecturer against prevailing modes of theology and apologetics—the later writings demonstrate a calm assurance of what de Lubac insists to be explicit conciliar justification for his arguments. "Nature and Grace" and *Athéisme et sens de l'homme* both proceed by way of a commentary on *Gaudium et spes*, Vatican II's *Pastoral Constitution on the Church in the Modern World* (1965). According to de Lubac, this document, the original schema on which he had some input as *peritus* (theological expert) to the council,[28] places the "seal of its authority" on the understanding of nature and grace championed by de Lubac and others throughout the 1940s and 50s.[29]

Whereas an attentiveness to the particularities of a theologian's context is offered as a general principle in "Apologetics and Theology," de Lubac's later writings follow *Gaudium et spes* in delineating modern atheism as the church's primary interlocutor. According to de Lubac, "the main doctrinal task to which the Constitution *Gaudium et Spes* summons and stimulates us is a confrontation with contemporary atheism."[30] As will become apparent in what follows, de Lubac was hardly a mere spectator to this struggle with philosophical atheism and the corresponding secularist ideologies of the nineteenth and twentieth centuries. Much of de Lubac's own theological output was developed on the frontlines of the church's confrontation with atheistic humanism.

Finally, with respect to the properly doctrinal content of the church's apologetics, de Lubac insists that a confrontation with atheist humanism ought to consist primarily in the articulation of a Christian anthropology.[31] As de Lubac argues elsewhere, the prevailing atheism(s) of the nineteenth and early twentieth centuries—the atheisms set forth, for example, by Auguste Comte, Ludwig Feuerbach, Karl Marx, and Friedrich Nietzsche—were nearly universally predicated on *humanist* grounds.[32] That is, the rejection of God was stipulated as the necessary condition for the exaltation of humanity. At the very least, therefore, the Christian must be able "to show by a sort of peaceful competition, in deeds as well as words, that 'we also, we Christians, we, more than anyone else have the cult of man.'"[33] In other words, the Christian must demonstrate that, rather than denigrating the human subject or the greater human totality, the church's teaching with respect to the nature of human beings and their common destiny and the church's own form of social existence secure the dignity and the intrinsic value of humanity in a manner that atheist humanism is ultimately incapable of securing. As de Lubac argues already in his first book, *Catholicism* (1938), those who insist that nothing short of humanity is worthy of adoration "are obliged to look higher than the earth in the pursuit of their quest. . . . For a transcendent destiny that presupposes the existence of a transcendent God is essential to the realization of a destiny that is truly collective, that is, to the constitution of this humanity in the concrete."[34]

However necessary, de Lubac is nevertheless adamant that this "peaceful competition" with the various humanisms on offer throughout the nineteenth and twentieth centuries in no way exhausts the church's confrontation with contemporary atheism. As de Lubac argues in both the 1966 lecture and in *Athéisme et sens de l'homme*, the struggle with atheism is at root a thoroughly *hermeneutical* enterprise. That is, in her development of a "Christian anthropology," and in conversation with the atheism of her interlocutors, the church continually navigates three interrelated lines of interpretation: a hermeneutics of contemporary atheism, a hermeneutics of the Christian scriptures, and a hermeneutics of human existence. The first line of interpretation—the effort to understand the church's interlocutor—is true of any intellectual exchange. Mutual understanding is a necessary condition for any constructive dialogue. Discourse entails the search for points of convergence and of divergence. In the case of the church's confrontation with contemporary atheism, this effort at understanding is particularly apposite. For the primary assault waged by atheist humanism *against* Christianity is not, according to de Lubac, the logical refutation of a metaphysical assertion or a considered dismantling of the traditional proofs of God's existence. It is rather an effort to *understand* the Christian mysteries in terms of atheist humanism's own immanentist dialectic. According to Feuerbach, for instance, the divine being is nothing other than the projection of a "purified" human nature into infinite objectivity. Theology is therefore wholly reducible to anthropology.[35] According to de Lubac, "in order not to be 'understood' in this sense, only one way is open: to do some understanding. Therefore the Christian must understand atheism." In confronting the atheistic reduction of theology to anthropology, the Christian must work to convey the extent to which all anthropology supposes a theology.[36]

The second line of interpretation concerns what we have referred to as the properly *theological* task of Christian apologetics. As de Lubac argues in his inaugural lecture, there is no better way for giving an explanation of the Christian faith than to work for its understanding. The task of fundamental theology begins in an encounter with the Word of God, an encounter with the person of Jesus Christ through the mediating witness of scripture within the community of the church. The Christian anthropology that the theologian seeks to develop in conversation with contemporary atheism is wholly contingent on this encounter. For according to de Lubac, "In revealing to us the God who is the end of man, Jesus Christ, the Man-God, reveals us to ourselves, and without him the ultimate foundation of our being would remain an enigma to us."[37] It is in looking to scripture, therefore, and to the person and works of Jesus

Christ in particular that the theologian comes to understand the vocation of human beings in terms of their common ordination to graced fellowship with God.

Finally, according to de Lubac, a confrontation with contemporary atheism entails what he refers to as a hermeneutics of human existence.[38] Drawing on the philosophy of Paul Ricoeur, de Lubac insists:

> "Behind the question of autonomy, behind that of enjoyment and power, arises the question of meaning and non-sense. The thinking of the modern world is marked by both increasing rationality and increasing absurdity. . . . Of course it is true that people today lack justice, and they certainly also lack love. But what they lack above all is meaning." *The primordial function of the Christian community is to be for them a "witness and agent of fundamental meaning."*[39]

As I will argue throughout this book, for de Lubac, a hermeneutics of human existence consists primarily in *an interpretation of human existence in the light of humanity's supernatural vocation.* It is something of a mediating discourse between the two lines of interpretation mentioned above, between a hermeneutics of contemporary atheism and a hermeneutics of the biblical writings. As an apologetic endeavor, the church's hermeneutics of human existence is necessarily public. It seeks to be intelligible to the unbeliever as well as the believer. As such, it often avails itself of the insights of philosophy, of what Maurice Blondel referred to as the "method of immanence." It attempts to demonstrate, by way of reflection on the dynamism of human thought and action, an "intrinsic relationship between rational speculation and supernatural revelation."[40] On the other hand, however, the church's hermeneutics of human existence everywhere presupposes the faith of the church. It is always an "understanding of faith." It is not, therefore, a theology *incognito*—a statement of faith masking itself as a purely rational demonstration. It is rather *the unveiling of the meaning of human existence in the light of the gospel and a corresponding demonstration of the absurdity of human being in abstraction from this truth.*

In both the opening to his 1966 lecture and in the introduction to *Athéisme et sens de l'homme*, de Lubac insists that he is simply "following in the wake of the Council," taking up certain problems delineated throughout *Gaudium et spes* "in order to give an account both of its teachings and of the temper of mind that it urges upon us." De Lubac's remarks are therefore "entirely prospective, in the sense that I do not pretend to bring forward a ready-made theory, or even propose a definitive conclusion, but simply to point to a direction for research."[41] One of my central aims throughout this book is to demonstrate the extent to which de Lubac need only have gestured in the direction of his own body of writing. As I intend to demonstrate, de Lubac's entire oeuvre is shot-through with this hermeneutical enterprise. From his inaugural lecture in 1929 to those writings published in the final decade of his life, de Lubac was continually devoted to what he perceived to be the principal theological task facing the church today. In his confrontation with contemporary atheism, and in his numerous writings on nature and grace, theological epistemology, historiosophy, and even on Christian mysticism, de Lubac sets out to develop the theological and philosophical resources necessary for the direction of research indicated in his commentaries on *Gaudium et spes*. A theological hermeneutics of human existence is central to de Lubac's corpus.

THE PARADOX OF HUMAN EXISTENCE: NEITHER EXTRINSICISM NOR INTRINSICISM

Hans Urs von Balthasar notes in his own introduction to de Lubac's theology that "whoever stands before the forty or so volumes of Henri de Lubac's writings . . . feels as though he is at the entrance to a primeval forest. The themes could hardly be more diverse, and the gaze of the researcher glides seemingly without effort over the whole history of theology—and of thought itself."[42] At the very least, this book attempts to offer a means of navigating this primeval forest, a way of locating the seemingly disparate themes canvassed in de Lubac's work around an often tacit theological agenda. Without presuming to flatten the entire corpus under the weight of a single organizing principle—de Lubac himself disparaged any such effort to seek a "gnoseological" synthesis in his writings[43]—I will nevertheless attempt to demonstrate that an analysis of de Lubac's hermeneutics of human existence opens a number of important vistas from which to survey his writings as a whole. Or rather, I will seek to show the extent to which this hermeneutical enterprise occupied de Lubac throughout his entire career.

In addition to offering a critical analysis of de Lubac's hermeneutics of human existence and its relation to a number of other important themes in his work, I hope to advance and defend a particular reading of de Lubac's theology of nature and the supernatural at variance with what is quickly becoming the "majority reading" of de Lubac on this score in the Anglophone literature. De Lubac's construal of fundamental theology—within which a hermeneutics of human existence enjoys a privileged status—entails the rejection of extrinsicist accounts of the relation between nature and the supernatural. Specifically, de Lubac admonishes a theological trajectory dating back to Denys the Carthusian (1402–71), and introduced into the Thomist commentarial tradition by Thomas de Vio (1469–1534) and Francisco Suárez (1548–1617), which states that human beings are teleologically ordered to a purely natural beatitude in strict correspondence to their natural capacities. According to this theory, human beings have an absolute desire for a connatural finality, and the fulfillment of this desire is in important respects *owed* to human beings by God on account of their created nature.[44] It is only by grace, therefore, that humans are ordered to a further *supernatural* end (the beatific vision), and the desire for this end is itself contingent on the prior bestowal of grace. In contradistinction to this "theory of pure nature," de Lubac advances what he refers to as a *paradoxical* account of human existence whereby human beings are naturally ordered to a strictly supernatural finality.[45] That is, only the supernatural enjoyment of God—the eschatological perfection of human being in the beatific vision and the restoration of human fellowship in the *totus Christus*—can satisfy the absolute longing of human beings. This paradoxical teleology is the ontological ground for de Lubac's distinctly theological approach to Christian apologetics. Only doctrine conquers the intelligence because only the revelation of God satisfies the desire of nature. Thus, as de Lubac insists, "to remind man what constitutes his final end is not to tell him something that substantially fails to interest him. . . . It is rather to illuminate the total meaning of his being by helping him to find and then to interpret the inscription written into his heart by his Creator."[46]

We've already seen how de Lubac's theology of nature and grace—and his insistence on a natural desire for the supernatural in particular—elicited a storm of controversy among the proponents of pure nature. This controversy—exacerbated by the promulgation of Pius XII's encyclical *Humani generis* (1950), which was generally believed to have implicated de Lubac's writings—eventually led to the removal of a number of de Lubac's publications from all Jesuit libraries and the suspension of his teaching duties for nearly a decade. According to his critics, de Lubac's rejection of extrinsicism forced him to adopt a theologically problematic *intrinsicism* that elided the necessary distinction between nature and grace and ultimately compromised the gratuity of the supernatural. From his earliest writings on the supernatural, however, de Lubac was adamant that an affirmation of humanity's natural desire for the supernatural in no way mitigates the gratuity of the supernatural. For it is God who freely instills in human beings this desire for himself. In fulfilling our desire, therefore, God "answers his own call. . . . In no sense and under no title, neither natural nor moral, do we have any rights over God. *Deus nulli debitor est quocumque modo* [God is no one's debtor in any way]."[47] To suggest otherwise is to overlook the sheer contingency of all created being. De Lubac is just as adamant, moreover, that the denial of pure nature in no way collapses the necessary distinction between nature and the supernatural. De Lubac goes on to write in *Surnaturel*: "No confusion of the natural and the supernatural is admissible; no explanation of the latter that harms its perfect transcendence."[48] De Lubac makes the same point more forcefully in an essay published three years after the publication of *Surnaturel* (and shortly *before* the promulgation of *Humani generis*): "The fact that nature is not conceived as an order able to come definitively to an end upon itself, but as having a supernatural finality, does not mean as a further consequence that it already has the least supernatural element in itself or as part of its property."[49] De Lubac reaffirms this basic principle throughout his writings on the supernatural, insisting at a number of places on the radical heterogeneity between nature and the supernatural.[50] For all of his protests to the contrary, however, de Lubac's thesis continues to receive a radically intrinisicist inflection by both his critics *and his theological proponents* alike. Thus, whereas de Lubac insists that "between the existent nature and the supernatural to which God destines it, the distance is as great, the abyss is as profound, the heterogeneity is as radical as between non-being and being,"[51] it has become commonplace to locate de Lubac's truly revolutionary insight in his supposed affirmation that *nature itself is always already graced.*[52]

As we will see in what follows, there is some warrant for this particular construal of the *Surnaturel* thesis. De Lubac's constant polemic against a "two-tiered" account of nature and the supernatural often prevented him from drawing neat conceptual distinctions between nature and the means by which nature participates in its own supernatural finality. So, for instance, in a lecture delivered in 1942, de Lubac insists that "the whole natural order, not only in man but in the destiny of man, is already penetrated by something supernatural that shapes and attracts it."[53] There is moreover a sense in which the denial of a "graceless nature" is absolutely central for de Lubac's construal of the relation between nature and the supernatural, if by that one means the denial of "a world outside the Christian dispensation."[54] According to the advocates of pure nature, "a world could have existed in which man, without prejudice perhaps to another desire, had restricted his reasonable ambitions to some inferior beatitude."[55] That is, it is possible to imagine an order within which human beings might obtain a purely natural finality without recourse to divine grace. According to de Lubac, however, regardless of whether or not such a counterfactual assists the theologian in her articulation of the gratuity of the supernatural (de Lubac is convinced that it does not), it is nevertheless the case that in our actual world, "the ambitions of man cannot be so limited."[56] The drama of human existence unfolds within the larger drama of God's providential and salvific economy, that "order" within which God has acted to reconcile us to himself and to one another in the person and works of Jesus Christ. In this order, nothing short of the beatific vision can satisfy the longings of human nature. In this order, it is only by grace that human beings attain their supernatural finality.

If this appeal to the condition of human existence within the actual economy of God's reconciling work is all that is meant by the insistence that nature is always already graced, then such a position certainly finds traction in de Lubac's own writings on nature and the supernatural. In recent years, however, this summary of the *Surnaturel* thesis has become closely allied with a radical ontology according to which nature always intrinsically, if only inchoately, participates in the supernatural that fulfills it. As Edward T. Oakes has argued, such intrinsicism "so *fuses* nature and grace that anything natural becomes, by the very fact that it *is* natural, a form of grace." According to this view, "grace more or less automatically wells up from within nature rather than confronting it extrinsically from the outside."[57] The most influential proponent of this particular reading of de Lubac is John Milbank, whose own book on de Lubac, *The Suspended Middle* (now in its second edition), and whose frequent use of de Lubac in the articulation of his own "Radical Orthodoxy,"[58] has done more to introduce de Lubac's theology to an English-speaking audience than perhaps any other contemporary theologian. Milbank's interpretation of de Lubac turns especially on the latter's insistence on a natural desire for the supernatural. According to Milbank, "while Creation is the gift of independent existence and grace is the irresistible gift of nonetheless free and deified existence . . . the natural desire of the supernatural is the gift of the bond between the two." The natural desire of/for the supernatural is "the dynamic link" between nature and grace, "such that this link is at once entirely an aspect of the Creation and entirely also the work, in advance of itself, of grace which unites human creatures to the Creator."[59] In stating the *Surnaturel* thesis in this way, however, Milbank is confronted with a rather troublesome exegetical hurdle, namely, de Lubac's insistence that the desire for God is "a longing 'born of a lack,' and not arising from 'the beginnings of possession.'" According to de Lubac, the radical heterogeneity of nature and the supernatural is traversed only by the gift of sanctifying grace. The desire for this gift is nothing more than a "passive aptitude" [*aptitude passiva*].[60] Milbank attempts to circumvent this hurdle by way of a rather ingenuous corruption narrative according to which de Lubac was forced to rework his original *Surnaturel* thesis under the weight of Roman censure. According to Milbank, the above quotation (taken from de Lubac's 1965 publication *Le mystère du surnaturel*) was simply a concession to *Humani generis*, the promulgation of which provoked in de Lubac "severe theoretical incoherence."[61]

We will return throughout this book (particularly in chapter 2) to address what I take to be the historical and exegetical deficiencies of Milbank's corruption narrative. It is, however, worth flagging from the outset some of the more problematic *theological* implications of this particular reading of de Lubac's work. That is, even if it could be demonstrated that de Lubac had indeed espoused this form of intrinsicism, there are good theological reasons why we ought to avoid following him along this path.

First, as Edward T. Oakes has argued, it is not at all clear that such intrinsicism prevents the kind of autonomy afforded to nature by the proponents of pure nature.[62] For if nature itself is always already *supernaturalized*, what need is there for a further revelation, for a new ontic or noetic condition that interrupts, or at the very least elevates and perfects, the order of nature? What does nature receive that it does not always already contain?

Second, and correlatively, it would appear that such intrinsicism ultimately mitigates the novelty of the Christ event and the church's kerygma. "Omnem novitatem attulit, semetipsum afferens."[63] *Christ brought total newness in bringing himself.* This Irenaean axiom, quoted by de Lubac throughout his writings,[64] provides the counterbalancing "apocalyptic" tenor to de Lubac's otherwise intrinsic (though not intrinsic*ist*!) construal of the relation between nature and the supernatural. Thus, in terms of the relation between reason and faith, it is insufficient to claim that, as Milbank does, "faith and reason are not essentially distinct, since both are but differing degrees of participation in the mind of God."[65] According to de Lubac, such assertions risk reducing the Christian *novum* to "a transcendental condition of man's understanding of himself," thereby evacuating revelation of anything "beyond the actuality of our existence."[66] The newness of faith, like the newness of Christ, presupposes the original giftedness of created nature. But the dynamism of faith is not simply the continuation of the dynamism of reason.[67] Reason finds its fulfillment only in revelation, but according to de Lubac, the latter always "upsets" our instinctive logic, "liberating" our understanding by "overturning" the arrangement of all of our previous ideas.[68]

Third, to insist that nature is always already graced is to soften de Lubac's insistence on the radical ontological transfiguration brought about by sanctifying grace. According to de Lubac, "The supernatural . . . is that divine element which man's effort cannot reach (no self-divinization!) but which unites itself to man, 'elevating' him . . . , penetrating him in order to divinize him, and thus becoming as it were an attribute of the 'new man' described by St. Paul."[69] De Lubac thus retains the Thomistic understanding of grace as an "accidental form,"[70] relating this understanding directly to patristic and "Petrine" accounts of divinization.[71] But this accidental form always remains for de Lubac the prerogative of a recreated creature. It is in no way a constitutive element of humanity's "natural" mode of being.

Fourth, as Andrew Swafford has recently pointed out,[72] intrinsicist construals of the relation between nature and the supernatural risk relativizing the historical means by which grace is mediated within the economy of salvation. That is, an emphasis on the graced status of human nature by virtue of a general participatory ontology detracts—or at the very least distracts—from the supernatural unification of humanity accomplished in the person and works of Jesus Christ and extended historically through the sacramental ministry of the church. This will become especially clear in our treatment of de Lubac's theology of history in chapter 4.

Fifth, an intrinsicist reading of de Lubac does little justice to the personalist register within which de Lubac's theology of the supernatural unfolds. The desire for God is the desire for "the free and gratuitous communication of a personal Being."[73] The supernatural is not simply an elevated mode of participation in uncreated Being. It is, as Maurice Blondel insists, "an entirely gratuitous relationship, one which, so to speak, is totally 'un-naturalizable.'"[74] And although it is certainly true that all creatures enjoy a particular relation to their Creator simply by virtue of the being that they receive from God—all created beings are "beings by participation"[75]—there is nevertheless an infinite qualitative distinction between humanity's natural mode of being in relation to God and the graced fellowship enjoyed by the "children of God."[76] As de Lubac argues at length in his treatment of Christian mysticism (to which we will devote ourselves in chapter 5), the "union of likeness" enjoyed by those united to Christ by the Holy Spirit is not to be confused with "the union that already exists between God and his creatures."[77]

Finally, by way of summation, intrinsicist construals of the *Surnaturel* thesis tend to overlook de Lubac's insistence on the necessity of *metanoia*, "without which there is no entry into the Kingdom."[78] De Lubac argues in an important 1947 lecture: "It is the same for Humanity, taken as a whole, as for each individual. Let it develop thus indefinitely in its order, let it cross more and more elevated thresholds: it cannot reach completion without a totally different process—or rather a 'passion': a turning around of the whole being, a mysterious passage through death, a revival and a recasting that are nothing other than the evangelical *metanoia*."[79] De Lubac's emphasis on the necessity of *metanoia* is inspired, first and foremost, by his reticence to consider human nature in abstraction from the present economy. That is, just as de Lubac refuses to reason from a hypothetical order of pure nature, so he maintains that in humanity's present state, it is always "sinful man" that is called by God to the supernatural. Between this disordered nature and divine grace, there is not only a radical heterogeneity but also a "violent conflict." "Consequently the call of grace is no longer an invitation to a simple 'elevation,' not even a 'transforming' one. . . . [In] a more radical fashion it is a summons to a 'total upheaval,' to a 'conversion' (of the 'heart,' i.e., of all one's being)."[80] And yet, according to de Lubac, "even for an innocent and healthy nature," this passage from nature to the supernatural "could never take place without some kind of death."[81] Such is the radical incommensurability between human nature and humanity's supernatural finality. Such is the irresolvable paradox of human existence. It is precisely this paradox that de Lubac seeks to render intelligible (to both believer and unbeliever) by means of a theological hermeneutics of human existence. Or rather, according to de Lubac, it is only a theological exposition of this paradox that renders intelligible the drama of human existence.

AN ENDURING CONTROVERSY

Much of what follows is concerned with defending de Lubac's project from the good intentions of his intrinsicist supporters, but I likewise seek to offer an alternative to the revived accounts of pure nature as set forth by a new generation of neo-Scholastic critics. In recent years, de Lubac's thesis has received a flurry of renewed attention and opposition. Beginning especially with the publication of Lawrence Feingold's *The Natural Desire to See God according to St. Thomas and His Interpreters* (2001), de Lubac's work on nature and the supernatural—which garnered wide support throughout the latter decades of the twentieth century—has become once more the subject of ardent debate.[82] It is beyond the scope of this work to respond in full to all the criticisms leveled against de Lubac's theology of nature and the supernatural by today's proponents of pure nature. The literature devoted to this important controversy shows no sign of abating, and others have already entered the fray in de Lubac's defense.[83] My goal is rather to advance a particular interpretation of de Lubac's overall project that is often obscured or distorted by the necessarily limiting scope of theological polemics.[84] Much as, for instance, Przywara's work on the *analogia entis* was until recently read almost exclusively against the backdrop of Barth's critique, so de Lubac's hermeneutics of human existence is all too often obfuscated amidst arguments for and against the theory of pure nature.

Nevertheless, in offering a reinterpretation of de Lubac's theology of nature and the supernatural, and especially in countering intrinsicist readings of his work, we will, I hope, go some way toward diffusing some of the more serious accusations currently leveled against his project. According to Bernard Mulcahy, for instance, in a book tellingly subtitled *Not Everything Is Grace*, de Lubac is guilty of "soteriological Arianism," whereby the necessary distance between nature and sanctifying grace is abrogated and salvation is understood as "a relatively minor 'adjustment internal to the contingent order.'"[85] As I have already indicated, and as I will argue throughout, such a reading does little justice to de Lubac's express teaching on the radical heterogeneity between human nature and the economy of grace, a heterogeneity analogous, de Lubac argues, to the relation between being and nonbeing. Mulcahy likewise charges de Lubac with failing to distinguish between a natural and a supernatural knowledge of God, suggesting that for de Lubac all such knowledge is, strictly speaking, supernatural.[86] To the contrary, as I hope to demonstrate at length in my treatment of de Lubac's theological epistemology in chapter 3, de Lubac clearly defends the possibility of a natural knowledge of God arising both "objectively," by means of attention to God's revelation in the external world, and "subjectively," through reflection on the natural dynamism of reason itself. Indeed, for de Lubac, following Aquinas, "all knowers know God implicitly in all they know."[87] What de Lubac denies is that such a natural knowledge could ever fully satiate the desire of nature. Finally, Mulcahy accuses de Lubac of advocating for a nominalist understanding of nature, according to which " 'humanity' is made up of many natures, one for each individual."[88] This accusation (a somewhat surprising claim considering de Lubac is often charged with the "re-Platonizing of theology"[89]) stems from a misunderstanding of de Lubac's assertion that although God *could* have created human beings with a strictly natural end (that is, in a hypothetical state of pure nature), humanity's "concrete nature" is teleologically ordered to the beatific vision. As such, "in me, a real, personal human being, in *my* concrete nature, the 'desire to see God' could not be eternally frustrated without essential suffering. . . . For my finality, of which this desire is the expression, comes to me from my nature. And I do not have any other real end, that is to say, any other end actually assigned to my nature, except to 'see God.' "[90] As we will explore in further detail in chapter 2, far from disallowing any real distinction between human nature and the concrete individual, de Lubac is rather insisting on an intrinsic relation between being and finality. That is, according to de Lubac, a change to a creature's end (*telos*) would constitute a change to a creature's nature.

This, of course, brings us to the very heart of the controversy between de Lubac and the proponents of pure nature and to the readings of Aquinas employed on either side of the debate. According to Steven A. Long, one of de Lubac's most influential and exacting critics, de Lubac is right to insist on an intrinsic relation between human being and finality. However, according to Long, "St. Thomas's clear and classical teaching is that human nature is defined in its species in relation to the *natural and proportionate end* as distinct from the supernatural beatific end."[91] The end to which human beings are ordered *by nature* is a strictly natural/ philosophical contemplation of God as "First Cause," what Feingold succinctly describes as a state of beatitude realized "in a way *proportionate to man's nature*, in a *loving contemplation of God* as grasped through His work of creation."[92] In relation to the beatific vision, therefore, human beings possess only a passive obediential potency, "an aptness that exists only in relation to the active power of God and is simply speaking disproportionate to finite nature."[93] An additional, *supernatural* finality, to which the desire for the supernatural necessarily corresponds, is given only in baptism with the new form of sanctifying grace.

Once more, I am not herein primarily concerned with defending de Lubac's reading of Aquinas against his contemporary critics. Attention will be given throughout chapter 2 to de Lubac's interpretation of Aquinas in relation to the theory of pure nature, but my principal aim in that chapter is to locate de Lubac's own theology of nature and the supernatural within the broader logic of his hermeneutics of human existence. Moreover, as advocates of pure nature have recently noted, the exegetical disputes concerning Aquinas's construal of the natural desire for God stem in large part from a tension *within* the writings of Aquinas themselves. According to Long, "It is without doubt true that there is a problem in the very texts of Aquinas, and a problem which seemingly does not allow much room for maneuver with respect to its solution because the doctrinal points that constitute the elements of the problem—one is almost tempted to say 'constitute the contradiction'—are starkly and clearly stated in St. Thomas's text."[94] Whereas proponents of pure nature have sought to resolve this problem by reading Thomas "forward"—that is, by interpreting the Thomistic corpus through the conceptual distinctions and apparatuses developed throughout the sixteenth- and seventeenth-century commentarial tradition—de Lubac's intent was always to throw into relief the traits in which a preceding theological consensus (a tradition exemplified in both Greek and Augustinian currents) finds in Thomas "its most eminent witness."[95]

De Lubac's interpretation of Aquinas aims to synthesize a vast terrain of material on humanity's vocation, the nature and means of attaining happiness, and the intellect's desire for knowledge. According to Aquinas, all things are subject to divine providence and hence purposively ordered toward some end.[96] Human beings, like the birds of the air, the lilies of the field, and all else that participates in existence, are lovingly called into being and directed to God as their *principium et finis.* What distinguishes humans from birds and lilies is the capacity for self-determination, that is to say, whereas other creatures are directed to an end "by natural inclination, as being moved by another and not by themselves," humans are capable, not only of apprehending an end, but of directing and leading themselves to that end.[97] On the other hand, whereas other creatures can attain their end through the actualization of their own natural powers (e.g., a lily seed has a natural potency to become a flowering lily), humans are naturally incapable of procuring their end.[98] This is because, as Aquinas argues in a number of places, the final perfection of human beings resides in "the perfect knowledge of God," "the vision of the Divine Essence," of which humans are wholly incapable "unless God by His grace unites Himself to the created intellect as an object made intelligible to it."[99] Thus, by a paradox perfectly in keeping with the gospel's elevation of humility, human nobility resides precisely in the *insufficiency* of human nature to procure its end without recourse to divine assistance. Aquinas notes, "The nature that can attain perfect good, although it needs help from without in order to attain it, is of more noble condition than a nature which cannot attain perfect good, but attains some imperfect good, although it need no help from without in order to attain it."[100]

In order to demonstrate that human beings are teleologically ordered to the vision of the divine essence, and to defend the possibility of the beatific vision against its philosophical and theological detractors,[101] Aquinas appeals to the natural dynamism of the human intellect's desire for knowledge. According to Aquinas, "there resides in every man a natural desire to know the cause of any effect which he sees; and thence arises wonder in men. But if the intellect of the rational creature could not reach so far as to the first cause of things, the natural desire would remain void. Hence it must be absolutely granted that the blessed see the essence of God."[102] In other words, the blessed *must* see God in his essence, otherwise they would not enjoy perfect blessedness (that which human beings desire as their "perfect and crowning good").[103] However much we may learn, there remains a desire to know other things, "a natural desire for a more perfect knowledge." For every encountered effect, the intellect desires to know its cause. For every discovered cause, the intellect desires to know its essence. The intellect's desire to know cannot be at rest, therefore, until it knows the first cause *by its essence.* Since the first cause is God, Thomas argues, "the final end of the intellectual creature is to see God essentially."[104]

Do we not have here a clear example of Aquinas's articulation of a natural desire for the supernatural and thus a vindication of de Lubac's position? How do proponents of pure nature seek to reconcile Aquinas's account of the intellect's natural desire to know God essentially with their insistence on a purely natural human finality? According to Feingold, the solution lies in a distinction between an *innate appetite* and an *elicited desire.* Whereas the former "*flows from the very essence of a thing* . . . and inclines each thing to its proper and proportionate end," an elicited desire is a conscious movement of the will set in motion by an object presented to the intellect or senses. "The desire is said to be 'elicited' in that it is 'drawn out,' as it were, by the desirability of the known object."[105] In the case of the desire to see God, Feingold argues, Thomas intends only an elicited desire aroused by *prior knowledge* of other objects. The desire for God is not therefore inscribed upon the very nature of humanity but is rather the wonder resulting from intellectual encounters with God's created effects.[106]

It is worth noting, as Feingold himself grants, that Aquinas nowhere explicitly distinguishes between an innate appetite and an elicited desire in the manner presented by Feingold.[107] For Thomas, the desire to see God is simply a "natural desire" (*desiderium naturale*), indeed, the "desire of nature" (*desiderium naturae*).[108] The distinction between an innate and elicited desire for God was first introduced into the Thomist commentarial tradition by Francisco Suárez in the late sixteenth century.[109] Moreover, it is not entirely clear how defining the desire to see God as an elicited desire actually protects the gratuity of the supernatural in the manner intended by proponents of pure nature. For even in Feingold's account, the desire for God is a *naturally* elicited desire. It is one thing to argue, as Feingold does elsewhere, that the desire for the beatific vision is granted to human beings only through the grace of baptism.[110] Such a position, even though it disallows anything like an intrinsic relation between human being and humanity's supernatural finality, clearly safeguards the gratuity of the beatific vision. But to insist that the intellect is naturally/necessarily stimulated to desire to know the cause(s) of

God's effects in the world is to maintain that the dynamism of reason (presupposing some degree of intellectual apprehension) remains restless until it arrives at the knowledge of the divine essence, a knowledge granted only by the light of glory in the beatific vision. Finally, there are grounds within Aquinas's own corpus to argue, along with de Lubac, that the elicited desire for a more perfect knowledge is but "the sign of a genuine natural desire, that is, of an appetite of nature."[111] In this sense, reason's (elicited) desire to know corresponds precisely to humanity's (innate) desire for happiness.

Aquinas himself seems to make this relation explicit in *Summa theologiae* Ia IIae, q. 3, a. 8, where he argues that "final and perfect happiness can consist in nothing else than the vision of God." According to Aquinas, insofar as happiness resides in the attainment of humanity's last end, and insofar as all humans share an absolute and innate desire for their own perfection, no man is perfectly happy "so long as something remains for him to desire and seek."[112] Thus (and here Aquinas appeals directly to the natural dynamism of reason's desire to know), even should the intellect arrive at the knowledge of God's existence, there remains a desire to know more. "[The intellect] is not yet perfectly happy. Consequently, for perfect happiness the intellect needs to reach the very Essence of the First Cause. And thus it will have its perfection through union with God as with that object, *in which alone man's happiness consists.*"[113] This is not to suggest that in desiring happiness, all humans consciously/explicitly desire the beatific vision as the realization of their happiness. Thomas is careful to distinguish between "the general notion of happiness" and "that in which happiness consists."[114] All humans necessarily desire happiness, but not everyone knows/acknowledges that perfect beatitude resides ultimately in God. Thus some mistakenly desire wealth as their consummate good, while others desire pleasure or other things.[115] Nevertheless, insofar as nothing satisfies the desire for happiness short of the perfect good, all humans (at least implicitly) desire God in desiring their own perfection and the satisfaction of their will. Nor is Aquinas (or de Lubac!) suggesting that humans are entirely incapable of attaining some degree of happiness without the assistance of divine grace. In designating man's happiness as the acquisition of his final end and the attainment of his supreme perfection, Aquinas nevertheless distinguishes between an *imperfect happiness* (that which "partakes of some particular likeness to happiness") and a *perfect happiness* ("that which attains to the true notion of happiness").[116] The former can indeed be enjoyed in this life, but perfect happiness can only be attained in the life to come.[117] Whereas imperfect happiness is impermanent, perfect happiness is eternally secured.[118] Finally, whereas imperfect happiness can be acquired *by man's natural powers*, perfect happiness consists in nothing short of the beatific vision, which infinitely surpasses all created substance and is thus only ever received as a gift of grace.[119] Thus, as de Lubac summarizes the teaching of Aquinas on humanity's twofold beatitude, "the first of these two 'beatitudes,' which is 'proportionate to our nature,' is not a transcendent beatitude, a final or definitive end of the created spirit in a hypothetical world of 'pure nature.' Rather, it is an imperfect 'beatitude,' terrestrial and temporal, immanent to the world itself."[120]

The exegetical terrain covered in this debate is vast, and the areas of divergence assume a high degree of technical precision and abstraction, but the sheer longevity of this controversy attests to its enduring theological significance. The ecclesial and theological landscape has no doubt changed a great deal since the initial publication of *Surnaturel*, and the reemergence of pure nature presents a valuable opportunity to reassess prevailing assumptions concerning the relation between nature and grace. As Edward T. Oakes notes, whereas de Lubac and others criticized the predominant (neo-Scholastic) account of grace in the first half of the twentieth century for being overly extrinsic, after Vatican II grace came to be seen by many as "so intrinsic to man that the supernatural gifts of revelation, the church, and the sacraments seemed, at best, merely symbolic reminders of an already realized redemption."[121] This move toward collapsing the supernatural into the order of nature is often attributed directly to de Lubac's assault on pure nature, but he himself devoted as much energy after Vatican II to refuting theological intrinsicism as he did before the council to challenging extrinsicism. As we will seek to demonstrate in the conclusion, de Lubac was convinced that both the theory of pure nature and certain trends in postconciliar theology mitigate the necessity of the supernatural. His account of the paradox of human nature was thus intended as a *via media* between these two theological alternatives.

BEING AND MYSTERY

We will begin our investigation of Henri de Lubac's hermeneutics of human existence with an analysis of his hermeneutics of atheist humanism. As we have seen so far, de Lubac insists that a confrontation with contemporary atheism must entail an effort at *understanding*, an attempt to interpret and effectively "out-narrate" atheist construals of the relation between anthropology and theology by means of the church's own theological hermeneutics of human existence. In chapter 2, we will devote ourselves to a critical evaluation of de Lubac's controversial *Surnaturel* thesis, focusing in particular on his paradoxical construal of the natural desire for the supernatural. According to de Lubac, "The infinite seriousness of this desire placed in me by my Creator constitutes the infinite seriousness of the drama of human existence."[122] De Lubac's interpretation of the *desiderium naturae* thus serves as the crux of his hermeneutics of human existence, providing the ontological grammar for considering humanity's natural vocation in terms of a wholly gratuitous supernatural finality. In addition to locating the *desiderium naturae* within the broader logic of de Lubac's hermeneutics of human existence, this chapter seeks to demarcate the theological significance of de Lubac's paradoxical account of human nature from both the extrinsicism of his neo-Scholastic opponents *and* the intrinsicism of his later interpreters. In chapter 3 we will turn our attention to an investigation of the dynamism of human *reason*. That is, we will trace the paradox of humanity's supernatural vocation throughout de Lubac's construal of the relation between reason and revelation, demonstrating the extent to which, for de Lubac, only the supernatural revelation of God satisfies the dynamism of human reason. Having considered the drama of human existence in largely individualistic terms in chapters 2 and 3, we will turn in chapter 4 to de Lubac's theology of history, to an investigation of the irreducibly social and historical conditions of human existence. In so doing, we will note a certain analogy between the drama of history taken as a whole and the drama of human existence: history itself is teleologically ordered to the gratuitous disposal of a wholly supernatural finality. According to de Lubac, the meaning of history resides first and foremost in the supernatural restoration of human fellowship with God and among human beings in the person and works of Jesus Christ and in his body, the church. It is this history of the reunification of humanity in the *totus Christus* that constitutes the narrative within which each individual drama finds its meaning. In chapter 5, we will consider de Lubac's hermeneutics of human existence through the lens of his account of Christian mysticism. For de Lubac, mysticism names a particular mode of being in relation to the mystery of Christ. It is the condition of human existence under the purview of grace, a participation *in via* in the graced perfection of humanity's supernatural finality. De Lubac's account of Christian mysticism thus brings into relief the integral relation between the paradox of human existence (as treated in chapters 2 and 3) and de Lubac's Christocentric theology of history (as treated in chapter 4). That is, de Lubac here portrays the dynamism of human existence explicitly in terms of the Christologically mediated transformation of human being into the "likeness" of God. By way of conclusion, we will consider de Lubac's response to certain trends in postconciliar theology, for it is in his engagement with such thinkers as Karl Rahner, Edward Schillebeeckx, and proponents of liberation theology that de Lubac devotes himself most clearly and forcefully to refuting the theological errors of intrinsicism.

The word "mystery" employed throughout this work is consecrated terminology in the Lubacian lexicon. A number of de Lubac's own writings bear the word (or the adjective *mystical*) in their titles,[123] and mystery carries tremendous theological freight throughout de Lubac's corpus. The range of meaning invested in this term, and the role that it plays in de Lubac's theology of human existence in particular, will be addressed at length herein, particularly in my treatment of Christian mysticism in chapter 5. There is, however, another reason for highlighting the significance of mystery in de Lubac's hermeneutics of human existence. As Paul Ricoeur notes, particularly with reference to the philosophy of his mentor Gabriel Marcel, the word "mystery" as applied to human being can be understood in one of two senses. First, we may understand the mystery of human being as referring to humanity's "rootedness in being or in the sacred." On the other hand, we may understand this mystery as "an 'irreducible opacity' to man's being which resists all attempts to schematize it."[124] As we will see throughout, both meanings are closely allied in de Lubac's hermeneutics of human existence. In the first sense, "being in mystery" refers to humanity's supernatural vocation, to the "natural desire for the supernatural" and the "transcendental affirmation of God" at the heart of human existence. It refers to the paradox of a creature destined for an end that infinitely surpasses the capacities of its nature to attain. It refers to the revelation and the fulfillment of human being in the life, death, and resurrection of Jesus Christ. Just for this reason, however, human being is also an enigma. The dynamism of human existence remains unintelligible in abstraction from the one who creates, and who alone can satisfy, the desire of our nature: "Man, made in the image of the incomprehensible God, is ultimately incomprehensible to himself."[125] Conversely, it is only the revelation of God that reveals us to ourselves.

ONE

A Hermeneutics of Atheist Humanism

A CONFLICT IN CONTEXT

According to de Lubac, a theological hermeneutics of human existence receives its contemporary urgency from the church's confrontation with modern atheism. The exigency of the church's apologetics is not, of course, a distinctly modern phenomenon. The church's beliefs have never ceased to elicit opposition, and every age witnesses "the principle of assaults against the faith renewed."[1] However, though such opposition remains (and will no doubt continue to remain) an abiding feature of the church's earthly pilgrimage, the assaults waged against the faith vary greatly. De Lubac mentions, for instance, challenges pertaining to the historicity of the events recorded in scripture, metaphysical denunciations of transcendence, and political opposition to the church's influence in temporal matters. However constant the object of the church's faith may be, the church is therefore called to employ a diversity of apologetic strategies to respond to the various consternations of the world around her.

Writing on the subject of the church's "Spiritual Warfare" in 1943, months after the German army extended its occupation to the southern zone of France, de Lubac argues that the "principal attack" against Christianity today "is no longer a problem of the historical, metaphysical, political or social order. It is a *spiritual* problem. It is the total human problem."[2] Contemporary atheism sets itself against both the Christian God and the Christian ideal of humanity. Or, rather, it seeks to dispense with the former in order to overcome the latter. In so doing, it attempts to restore to humanity its rightful dignity, to liberate immanence from the tyranny of transcendence. In his many writings on contemporary atheism, de Lubac readily grants that there is a necessary relation between the Christian idea of God and the Christian ideal of humanity. He is, however, adamant that only the former establishes the absolute value of the human person and society. Jean Daniélou summarizes de Lubac's argument: "Atheist Humanism is self-destructive. There can be no real Humanism without a foundation in something beyond man."[3]

Like the majority of French Catholics in the first half of the twentieth century, de Lubac's engagement with contemporary atheism was as much a social and a political reality as an intellectual and religious concern. Tensions between the Catholic Church and the French government, recurrent from at least the time of the Revolution (1789–99) and only partially dispelled by the Concordat of 1801, were exacerbated under the Third Republic (1870–1940) and brought to a head in the aftermath of the Dreyfus Affair (1894–1906). As Georges Chantraine notes in his biography of de Lubac, these mounting hostilities between the laicism of the Third Republic and the Catholic Church in France had an enormous effect on de Lubac's immediate family in the years leading up to his birth.[4] On March 29, 1880, Jules Ferry, minister of education and soon to be prime minister, instigated a series of decrees dissolving a number of "unauthorized" religious congregations in France (including the Society of Jesus). At the time, a large portion of the nation's children were educated in church schools by members of religious orders, and the decrees of March 29 were part of a larger attempt to protect French youth from the illiberal and ultimately antirepublican influence of the Roman Catholic Church. Among the many Catholic protestors against the decrees was a nineteen-year-old Maurice de Lubac, who, while escorting a group of Capuchin fathers from Lyon, became involved in a brawl and injured a counterprotester by striking him in the face with the hilt of his sword. De Lubac was fined for carrying an unauthorized weapon and encouraged by his employer, the Banque de France, to take up his post somewhere outside of Lyon on account of his conviction. De Lubac was sent first to Lille, then to Verdun, and finally to Cambrai where, on February 20, 1896, his wife, Gabrielle, gave birth to their third child, Henri.

Shortly after de Lubac's birth, hostilities between the Third Republic and the Catholic Church in France were exacerbated during what is commonly referred to as the Dreyfus Affair or the Dreyfus Revolution. On December 22, 1894, a Jewish artillery captain by the name of Alfred Dreyfus was convicted of treason and sentenced to life imprisonment for allegedly betraying military secrets to the German embassy in Paris. The case became something of a lightning rod for political debate and public outcry when, in 1897, it was discovered that the principal document used by the military to incriminate Dreyfus had been a forgery. Those in support of Dreyfus (the *Dreyfusards*)—largely those on the ideological and political left—charged the military with anti-Semitism and obscurantist authoritarianism. Those opposed to Dreyfus (the *anti-Dreyfusards*) meanwhile hearkened back to the nationalist and militarist ideals of the *ancien régime.* The Catholic Church in France found herself, for the most part, on the side of the anti-Dreyfusards. Thus, by the time Dreyfus was pardoned in 1899 (he was not formally acquitted until 1906), the church's reputation in France was severely tarnished. Whatever her reasons for opposing Dreyfus[5]—there were certainly a number among her ranks who warranted the charge of anti-Semitism—the church's involvement in the Dreyfus Affair seemed to set her squarely against the proponents of liberty and equality in France. Writing in 1931, Roger Soltau powerfully expresses the typical republican interpretation of this affair:

> The Dreyfus case, complex as it was in many ways, reduced itself ultimately to a simple choice between the two conceptions of society which had, ever since the Revolution, been struggling for mastery in the French mind: the one, the basing of society and civilization on certain elemental individual rights, which no danger of upheaval or reasons of State could shake in their sanctity, the other based on authority as external and prior to individual citizens, superior to and judge of the rights of these and the desirability of their exercise. It was the declaration of the Rights of Man versus the *ancien régime*, the Reformation and the Revolution as against the Church, and it suddenly

> forced every thinking man to choose the side to which he really belonged.[6]

With the majority of public opinion, and the overwhelming testimony of the evidence, firmly on the side of Dreyfus, the conception of society that emerged victorious from the affair was that of the liberal republicans. Thus, having secured the *ideological* victory, the republican government, under both the centrist prime minister Pierre Waldeck-Rousseau (1899–1902) and the more radical Emile Combes (1902–5), promulgated a series of rigid anticlerical policies, culminating in the so-called *lois d'exception* of 1901 and 1904. In accordance with these measures, about 20,000 members of religious communities were expelled from France, and approximately 10,000 congregation schools were forcibly closed. As a result, students seeking religious training were obliged to pursue their studies elsewhere.[7] It was for this reason that de Lubac underwent his own education largely abroad, first at St. Mary's College in Canterbury (1920), then in Jersey (1920–23), and finally at Ore Place, Hastings (1924–26), before concluding his formal theological training at Fourvière, Lyon (1926–28). Having therefore received his philosophical and theological formation "in exile" from the laicization of the Third Republic, it is scarcely surprising that some of de Lubac's earliest theological reflections are concerned with the phenomenon of contemporary atheism.[8]

The cultural and political marginalization of the church under the Third Republic in the late nineteenth and early twentieth centuries is crucial for understanding the tremendous ecclesial support given to Maréchal Pétain (1856–1951) and the Vichy regime during World War II. Following the fall of Paris and the armistice at Compiègne in 1940, which officially placed the north and west of France under German control, Pétain was appointed prime minister of France, governing the country's "free zone" from Vichy in collaboration with Hitler's Reich. As Joseph Komonchak notes, the prestige gained by Pétain during his time as a military commander in World War I, his appeal to the traditional values of "Work, Family and Country," and his political opposition to the anticlericalism of the Third Republic help to explain the allegiance given to Pétain by many in the church in France.[9] For those on the margins after the Dreyfus Affair, the Vichy regime seemed to offer the promise of an end to secular republicanism and the restoration of a political arrangement more favorable to the Catholic Church.[10]

In a letter written to his Jesuit superiors on April 25, 1941, de Lubac decried the "Hitlerian virus" sweeping France, expressing outrage at the number of clergy who had offered their public support to the "miracle" of the Vichy government.[11] In addition to insisting on the threat posed by Nazism to the church, de Lubac disparaged the propagation of anti-Semitism throughout occupied France, notifying his superiors that "this anti-Semitism is already gaining ground among the Catholic elite, even in our religious houses."[12] Over the next three years, de Lubac played a leading role in the "spiritual resistance" to Nazism. From Lyon, the "capital of the Resistance," de Lubac wrote and lectured frequently on the dangers of Nazi ideology.[13] He recalls one instance when, by coincidence, a German squad conducted a raid on a house at the very moment that he was giving a presentation on Nazism in a room on the first floor.[14] Along with such figures as Pierre Chaillet, Gaston Fessard, Jean Daniélou, and Yves de Montcheuil, de Lubac contributed regularly to the production and distribution of the *Cahiers du Témoignage chrétien*, a clandestine series of pamphlets intended to encourage Christians to oppose and to organize resistance to Nazism on spiritual grounds.[15] Of the contributors to the *Cahiers*, Father Chaillet narrowly escaped being arrested by swallowing incriminating papers moments before his interrogation by the Gestapo, and Father de Montcheuil was tragically executed in 1944. De Lubac himself was hunted by the Gestapo and forced to flee Lyon in 1943. He remained hidden away in Vals until the departure of the German army in 1944.

In the 1941 "letter to his superiors" and in numerous published reflections on the war years, de Lubac insists that his principal motivation during the resistance was not political but spiritual. That is, de Lubac was not primarily concerned with the economic and political conditions that led to the collaboration between France and Hitler's Germany. Rather, he was motivated by what he believed to be the inherently anti-Christian, and hence *inhuman*, ideology of the Third Reich: "The war of conquest being waged today by Hitler's Germany is for it only one stage conducted in the forward progress of a revolution which, before being an anti-

French, for example, or an anti-English fight, is an anti-Christian revolution."[16] In their eagerness to overcome the laicism of the Third Republic, many in the Catholic Church had thus courted a more insidious form of captivity. Much of de Lubac's wartime effort was devoted to unmasking the "neopagansim" of such Nazi ideology.[17] As we will see in what follows, this involved him in something of a genealogical exercise, an attempt to demonstrate the extent to which the contemporary crisis owes its genesis to an intellectual "crisis" a century earlier. That is, according to de Lubac, the dissolution of humanity in the twentieth century was something of an aftershock caused by the death of God in the nineteenth.

Such is the argument set forth by de Lubac at length in a number of lectures throughout the Occupation, lectures eventually compiled and included in the first part of his massively influential *The Drama of Atheist Humanism*. To speak of this work as genealogical is not *entirely* apposite. De Lubac traces the well-known intellectual trajectory from Hegel to Marx by way of Ludwig Feuerbach, and the more contentious influence of Feuerbach upon Nietzsche by way of Schopenhauer and Wagner, but *The Drama of Atheist Humanism* is not primarily devoted to the genetic relations between the various advocates of atheist humanism in the nineteenth century. Moreover, the political climate during the Occupation largely prevented de Lubac from making explicit the relation between the authors treated and Nazi neopaganism; there is not a single overt reference to Hitler or Nazism in *The Drama of Atheist Humanism*.[18] The drama that de Lubac narrates is less a "history of philosophy" in the technical sense than the charting of an *idée-force*, the interpretation of a pervasive "mystical immanentism" that, according to de Lubac, has three principal aspects that can be symbolized by the philosophies of Auguste Comte, Ludwig Feuerbach, and Friedrich Nietzsche.[19]

Before devoting ourselves to the various "acts" making up the drama set forth in de Lubac's interpretation of contemporary atheism, it is worth noting the prevalence of "humanist" discourse in France in the immediate aftermath of World War II. For it was this discourse that provided an immediately recognizable and culturally pertinent grammar for de Lubac's refutation of modern atheism. As the historian Michael Kelly has argued extensively, humanism was *the* dominant ideological tendency in France during the era of reconstruction.[20] Still reeling from the German occupation and the collapse of the Vichy regime, the French political and intellectual elites sought a unifying ideological framework through which to rebuild national identity and cultural unanimity. It was in this context that "humanism emerged suddenly and unexpectedly as the uncontested framework of values within which the debates and struggles of the period were expressed."[21] The humanist mantle was taken up by Catholics, Marxists, and existentialists alike as a means of galvanizing public opinion and criticizing rival ideologies. Thus, in 1945, the French Socialist Party (SFIO) adopted the humanist epithet in a shrewd attempt to unite to itself the most extreme wings of the Catholic Social Democrats (MRP) and the Communist Party (PCF).[22]

As Kelly notes, the groundwork for this ideological framework was already laid during the prewar and Occupation years. By the mid-1930s, for instance, the PCF had employed the rhetoric of humanism in a broad platform based on antifascism and social progress.[23] Around the same time, the philosophical significance of humanism was being advanced by such leading Catholic intellectuals as Emmanuel Mounier and Jacques Maritain.[24] In his widely influential *Integral Humanism*, Maritain spoke of the need for a "new Christendom" characterized by an integral or theocentric humanism. "We see this new humanism," wrote Maritain, "which has no standards in common with 'bourgeois' humanism . . . as oriented toward a socio-temporal realization of the Gospel's concern for human things . . . and toward the ideal of a fraternal community."[25] During the Occupation, the language of humanism—the opposition to totalitarianism on behalf of "man" or "humanity"—became a powerful rhetorical tool for the Resistance. It was partly for this reason that humanism came to the fore after the Liberation as a positive means of reconstructing French cultural identity. Humanism provided a point of contact among otherwise diverse political groups that found themselves suddenly allied in their opposition to the Vichy regime. Ironically, it also provided a convenient "ideological umbrella" for those Catholics who had supported Pétain's government during the Occupation. Kelly notes that "those whose wartime situation had been, like that of the church itself, highly ambiguous, were given a moral language in which to express attitudes which could not be stated politically. . . . In this way, Humanism opened the door to allow people who had 'backed the wrong horse' under the occupation to be reintegrated into the nation."[26]

In addition to providing an ideological framework for *unifying* France after the Liberation, humanism also served as a common discourse within which the various ideologies and political parties *competed* for cultural and political influence. Thus, although Catholics, communists, and socialists all agreed on the importance of humanism for the future of France, "each claimed to possess the *only* philosophy capable of providing man with the dignity he deserved. . . . Thus, every claim to humanism emphasized . . . the absolute impossibility of arriving at a proper care for man in *any* other way."[27] According to the communists, for instance, a true humanism presupposes the overcoming of humanity's alienation from the means of production. Only Marxist economics, therefore, provides the means of establishing genuinely human relations.[28] For Catholics, any humanism that fails to account for the transcendent dimension of humanity is ultimately—as Maritain insists—an *inhuman* humanism, or, as the Russian émigré Nicholas Berdyaev refers to it, antihumanism.[29]

Given the prevalence of humanist discourse after the Liberation and de Lubac's own liberal use of such thinkers as Maritain and Berdyaev, it is tempting to see in de Lubac's engagement with contemporary atheism a mere defense of humanism on wholly theological grounds. However, de Lubac was far more reluctant to identify his own engagement with atheist humanism as itself humanist. Unlike a number of his contemporaries, de Lubac nowhere develops a positive sociopolitical alternative to secular humanism in a manner similar to Maritain's "new Christendom" or Berdyaev's "personalist socialism." In this chapter, I will offer instead an interpretation of *The Drama of Atheist Humanism* (and some of de Lubac's other writings on contemporary atheism) according to the program set forth in "Nature and Grace" and *Athéisme et sens de l'homme*, that is, as a means of confronting atheistic renderings of Christianity by way of a theological hermeneutics of contemporary atheism. De Lubac's confrontation with atheist humanism entails a demonstration of both its indebtedness to the claims of Christian theology and its inability to secure a positive account of humanity without recourse to some form of transcendence. The drama of atheist humanism begins with the rejection of Christianity on humanist grounds, proceeds by way of the transfiguration of the Christian kerygma according to the logic of its own immanentist dialectic, and eventually culminates in its own dissolution.

In addition to offering an analysis of de Lubac's confrontation with contemporary atheism, we will attempt, in the final part of this chapter, to move with and beyond de Lubac by placing his work in conversation with another important intellectual development in postwar France. That is, I will argue that de Lubac's hermeneutics of atheist humanism anticipates, and sheds significant light upon, the rise of philosophical antihumanism in the latter half of the twentieth century. The ideological landscape of postwar France witnessed both the apex of humanist discourse and the emergence of what Emmanuel Levinas referred to as "an atheism that is not humanist."[30] Given the atrocities of the first half of the century, a diminished confidence in the humanist enterprise is scarcely surprising. The pretensions of human beings to a privileged place in the universe, for instance, became somewhat difficult to stomach in the wake of two world wars and the nightmare of Auschwitz.[31] But to reduce the critique of humanism to a mere disgust with totalitarianism or skepticism with regard to human progress would be to overlook the more significant (and radical) philosophical claims of antihumanism. Whereas the vast majority of philosophies leading up to the twentieth century make some sort of an appeal to the notion of a shared humanity, antihumanism rejects outright "the very possibility of an irreducible or given *human nature* . . . or of something in man that is *essentially* or *fundamentally human* and that forms the core of human existence."[32] The various humanisms of the nineteenth century locate the source of meaning in humanity itself or in individual human beings, but antihumanism reduces the human to the inhuman, locating meaning rather in the structures of language, culture, or the totality of being. Whereas Feuerbach, for example, reduces the dignity of God to the dignity of man, Heidegger subsumes the dignity of man to the dignity of being. Whereas Marx declares that "man is the highest being for man,"[33] Foucault insists that "man is an invention of recent date. *And one perhaps nearing its end*."[34] Thus, we might say that if the "death of God" served as the rallying cry for atheist humanism, "the death of man" soon took its place as the slogan of that atheism that is not humanist. In the decades immediately following its publication, the principal thesis of *The Drama of Atheist Humanism* was therefore corroborated by the existentialism of Sartre, the fundamental ontology of Heidegger, and the adherents of structuralist anthropology: "Where there is no God, there is no man either."[35]

THE DRAMA OF ATHEIST HUMANISM

Act One: Resentment

De Lubac's interpretation of atheist humanism occurs largely in three acts. The first act runs within a typical Promethean register. Originally, de Lubac argues, the deposit of Christian faith was regarded as *securing* the dignity of human beings, liberating them from the ontological slavery of Fate. By the nineteenth century, however, what was once lauded as humanity's true source of liberation became, in the eyes of many, the perpetrator of a more insidious form of captivity. As de Lubac laments, "that same Christian idea of man that had been welcomed as a deliverance was now beginning to be felt as a yoke. And that same God in whom man had learned to see the seal of his greatness began to seem to him like an antagonist, the enemy of his dignity."[36] The atheist humanism of the nineteenth century, as set forth by such diverse thinkers as Comte, Feuerbach, Marx, and Nietzsche, was more than a merely *critical* atheism. That is, "it [did] not profess to be the simple answer to a speculative problem and certainly not a purely negative solution." Rather, according to de Lubac, the problem posed by such thinkers was a human problem: "It was *the* human problem—and the solution that is being given to it is one that claims to be positive. Man is getting rid of God in order to regain possession of the human greatness that, it seems to him, is being unwarrantably withheld by another."[37] Like Jacques Maritain, de Lubac thus distinguishes between two forms of atheism: a *negative* and a *positive.* Whereas the former entails a mere rejection of belief in God, the negation of a metaphysical assertion, the latter "is built upon resentment and begins with a choice."[38] Positive atheism, in other words, is "*anti*theism, or, more precisely, anti-Christianism."[39] As such, it is little wonder that a young Marx considered Prometheus "the noblest of saints and martyrs in the calendar of philosophy."[40] For despite the many and often contentious differences among the various advocates of atheist humanism in the nineteenth century, each were in resolute accord in their rejection of God, a rejection predicated on positive, humanist grounds.

The chief protagonists of this anthropological revolt were, by de Lubac's account, Feuerbach (1804–72) and Nietzsche (1844–1900). In *The Essence of Christianity*, Feuerbach insists that "the divine being is nothing else than the human being, or, rather, the human nature purified, freed from the limits of the individual man, made objective—that is, contemplated and revered as another, a distinct being. All the attributes of the divine nature are, therefore, attributes of the human nature."[41] According to Feuerbach, religion is nothing but the relation of man to his own nature. Man projects his being into objectivity, thereby making himself an object to that image of himself now considered as the divine subject. This psychological-projectionist account of religion was not simply a descriptive exercise. For insofar as religion is "the disuniting of man from himself," man ultimately denies to himself that which he attributes to his God.[42] "To enrich God," Feuerbach writes, "man must become poor; that God may be all, man must be nothing. But he desires to be nothing in himself, because what he takes from himself is not lost to him, since it is preserved in God. Man has his being in God; why then should he have it in himself?"[43] It is this denigration of human dignity—the sacrifice of human greatness at the altar of divine being—that Feuerbach's projectionist account of religion intends to dispel. Thus, according to de Lubac, Feuerbach's sole aim was "to reveal to mankind its own essence in order to give it faith in itself."[44] Feuerbach's efforts swiftly garnered a host of eager disciples, the most notable of which was undoubtedly Marx. For despite his many (and often severe) criticisms of Feuerbach, and his eventual break with the Young Hegelians, Marx remained ever indebted to Feuerbach's fundamental critique of religion.[45] De Lubac thus echoes Paul Vignaux's assertion that "Marx traces his spiritual descent from the humanist religion of Feuerbach."[46]

De Lubac's reading of Nietzsche, who receives the lion's share of his attention at this stage in the drama of atheist humanism, follows closely upon his interpretation of Feuerbach. Nietzsche, who published his first work in the year of Feuerbach's death, was hardly a sympathetic interpreter of the latter, but de Lubac suggests that he nevertheless received from Feuerbach more than he may have cared to admit through his two masters, Schopenhauer and Wagner.[47] Thus, in a passage reminiscent of Feuerbach's own project, de Lubac relates Nietzsche's critique of religion as follows:

> God, according to Nietzsche, is nothing more than the mirror of man, who, in certain intense, exceptional states, becomes aware of the power that is in him or of the love that exalts him. . . . Man, not daring to ascribe such power or love to himself, makes them the attributes of a superhuman being who is a stranger to him. He accordingly divides the two aspects of his own nature between two spheres, the ordinary weak and pitiable aspect appertaining to the sphere he calls "man," while the rare, strong and surprising aspect belongs to the sphere he calls "God." Thus by his own action he is defrauded of what is best in him.[48]

For Nietzsche, religion is therefore the self-debasement of man, relegating everything that is great in him to an alleged bestowal of divine grace.[49] Human beings must therefore rid themselves of God so as to regain possession of their own greatness. God must die that man might truly live. "You higher men," Nietzsche declares through the mouth of Zarathustra, "this god was your greatest danger. It is only now, since he lies in his grave, that you are resurrected. . . . Well then! Well now! You higher men . . . God died: now *we* want—the overman [*Übermensch*] to live."[50] It is this proclamation of "the death of God" that delineates Nietzsche as the great prophet of atheist humanism and, as we shall see, precursor to the antihumanism of the twentieth century. Like Feuerbach, Nietzsche is scarcely content with refuting the traditional "proofs" of God's existence. Rather, Nietzsche declares that "the question of the mere 'truth' of Christianity . . . is of secondary importance."[51] It is not against a *belief* in God that Feuerbach and Nietzsche are revolting, but rather the particular ideal of human beings that such a belief engenders. For "perhaps man would rise higher and higher," writes Nietzsche, "from the moment when he ceased to flow into God."[52] It is only through the crucible of theocide that humanity begins the long march toward self-realization.

Act Two: *Dépassement*

The second act of de Lubac's interpretation of atheist humanism involves what he refers to as a *dépassement* (overtaking). Though not entirely absent from *The Drama of Atheist Humanism*,[53] this line of interpretation appears most clearly in de Lubac's *Athéisme et sens de l'homme* (1968), a "commentary" on *Gaudium et spes.* According to de Lubac, the revolt waged by atheist humanism against the Christian God is typically complemented by a corresponding movement of overtaking, by which he means the transformation of the Christian mystery into the immanentist religion of atheist humanism. Thus, according to de Lubac, "contemporary atheism considers itself capable of absorbing into itself the Christian substance and of transforming 'without violence' the believer, now 'fully adult,' into an atheist."[54] Rejection is coupled with an act of reinterpretation, and the "fancies of theological illusion" are granted a more basic human meaning. De Lubac likens this transposition to the church's understanding of the relation between the Old and New Testaments. Just as ancient and medieval exegetes saw in the New Testament the disclosure of the true meaning of the Old, so the champions of atheist humanism have adopted a similar hermeneutic in their reading of the Christian faith. The essential reproach that the atheist humanist addresses to the Christian mystery is thus "similar to the one which Origen once addressed in the name of this mystery to the Jewish religion: he reproaches the figure for its refusal to disappear in the face of the truth that fulfils it. All theology is for him reducible to anthropology."[55] The atheist humanist presumes an understanding of the Christian faith, even claiming to exalt its role, all the while rejecting its mythological assertions in favor of their underlying anthropological truths.[56]

De Lubac traces this tendency to the philosophy of Hegel; though, as de Lubac intimates, there is a certain irony in Hegel's role as progenitor of this distinctly *atheistic* movement of thought.[57] For according to Hegel, "God is the one and only object of philosophy." As such, philosophy's primary concern is

> to occupy itself with God, to apprehend everything in him, to lead everything back to him, as well as to derive everything particular from God and to justify everything only insofar as it stems from God, is sustained through its relationship with him, lives by his radiance and has [within itself] the mind of God. Thus philosophy *is* theology, and [one's] occupation with philosophy—or rather *in* philosophy—is of itself the service of God.[58]

To what extent then does Hegel's thinking anticipate the hermeneutic of atheist humanism? How does the Hegelian "service of God" lend itself to the overtaking mentioned above? For Hegel, God is absolute *spirit* (*Geist*). As spirit, "God *is* essentially in his community . . . he is objective to himself and is such truly only in self-consciousness [so that] God's very own highest determination is self-consciousness. Thus the concept of God leads of itself necessarily to religion."[59] Religion then, as conceived by Hegel, is not merely a mode of human cognition or feeling, but the very process whereby the self-consciousness of absolute spirit is actualized in and through the medium of finite consciousness. It is, as it were, "the highest determination of the absolute idea itself."[60] For Hegel, God is not the infinite as set wholly over and against the finite. Rather, the divine spirit becomes absolute spirit precisely in and through the mediation of finite spirit: "It is in the finite consciousness . . . that the divine self-consciousness thus arises. Out of the foaming ferment of finitude, spirit rises up fragrantly."[61] It is not difficult to imagine how Hegel's idealist rendering of the Christian kerygma might lend itself to the overtaking proffered by the advocates of atheist humanism. For if the absolute spirit is mediated through finite consciousness—if God ultimately *becomes* God in and through religion—then one might just as easily dispense with the postulate of transcendence, thereby relegating the mystery of the infinite to the realm of human consciousness. The self-consciousness of absolute spirit is thus subsumed under the self-consciousness of finite spirit, rendering the former superfluous. One sees this most explicitly in the work of Hegel's student, Feuerbach.

For Feuerbach, as was intimated above, religion is identical with self-consciousness. As such, "the consciousness of the infinite is nothing else than the consciousness of the infinity of the consciousness; or, *in the con-*

sciousness of the infinite, the conscious subject has for his object the infinity of his own nature."[62] Having therefore rid himself of that "residue of transcendence that still betrayed the Hegelian philosophy of religion,"[63] Feuerbach devotes chapter after chapter of *The Essence of Christianity* to showing the ways in which "the object and contents of the Christian religion are altogether human."[64] Feuerbach's projectionist hermeneutic is applied to an impressive array of theological illusions, from the mystery of the Resurrection to the doctrines of providence and creation. Of particular importance to Feuerbach's psychological overtaking of the Christian faith is the doctrine of the Incarnation. As a morally perfect being, Feuerbach explains, God is nothing other than the moral nature of man posited as an absolute. But consciousness of the absolutely perfect moral nature entails with it a consciousness of one's own moral ineptitude. It is therefore "a dispiriting consciousness, for it is the consciousness of our personal nothingness, and of the kind which is the most acutely felt—moral nothingness."[65] Man is placed in a state of disunion with himself, a sinner in contradiction to a just and angry God. It is thus only insofar as he is conscious of *love* as the highest truth—only insofar as he regards God as not merely a moral law but a personal, loving being—that man is ultimately delivered from this state of disunion. Love is therefore the principle of reconciliation between God and man and the essential truth behind the idea of the Incarnation. For according to Feuerbach, "love determined God to the renunciation of his divinity. Not because of his Godhead as such, according to which he is the *subject* in the proposition, God is love, but because of his love, of the *predicate*, is it that he renounced his Godhead; thus love is a higher power and truth than deity. Love conquers God. It was love to which God sacrificed his divine majesty."[66] The Christian idea of the Incarnation, therefore, is not merely subjected to Feuerbach's projectionist hermeneutic as one doctrine among others, but rather contains within itself the very justification of such an anthropological overtaking. For "as God has renounced himself out of love, so we, out of love, should renounce God; for if we do not sacrifice God to love, we sacrifice love to God."[67]

Like Feuerbach and Nietzsche, though with drastically different results, the positivist philosopher Auguste Comte (1798–1857) attempts to eliminate the idea of God "by explaining what illusion accounts for that belief and what role that belief has temporarily played."[68] In so doing, Comte makes use of his influential "law of the three states," in which every branch of knowledge necessarily passes through three successive stages: the theological or fictitious state, the metaphysical or abstract state, and the scientific or positive state. In the first two states (the theological and metaphysical), man is largely consumed with the question of *why*, searching in vain for something absolute that is the ultimate cause of everything in the world. Thus, even though the answers given may differ substantially, the questions put by man in the theological and metaphysical states are ultimately the same. In the positive state, however, man is no longer concerned with the causes of phenomena but seeks instead the laws according to which they occur.[69] The inquiry shifts from *why* to *how*, and the question concerning the Absolute becomes absolutely devoid of meaning. The positivism of Comte, therefore, insists, in a fashion similar to Immanuel Kant, that the problem of God is ultimately unsolvable. But whereas Kant sought to regain by faith that which had been denied to him by reason, Comte rules out belief in God altogether. This is not to say that Comte considered himself a "mere atheist." For according to Comte, "*Atheism represents no more than an inadequate emancipation*, since it tends to prolong the metaphysical state indefinitely by continually seeking new solutions of theoretical problems, instead of ruling out all accessible researches as inherently fruitless."[70] One must therefore transcend atheism too, relegating the very question of first or final cause to a more primitive state of human imagination.

Having rid himself of the very idea of God, Comte sought an alternative object of worship by which to fill the void. For "only what is replaced is destroyed." Humanity is thus substituted for God, and positivism comes to replace Christianity as the true religion of Humanity.[71] Whereas the overtaking waged by Feuerbach remained a principle of interpretation, a strictly psychological account of the religious phenomenon, Comtian positivism offers a more radical *dépassement*, complete with its own form of worship, dogma, and regime. Thus, Comte proffers nine "social sacraments" by which each of the successive stages of one's private life are incorporated into the public life of one's society.[72] Moreover, as in the church, the positivist religion contains its own cult of saints, with Caesar, Charlemagne, and St. Paul held in particular esteem, which composes a liturgical year.[73] There is even a positive equivalent to the Christian idea of the Trinity, by which Space, Earth, and Humanity constitute a religious triumvirate that, according to Comte, "closely links abstract reason with concrete reason."[74] Most importantly, the positivist religion contains its own clerical order, a priesthood of Humanity composed entirely of scientists. In contradistinction to that spirit of particularism and specialization that has come to reign among the various empirical sciences, the priests of positivism are driven by a "spirit of integration," in which all particular knowledge is subsumed under "one single science, namely, human or, rather, social science."[75] To these masters of synthesis, therefore, man's conduct and understanding are inexorably subjected. For "in all things it will decide what should be thought. . . . In the positive regime, in fact, there can be no more question of free thought or of freedom of conscience." The positivist doctrine is a faith, and its initiates are henceforth the "true believers" of Humanity.[76]

Without dwelling on the potentially despotic nature of Comte's positive sociocracy, there is, as de Lubac notes, something supremely artificial in his reconstruction of religion: "'It is a religion made, so to speak, on purpose'; it takes shape only by pushing 'the poetic license of worship . . . to the point of self-deception.'"[77] However, in offering Humanity to itself as an object of worship, in substituting the immanentist religion of positivism for Christianity, Comte is simply appropriating to the social sphere that same hermeneutic that Feuerbach applies so persuasively in the realm of psychology. Both thinkers are driven by a similar dialectic: religion, construed as "a vampire that feeds upon the substance of mankind,"[78] is substituted for a humanism that, in turn, feeds upon the substance of religion. Thus, according to de Lubac, the atheist humanism of such thinkers as Feuerbach and Comte is "a phenomenon parasitic on Christianity, which is grafted onto its dogma in order to empty it of its kerygmatic content. . . . It is, in other words, a gnosis that perverts the expressions of faith."[79] Having thus decried Christianity for conflating anthropology and theology, the advocates of atheist humanism, it would seem, have merely returned the favor.

Act Three: Annihilation

The third and final act of de Lubac's hermeneutical drama marks a significant shift in his engagement with atheist humanism. Having assumed, for the most part, the role of narrator in acts one and two, de Lubac's rhetoric shifts in act three to polemic, and the narrator dons a more prophetic persona. "It is not true," writes de Lubac, "that man cannot organize the world without God. What is true is that, without God, he can ultimately only organize it against man. Exclusive humanism is inhuman humanism."[80] These words, penned on Christmas 1943 while in hiding from the Gestapo, encapsulate de Lubac's commentary on the atrocities of the 1930s and 40s. For de Lubac, Europe was witnessing firsthand the "fire and slaughter" of a world organized without God and against humanity. As de Lubac notes, Nietzsche had himself predicted just such a tragic era. "Some day," wrote Nietzsche, "my name will be linked to the memory of something monstrous, of a crisis as yet unprecedented on earth, the most profound collision of consciences, a decision conjured up *against* everything hitherto believed, demanded, hallowed." Nietzsche thus saw himself as "the man of impending disaster." "For when the truth squares up to the lie of millennia, we will have upheavals, a spasm of earthquakes, a removal of mountain and valley such as have never been dreamed of . . . there will be wars such as there have never yet been on earth."[81] The gross inhumanity played out on the historical stage throughout the first half of the twentieth century was thus, according to de Lubac, the manifestation of a deeper crisis begun a century earlier. For all their differences, the various "humanisms" set forth by Feuerbach, Comte, and Nietzsche share a similar telos. The final act of the drama of atheist humanism is *the annihilation of the human person.* "If man takes himself as god," writes de Lubac, "he can, for a time, cherish the illusion that he has raised and freed himself. But it is a fleeting exaltation! In reality, he has merely abased God, and it is not long before he finds that in doing so he has abased himself."[82]

De Lubac's assessment of atheist humanism is by this point unashamedly theological. Human beings are derivative, originating in an act of divine creativity and ordered to the perfect enjoyment of their maker. The truth of human being therefore transcends itself, residing in the one in whose image we were created and after whose likeness we are continually being transformed. De Lubac insists as early as *Catholicism*: "If man, by an act of sacrilege, inverts the relationship, usurps God's attributes, and declares that God was made to man's image, all is over with him. The transcendence that he repudiates was the sole warrant of his own immanence. Only by acknowledging himself to be a reflection could he obtain completeness, and only in his act of adoration could he find his own inviolable depths."[83]

De Lubac thus subverts the Feuerbachian logic, arguing that it is not the projection of human being into infinite objectivity that denigrates the dignity of humanity, but rather the transmigration of divinity into finite subjectivity. Such claims are, of course, largely unconvincing in abstraction from a theological account of human existence. De Lubac's critique of atheist humanism everywhere presupposes an understanding of the human vocation in terms of humanity's supernatural finality. Thus, in defense of his assertion that "atheist humanism was bound to end in bankruptcy," de Lubac insists that "man is himself only because his face is illumined by a divine ray."[84] As John Webster remarks elsewhere on the content of Christian anthropology, "such claims, for all their loveliness, are culturally marginal."[85] It is difficult to imagine public consent, that is, to an argument predicated on the brightness of a divinely illumined face! For de Lubac, however, the adamant refusal to ground human being in itself is simply an ingredient within a believer's witness to the one "in whom we live and move and have our being."[86]

De Lubac's critique of *atheist* humanism must not, therefore, be misconstrued as simply a defense of *humanism* on theological grounds. As D. Stephen Long aptly notes, such a reading would invite a mere "instrumentalization of God for the preservation of humanism."[87] Were such the case, one would surely be hard-pressed in defending de Lubac from the charges of Jüngel and others concerning the "non-necessity" of God for the self-establishment of man.[88] In contradistinction to the humanist readings of his work, de Lubac cautioned against an uncritical acceptance of the humanist enterprise. In his 1950 publication *Affrontements mystiques* (Mystical confrontations), for instance, de Lubac questions the very merit of speaking of a Christian humanism. "More than one Christian contests it," notes de Lubac, "and for serious reasons: either this expression risks suggesting that Christianity would come merely to crown a humanism already constituted without it, or one is anxious to recall that the essential object of revelation is not man but God and that the Christian must seek God, not himself."[89] De Lubac thus acknowledges the potential impropriety of the expression "Christian humanism," but he is nevertheless emphatic that the Christian affirmation of God in no way necessitates the negation of humanity. On the contrary, the nobility of human beings resides precisely in their being in relation to God. It is not the affirmation of God but God's denial that eventuates in the dissolution of humanity: "Man without God is dehumanized."[90] According to de Lubac, the fruits of this dehumanization are already apparent in the various anthropologies proffered by the advocates of modern atheism. For Marx, the human being is dissolved into a larger matrix of social relations—subsumed, as it were, by the structures of a given sociopolitical arrangement.[91] For Comte, meanwhile, man has become, "like external nature, the object of positive science, submitted to the same methods of investigation."[92] Under the positive regime, moreover, individual rights are relinquished in obedience to that Great Being of temporal society, Comte's universal sociocracy.[93] Finally, in his rhapsodic pronouncements on the Eternal Return ("the unconditional and infinitely repeated circulation of all things"),[94] Nietzsche subjugates humanity once more to the ontological slavery of Fate, that blind destiny from which the Christian idea of man had long since proclaimed deliverance. In each of these thinkers, writes de Lubac, "we are confronted with what Nicholas Berdyaev . . . has rightly called 'the self-destruction of humanism.' We are proving by experience that '*where there is no God, there is no man either.*'"[95]

AN ATHEISM THAT IS NOT HUMANIST

Despite the unmistakably confessional nature of his polemic, de Lubac's critique of atheist humanism soon found an unlikely host of allies. To return to a quotation we saw above by Emmanuel Levinas, "contemporary thought holds the surprise for us of an atheism that is not humanist. The gods are dead or withdrawn from the world; concrete, even rational man does not contain the universe. In all those books that go beyond metaphysics we witness the exaltation of an obedience and a faithfulness that are not obedience or faithfulness *to* anyone."[96]

Levinas's pronouncement denotes a new form of atheism emerging particularly in France in the aftermath of World War II. Having liberated themselves from obedience to God, these new atheists sought deliverance from obedience even to the human subject. Thus, in his famous 1945 lecture "Existentialism Is a Humanism," Jean-Paul Sartre declared before a crowded audience at the Club Maintenant, "One may understand by humanism a theory which upholds man as the end-in-itself and as the supreme value. . . . That kind of humanism is absurd . . . an existentialist will never take man as the end, since man is still to be determined."[97] Sartre's lecture marks a significant point of transition between the legacy of atheist humanism and the emergence of philosophical antihumanism. Stefanos Geroulanos notes that "Existentialism Is a Humanism" is at once an accomplishment for antihumanism and, paradoxically, an attempt to maintain the moniker of humanism for Sartre's own existentialist project.[98] Of central import to Sartre's argument is what he refers to as the first principle of existentialism, namely, "man is nothing else but that which he makes of himself." Whereas, according to Sartre, all prior contributions to philosophy held to the idea that essence precedes existence—that is, man possesses an essential human nature, of which each individual serves as a particular example—Sartre declares that in the absence of God, man's existence must precede his essence. In other words, "man first of all exists, encounters himself, surges up in the world—and defines himself afterwards. If man as the existentialist sees him is not definable, it is because to begin with he is nothing. . . . Thus, *there is no human nature, because there is no God to have a conception of it.*"[99] Following in the wake of Sartre's "critique" of humanism, a litany of antihumanisms began to emerge, each dismissing the one that preceded it for its alleged failure to overcome the specter of humanism.[100] Thus, although Heidegger denounces Sartre's existentialism for its complicity in the tyranny of metaphysics,[101] Derrida faults Heidegger in turn for granting *human* beings a privileged relation to *being*.[102] Rather than narrating the unique contributions of each of these adherents of antihumanism, it is worth focusing briefly on an essay by the French writer and literary theorist Maurice Blanchot (1907–2003). Not only is Blanchot paradigmatic for a discussion of antihumanism (the above-mentioned quotation by Levinas, for example, is located in an essay devoted to the work of Blanchot), but his 1949 article "On Nietzsche's Side" was written directly in response to de Lubac's *The Drama of Atheist Humanism.*

As the title suggests, Blanchot's rejoinder to de Lubac takes the form of a defense of Nietzsche. Like de Lubac, Blanchot grants that for Nietzsche the negation of God entails the affirmation of *something.* However, for Blanchot this *something* is scarcely akin to the positive ideal of man set forth in de Lubac's reading of Nietzsche. According to Blanchot, "'God is dead' cannot live in Nietzsche as knowledge bringing an answer, but as the refusal of an answer, the negation of a salvation, the 'no' he utters to this grandiose permission to rest, to unload oneself onto an eternal truth, which is God for him. 'God is dead' is a task, and a task that has no end."[103] The radical ingenuity of Nietzsche's claim to theocide, according to Blanchot, does not reside in the bare affirmation of humanity, for such an affirmation would simply be the substitution of one absolute for another. Rather, the death of God heralds something far more courageous and unsettling: "The Death of God is less a negation aiming at the infinite than an affirmation of the infinite power to deny and to live to the end of this power."[104] The death of God is the refusal of all foundations, an act of what Geroulanos has termed "ontological revolt" whereby the individual is constituted by the very power of this negation.[105] As such, according to Blanchot, "the infinite collapse of God allows freedom to become aware of the nothing that is its foundation, without making an absolute of this nothing. . . . And the infinite ability to deny remains an ability to deny the infinite, and *escapes the temptation to place oneself outside of questioning, to turn petrified by choosing oneself as the inarguable value.*"[106] The denial of God is the denial of all certitude, the refusal to ground truth and morality even in the self or the nature of humanity. Thus, without granting de Lubac's recourse to the claims of theology, Blanchot accepts his critique of atheist attempts to supplant the transcendence of God with the "dogmatic affirmation of immanence."[107] In countering de Lubac's reading of Nietzsche, Blanchot ironically confirms his principal thesis that "where there is no God, there is no man either."

It is precisely here, in the refusal to secure an absolute in the resources of its own immanence, that the theological significance of antihumanism resides. De Lubac's pious (some might say *naïve*) prediction of the imminent collapse of atheist humanism was swiftly corroborated by some of the most influential inheritors of the antitheism of the nineteenth century. For the advocates of antihumanism, moreover, the death of man does not occur *in spite of* the negation of divinity, but rather, as de Lubac had insisted, as the very *consequence* of the death of God. The existentialism of Sartre, for example, is but one attempt at drawing the consequences of atheism right to the end. For according to Sartre, if God does not exist, "[man] cannot find anything to depend upon either within or outside himself."[108] For Blanchot, moreover, the adamant refusal to locate value within the confines of human subjectivity is indispensable to the ever-recurring task of theocide. The human subject simply cannot bear the freight of "truth" and "meaning" that humanity once attributed to its God.

It is surprising, given the proximity of the emergence of philosophical antihumanism to de Lubac's own hermeneutics of atheist humanism, that de Lubac nowhere relates the "death of man" after the Liberation to the genealogy of anti-Christian ideologies set forth in *The Drama of Atheist Humanism.* De Lubac's confrontation with contemporary atheism remained fixated after the war years on the progenitors of atheist humanism in the nineteenth century, likely on account of what he perceived to be the bourgeoning sympathy among young Roman Catholics, and the Jesuits in particular, for the philosophies of Feuerbach, Nietzsche, and especially Marx.[109] Nevertheless, de Lubac's hermeneutics of atheist humanism offers a compelling historical and "spiritual" narrative within which to delineate the theological significance of antihumanism as the inevitable consequence of the immanentist anthropology of atheist humanism. With de Lubac, albeit on wholly atheological grounds, the various proponents of philosophical antihumanism attest to the self-destruction of a humanity indignant of its divine derivation. The "death of man" is but a corollary to the "death of God."

CONCLUSION

We have begun to lay the groundwork for an exposition of de Lubac's hermeneutics of human existence by way of an analysis of his confrontation with atheist humanism. That is, we have sought to locate the context (both sociopolitical and ideological) within which, according to de Lubac, a theological hermeneutics of human existence derives its contemporary exigency. As we have seen, de Lubac insists on the volatility of strictly immanentist construals of human being. Any account of human existence or the ordering of human society built on the absolute rejection of transcendence is destined to end in failure. As will become apparent in the chapters that follow, this critique of secular immanentism is predicated on a particular theological anthropology and a particular theology of history according to which human beings—and the movement of history itself—attain their finality only under the condition of "a wholly different principle." For de Lubac, a true humanism (should we maintain the moniker) is a *converted humanism*—human beings must inevitably lose themselves so to be found in that humanity reconstituted in the person of Jesus Christ.[110]

TWO

The Desire of Nature

INTRODUCTION

In those often clandestine lectures delivered during the Occupation, de Lubac devoted himself not only to confronting what he believed to be the anti-Christian ideology funding Nazi neopaganism, but also to evaluating the "internal causes" of the present spiritual malaise. De Lubac was convinced that the church—and the church's present mode of theologizing in particular—bore significant responsibility for the contemporary crisis. In a lecture delivered to the École des cadres d'Uriage in 1941, de Lubac spoke of a twofold failure among Christians at the root of the modern transvaluation of European values.[1] For many, the faith had become merely habitual, a means to civic order in accord with Napoleon's purely utilitarian maxim: "A religion is necessary for the people." De Lubac thus implicates the faith of a whole faction of the "ruling" class for whom religion served a primarily conservative social agenda. De Lubac clearly had a number of Pétain's supporters in mind. On the other hand, for many a sincere believer, faith had become a strictly private affair. The religious life was reduced to "a kind of disincarnated mysticism, leaving the 'century' to its path to perdition. Justice and charity were understood only as purely individual obligations. The profound meaning of the church, which is fraternal community, was lost."[2] This privatization of the Christian faith, coinciding with the rise of political Machiavellianism and economic liberalism, effectively evacuated public discourse of any reasoned Christian account of the common good. The project of cultural construction was thus relegated to largely atheological—or explicitly anti-Christian—influences.

In a 1942 lecture to a gathering of Chantiers de Jeunesse chaplains,[3] de Lubac aimed his critiques more directly at the teaching office of the church, addressing the culpability of priests and theologians for the "disappearance of the sense of the sacred" in modern France. According to de Lubac, there are at least four internal causes for this "frightful lack of the sacred." First, there is a notable disproportion between the Christian's secular knowledge and his or her religious instruction. The former is that of an adult, the latter "has remained that of a child."[4] According to de Lubac, this disproportion, which has led many to abandon the faith altogether, results in large part from a lack of clarity and intellectual rigor on the part of priests and theologians. Second, "a polemical concern has outpaced the concern to build a complete and truly positive doctrine."[5] Not only has this concern for polemics led to a superficial understanding of the content of Christian belief, but it tends to cede too much territory to the church's opponents, bending the emphases and proportions of doctrine under the weight of largely external concerns. Third, de Lubac insists that the general appearance of contemporary theology and the church's preaching is often too abstract, too *rationalist*.[6] Theology all too often proceeds in the manner of an esoteric science, similar to other sciences with the sole exception that theology's first principles are derived from revelation rather than from reason or experience. The self-revelation of God is thus reduced to a set of propositions from which the theologian works to deduce and to convey a host of timeless theological concepts and conclusions. De Lubac's target here is the "manualist theology" that was being taught in most Roman Catholic seminaries in the first half of the twentieth century.[7] Fourth, and most significantly for our investigation of de Lubac's hermeneutics of human existence, de Lubac argues that the disappearance of the sense of the sacred was caused in large part by a particular construal of the relation between nature and the supernatural in a great deal of modern Roman Catholic theology. In an effort to avoid confusing the orders of nature and the supernatural, the former was granted a level of autonomy heretofore unrealized in the history of Christian thought, while the latter was relegated to "some distant corner" where, according to de Lubac, "it could only remain sterile." There was, therefore, "an unconscious conspiracy between the movement that led to laicism and a certain theology."[8] Theology concerned itself strictly with the supernatural truths of revelation, those truths available to faith and only extrinsically related to the order of nature. Secularism meanwhile took root and developed within an order wholly sufficient unto itself in isolation from the claims of the supernatural. The lines of demarcation were thus drawn and agreed upon by both parties, theology supplying the metaphysical warrant as it were for its own marginalization. As we will see in what follows, de Lubac insists that a confrontation with atheistic secularism thus entails a return to an earlier theological rendering of the relation between nature and the supernatural, one that takes seriously humanity's ontological ordination to the supernatural. Crucial to such a "traditional" account of nature and the supernatural is the affirmation of what de Lubac famously refers to as *a natural desire for the supernatural.* It was this particular theological vision that de Lubac sought to rehabilitate in his *Surnaturel*, that epochal text that was completed during the Occupation while de Lubac was hidden away from the Gestapo in Vals and that would come to introduce de Lubac to a wholly different kind of "warfare" throughout the late 1940s and 1950s.

WE SAW IN CHAPTER 1 THAT A PARTICULAR CONSTRUAL OF humanity's relatedness to God is essential to de Lubac's thesis regarding "the self-destruction of atheist humanism." Immanence receives its dignity, indeed its very intelligibility, only in its relation to transcendence. The significance of this relatedness is pervasive throughout de Lubac's confrontation with atheist humanism, but the precise nature and scope of this relation remain to be seen. The burden of this chapter is to begin to uncover the existential implications of humanity's ontological ordination to God by focusing in particular on de Lubac's controversial, and often misunderstood, thesis concerning humanity's natural desire for the supernatural. An investigation of this desire takes us to the very heart of de Lubac's hermeneutics of human existence. De Lubac argues on a number of occasions that "the infinite seriousness of this desire placed in me by my Creator constitutes the infinite seriousness of the drama of human existence."[9]

In engaging de Lubac's treatment of the *desiderium naturae* and the relation between nature and the supernatural more generally, we are of course venturing into well-trodden and highly contentious territory. De Lubac's writings on the supernatural span six decades, consisting of four monographs and numerous articles.[10] His work on the subject served as something of a fault line among mid-twentieth-century Roman Catholic theologians, dividing certain inheritors of the neo-Scholastic tradition from those theologians loosely (and pejoratively) associated under the epithet of the *nouvelle théologie.* Moreover, as we noted in the introduction, de Lubac's thesis has become once more the subject of serious debate. As with the controversies of the 1940s and 50s, the renewed controversy surrounding de Lubac's work on nature and the supernatural constitutes more (though certainly not less) than an exegetical dispute surrounding the proper interpretation of Thomas Aquinas. What is ultimately at stake in these debates is the very gratuity of the supernatural and the integrity of created nature.

It is beyond the scope of this chapter to provide an exhaustive account of these controversies. Nor is it my primary intent to defend de Lubac's reading of Aquinas from contemporary critics of his work. As we noted in the introduction, the exegetical disputes concerning Aquinas's construal of the natural desire for God stem in large part from an inherent tension within the writings of Aquinas themselves. That is, Thomas presents us with two seemingly contradictory series of texts. In the first series, Thomas argues that human beings are ordered to a single, supernatural finality (the beatific vision) and that, by virtue of this unique teleology, humans enjoy a natural desire for the vision of the divine essence. In the second series of texts, however, Thomas insists on a *twofold* happiness for humanity: one that is strictly proportionate to human nature, and another that surpasses human nature and is only ever attainable by grace. According to the latter series of texts, it would appear that humanity's ordination to the supernatural is strictly consequent upon the prior reception of grace and the theological virtues.[11]

The primary aim of this chapter is to locate de Lubac's own treatment of nature and the supernatural within the broader logic of his theology of human existence, looking especially at the ontological status of humanity's desire for the supernatural. In so doing, I hope to demarcate the theological significance of de Lubac's "paradoxical" account of human nature from both the *extrinsicism* of his neo-Scholastic opponents and the *intrinsicism* of recent interpretations of his work. A more thoroughgoing exposition of these two terms will emerge over the course of the discussion that follows, but we might provisionally describe the extrinsicist position as a defense of the gratuity of the supernatural by means of *a purely immanent account of human finality* and the intrinsicist position as a defense of the intrinsic relation between nature and the supernatural by way of *an account of human existence as always already suffused with grace.* Whereas the former was the chief recipient of de Lubac's polemic throughout his writings on nature and the supernatural, the latter has emerged in recent years as a leading interpretation of de Lubac's own theological project. Thus, rather than considering the natural desire for the supernatural as *a longing born of lack*, contemporary exponents of de Lubac's theology insist that the desire for grace is already "the work, in advance of itself, of grace which unites human creatures to the Creator."[12] We noted in the introduction that this particular reading has been developed most persuasively by John Milbank and is all but assumed by a host of contemporary treatments of de Lubac's work. Moreover, in the case of Milbank, this line of interpretation is reinforced by a larger "corruption narrative" according to which de Lubac, under the strain of hierarchical opposition, was forced to betray the original *Surnaturel* thesis in his subsequent treatments of the supernatural. This allows Milbank to denigrate the significance of those passages in the later writings that would appear to contradict his own reading of the earlier "uncorrupted" de Lubac. In an attempt to untangle de Lubac's own account of nature and the supernatural from the intrinsicism of Milbank and others, we must therefore demonstrate the relevant continuity between de Lubac's early and later treatments of the natural desire for the supernatural.

THE PROBLEM OF EXTRINSICISM

The "system of pure nature" to which de Lubac devotes his decades-long critique is less an isolated doctrine than a series of interrelated principles and theological convictions intended to safeguard the gratuity of the supernatural while also protecting the integrity of created nature. At the heart of this system lie both an affirmation and a negation. Negatively, the theory of pure nature denies the existence of a natural desire for the vision of God considered as an innate, unconditional appetite of human nature (not only a *desiderium naturale*, but a *desiderium naturae*).[13] Positively, the theory of pure nature refers to "the hypothesis of a possible universe in which nature would supposedly have known its complete development and its 'proportioned' end without ever [being] raised above itself."[14] Taken together, this system posits a twofold finality for human being, a purely *natural beatitude* corresponding to the natural desire of human beings and their connatural end and a *supernatural beatitude* surpassing the capacities of human nature and the limitations of natural desire. According to the advocates of pure nature, both ends reside strictly in the contemplation of God. However, whereas one's natural beatitude consists in the contemplation of God *according to his or her natural powers*, supernatural beatitude is possible *only by the light of glory* in the beatific vision. Thus, whereas the former is to a certain extent "owed" to human beings as a matter of right, insofar as it lies within the powers of human nature to attain, the latter is strictly gratuitous, exceeding the proportionality of created nature and only ever received in the form of a divine gift. The logic governing this twofold rendering of human finality is rather straightforward. According to the advocates of pure nature, "an end, without which a nature is inconceivable, cannot be an end which surpasses this nature; such an end is natural to it. It is the end which is due to it, and which God owes to Himself to give to it."[15] In order to protect the gratuity of the supernatural, therefore, one must insist that human nature entails a purely immanent teleology. Otherwise, the supernatural would be the logical (and hence necessary) complement of created nature.

De Lubac's misgivings about this theory began as early as his student days, first at St. Mary's College, Canterbury (1920), then while undertaking his philosophical training on Jersey (1920–23), and finally as a student of theology at Ore Place, Hastings (1924–26) and Fourvière (1926–28). During a semester studying the humanities at St. Mary's College, de Lubac encountered Pierre Rousselot's *L'Intellectualisme de saint Thomas*, where he discovered an alternative to neo-Scholastic readings of Aquinas, one that prioritized the intellect's need and *innate desire* for "that supernatural complement that takes place in the Beatific Vision."[16] This rendering of the dynamism of reason was soon reinforced by his reading of Blondel while under the tutelage of Auguste Valensin in Jersey (of which more shall be said shortly).[17] In Jersey, de Lubac also began studying Plotinus and Augustine on the desire for God. In notes taken during that time, de Lubac remarks: "The supernatural extends nature, raises it, [and] transforms it. . . . The mystery is in this continuity, which is at the same time a transformation in this survival [*survivance*] of divinized nature."[18] Finally, during his days as a student of philosophy at Ore Place, de Lubac was a member of La Pensée, a free "academy" within the scholasticate that met each Sunday under the patronage of Joseph Huby to debate a subject chosen by one of its members. As de Lubac recounts in his memoir, Father Huby encouraged the members to verify whether the doctrine of Thomas Aquinas on the subject of the supernatural "was indeed what was claimed by the Thomist school around the sixteenth century, codified in the seventeenth and asserted with greater emphasis than ever in the twentieth."[19] At Huby's behest, de Lubac thus embarked upon a course of study that would place him at odds with the regnant neo-Scholasticism of the manualist tradition. The subject of these investigations was, by de Lubac's account, central to the work of such contemporary "masters" as Maurice Blondel, Joseph Maréchal, and Pierre Rousselot, and also to the thought of Augustine, Bonaventure, and—as de Lubac would repeatedly argue—Thomas Aquinas. De Lubac likewise noted that the question surrounding the relation between nature and the supernatural was foundational to discussions with modern atheism and that "it formed the crux of the problem of Christian humanism."[20] Already during his student years, therefore, de Lubac was convinced of the theory's theological and historical shortcomings as well as its inability to respond adequately to the challenges presented to the faith by contemporary atheism.

The Secular and the Supernatural

According to de Lubac, there was an "unconscious conspiracy" between the rise of secularism and the theory of pure nature. Without offering anything as ambitious as the genealogies of modernity fashionable today, de Lubac is nevertheless adamant that extrinsicist accounts of the supernatural emerging especially in the sixteenth and seventeenth centuries helped pave the way for (and subsequently reify) the secular immanentism of the nineteenth and twentieth centuries. According to de Lubac, the advocates of pure nature advance a "dualistic" construal of the relation between nature and the supernatural. Nature and the supernatural constitute something like two self-contained orders, "the second being superadded in fact to the first, without any inner connection between the two other than there existing, in our nature, a vague and general 'obediential potency' for being so to speak 'elevated.'"[21] This "two-tier" approach to the problem of the supernatural results in the inevitable isolation of the supernatural from the everyday lived existence of human beings. De Lubac argues in his 1966 lecture "Nature and Grace":

> The supernatural gift henceforth appeared as a superimposed reality, as an artificial and arbitrary superstructure. The unbeliever found it easy to withdraw into his indifference in the very name of what theology was telling him: if my very nature as a man truly has its end in itself, what should oblige or even arouse me to scrutinize history in the quest for some other vocation perhaps to be found there? Why should I listen to a Church which bears a message having no relation to the aspirations of my nature? Should not the intrusion of some outside supernatural even be rejected as a kind of violence?[22]

De Lubac is certainly not alone in locating the bifurcation of nature and the supernatural at the origins of secular modernity. Charles Taylor has advanced a similar argument in his massive and massively influential intellectual history of secularity. Like de Lubac, Taylor delineates an "exclusive humanism" as the identifying marker of modern secularism.[23] Moreover, according to Taylor, the great invention of the West *behind* this self-sufficient humanism "was that of an immanent order of Nature, whose workings could be systematically understood and explained on its own terms. . . . This notion of the 'immanent' involved denying—or at least isolating and problematizing—any form of interpenetration between the things of Nature, on one hand, and 'the supernatural' on the other."[24] De Lubac's insistence on secularism's indebtedness to immanentist accounts of nature is thus largely uncontested, but it is not self-evident that modernity's "self-sufficient humanism" is primarily (or even remotely) the result of developments in late Scholastic Thomism. At the very least, de Lubac's argument is historically underdetermined. Be that as it may, de Lubac's principal concern in diagnosing a complicity between pure nature and secularism is not genetic but apologetic. That is, de Lubac is convinced that a commitment to the theory of pure nature hinders the church's ability to confront the hegemony of contemporary atheism. This is, of course, not a *sufficient* reason for rejecting the theory. As we will see, de Lubac's own refutation of pure nature goes well beyond its hindrance to fundamental theology. Nevertheless, it is not difficult to imagine how theological appeals to a purely natural teleology lend themselves all too easily to the immanentist (and ultimately nihilist) space carved out by secular humanism. As Jean-Yves Lacoste notes, accounts of pure nature run the risk of encouraging philosophy to adopt an eschatology of its own within the limits of being-in-the-world—that is, under the shadow of the "omnipresent certainty of death." Thus, "however pious the fairies that watched over its cradle, the idea of pure nature was in fact bound to deprive man of hope, leaving him unarmed before the disturbing reality of nihilism."[25]

A Recent Invention

In addition to hindering the church's ability to effectively confront the "exclusive humanism" of secular modernity, de Lubac is convinced that the theory of pure nature undermines the church's traditional rendering of the relation between nature and the supernatural. De Lubac's preoccupation with the task of *historical* theology throughout his career was motivated by a devotion to what he perceives to be the organic unity of the church's tradition. Without denying the great diversity of theological trajectories or the necessarily historical/contextual nature of all theology,[26] de Lubac nevertheless discerns an impressive uniformity in the church's polyphonic witness throughout history. Reflecting in 1975 on the "unity" of his own theological project, de Lubac writes: "Without claiming to open up new avenues of thought, I have sought rather . . . to make known some of the great common areas of Catholic tradition. I wanted to make it loved, to show its ever-present fruitfulness."[27] This enterprise is evident as early as *Catholicism*, where de Lubac endeavors "to bring to light certain permanent features . . . among the very diverse and sometimes contrary trends of Tradition."[28] It is apparent also in de Lubac's voluminous contribution to the history of premodern exegesis, where he canvasses a staggering array of theological voices in relative harmony on the "spiritual interpretation" of scripture.[29] It is this same concern for the common testimony of the church's tradition that informs his writings on the supernatural. For according to de Lubac, the theory of pure nature is ultimately at variance with the "unanimous Tradition" with respect to the doctrine of humanity's supernatural vocation, a tradition shared by thinkers as diverse as Irenaeus, Bonaventure, Duns Scotus, and Thomas Aquinas and summed up in the famous exclamation of Augustine: "Lord, you have made us for yourself, and our heart is restless until it rests in you."[30]

Without devoting too much attention to the historical argument developed in *Surnaturel* and built upon in the "twins" of 1965 (*Augustinianism and Modern Theology* and *The Mystery of the Supernatural*),[31] we might summarize de Lubac's findings as follows. Whereas contemporary advocates of pure nature trace their theological lineage to the writings of Thomas Aquinas, de Lubac is at pains to show that the theory actually emerged in the sixteenth century as the result of a conglomerate of ecclesial controversies and theological trends.[32] In particular, de Lubac notes three crucial factors at the origin of pure nature. First, pure nature was one of those abstract hypotheses resulting from medieval speculation on the *potentia Dei absoluta* (the absolute power of God).[33] Put simply, it was asserted that God *could have* created human beings without necessarily ordering them to a supernatural end. That God has not, in fact, determined to do so is quite beyond the point. The intent was simply to show that such a divine decree would not have been intrinsically impossible. Second, the theory of limbo led by way of analogy to the hypothesis of an intermediate state in which human beings, deprived of the beatific vision, would still be capable of enjoying a purely natural beatitude.[34] Serge-Thomas Bonino notes, "The paradox of limbo is that it is a definitive state where on the one hand the human person is deprived of his supernatural last end, which is the beatific vision of the divine essence, but where on the other hand he does not suffer from this."[35] Having thus granted the possibility of a state in which those infants that die unbaptized might fail to attain their supernatural end *without* thereby suffering the punishment of the damned, it became no less difficult to envisage a case in which "the first man could have died before receiving the infusion of sanctifying grace, and consequently before having to make the moral choice, which was original sin."[36] As with the appeal to God's absolute power, this construal of a purely natural human being remained strictly hypothetical. For as St. Thomas argues, there never was a time when human beings existed *prior* to the gift of sanctifying grace.[37] And just as Adam was not created in a state of *natura pura*, so the loss of original justice did not result in his return to a purely natural state, but in the *corruption* of his very nature.[38]

The third and final factor at the origin of the system of pure nature was, according to de Lubac, the most determinative: "The idea of 'pure nature' was virtually part of the speculations of the Humanists who in the fifteenth century developed the idea of a natural religion."[39] That is to say, whereas St. Thomas maintained that the ancient philosophers were incapable of discerning the true end of humanity,[40] certain theologians in the fifteenth century began to think of that end envisaged by the philosophers as in fact the *natural* end of human beings. According to de Lubac, this idea was first introduced into medieval theology under the auspices of Denys the Carthusian (1402–71). Greatly indebted to the Neoplatonist authors that he encountered in the library of Nicholas of Cusa (particularly Avicenna), Denys located human beings within a hierarchical universe in which every intelligence has as its last end the contemplation of the intelligence directly above it. Man's natural end is thus relegated to the contemplation of the lowest of the angelic natures, *as is his natural desire.* This correlation of man's end with his innate desire was axiomatic for Denys.[41] However, Denys was fully aware that this placed him in *contradiction* with the writings of St. Thomas. For according to Denys, "Saint

Thomas strives to prove in many ways . . . that the natural desire of no created mind can rest or be contented, except by the divine substance specifically, as if it is known."[42]

How then did the system of pure nature, developed initially in *opposition* to the writings of Aquinas, come to be so firmly entrenched in the Thomist commentarial tradition? The progenitor of this theological revolution was, according to de Lubac, the Dominican cardinal Thomas Cajetan (1469–1534). Without adopting the Neoplatonism of the Carthusian, Cajetan nevertheless maintained that human beings can have a natural desire only for an end connatural to them. However, whereas Denys developed this claim as a direct *refutation* of the teaching of St. Thomas, Cajetan put forward his thesis as an *explanation* of the writings of the Angelic Doctor.[43] This he accomplished through a rather ingenious interpretation of one of Thomas's most paradigmatic texts on the natural desire to see God: *ST* Ia, q. 12, a. 1. In this article, Thomas considers whether any created intellect can see the essence of God. He answers in the affirmative, supporting the claim that "the blessed see the essence of God" with two arguments: the first advanced on theological (and largely Neoplatonic) grounds;[44] the second based on the existence of a natural desire in human beings. According to the latter argument, every human being has a natural desire to know the cause of every encountered effect. Insofar as this desire is only ever satiated in the knowledge of the first cause, and insofar as the first efficient cause is God,[45] one must therefore conclude that there is in every human being *a natural desire to know/see the essence of God.* How does Cajetan presume to avoid this conclusion?

According to Cajetan, it is only *as a theologian* that Thomas is able to speak of humanity's natural desire to see God, thereby presupposing the effects of God's prior self-revelation. Cajetan notes that there are two ways that a rational creature can be considered: (1) simply speaking, or (2) as already ordered to beatitude. Thus, according to Cajetan,

> If he [the rational creature] is considered in the former manner, then his natural desire does not extend beyond the power of his nature. . . . However, if he is considered in the second way, then he does naturally

> desire the vision of God. The reason for this is that he knows certain effects, such as grace and glory, whose cause is God, as God is in Himself absolutely, and not just as universal cause. Once these effects are known, it is natural for any intellectual creature to desire knowledge of the cause.[46]

With this qualification in place, Cajetan is able to deny a natural desire for the vision of God *without* thereby denouncing the authority of St. Thomas. For Cajetan, the desire for the vision of God's essence is strictly consequent upon God's prior self-revelation. Without the aid of grace and glory, therefore, human beings can at most desire a *natural* knowledge of God, a strictly philosophical contemplation of God *as first cause*, corresponding to the natural capacities of human nature. Only those who, like St. Thomas, know *by faith* that human beings are ordered to the beatific vision can "naturally" desire a "supernatural" end.

Two Errors of Imagination

Having thus argued for a certain relationship between extrinsicist accounts of the supernatural and the immanentism of secular modernity, and having demonstrated the relative novelty of the theory of pure nature (thereby undermining neo-Scholastic appeals to catholicity and the authority of Thomas Aquinas), de Lubac finally presents his own understanding of the relation between nature and the supernatural as a necessary corrective to what he perceives to be the properly *theological* and *anthropological* deficiencies of appeals to pure nature. According to de Lubac, "the intelligence must free itself of two errors of imagination: thinking of God in the same way as man, and thinking of man in the same way as a 'natural being.' "[47] By de Lubac's estimation, the latter error of imagination is the result of an overextension of Aristotelian metaphysics, while the former is an unfortunate by-product of the logic of "giftedness" as appropriated uncritically in a theology of the supernatural.

The first error of imagination (thinking of God in the same way as man) has to do with a particular account of the gratuity of the supernatural. A gift, the argument runs, cannot be a gift if it cannot be denied. If therefore we are to maintain that grace is gratuitously bestowed to human beings strictly by virtue of the divine generosity, we must likewise insist that God could have created human beings without leading them to himself as their supernatural end. Otherwise, God would either be compelled by the very constitution of our nature to lend us his grace or altogether responsible for the frustration of our nature. To a certain extent, de Lubac readily acknowledges that we cannot exempt ourselves from such patterns of thinking. An appeal to the logic of giftedness is necessary insofar as it expresses "the radical distance that exists between my natural being and my supernatural end, in other words, between my condition as creature and divine filiation."[48] If the language of gift is necessary, however, it is also insufficient. For as with any analogy between created and uncreated being, we must bear in mind the infinite disproportion between the supernatural gift of God's own self and the gift that one human being makes to another.

In an attempt to underscore the superficiality of this analogy, de Lubac appeals to a similar analogy: that of the primordial "gift" that God makes to us in granting us being. For according to de Lubac, there is "a genuine parallelism between that first gift of creation and the second, wholly distinct, wholly supereminent gift—the ontological call to deification which will make of man, if he responds to it, a 'new creature.' "[49] In turning our attention to the gift of creation, de Lubac seeks to convey an unavoidable disruption in the language of giftedness as applied to any sort of "exchange" between the Creator and the created recipients of being. For in speaking of the gift that God makes to me in giving me being, I must necessarily conceive of myself as somehow preceding the event of my creation. There must be an "I," in other words, whose being precedes my existence in such a way as to be identified as the recipient of this gratuitous benefit. Taken univocally, therefore, the language of creation as a gift breaks down. The burden of de Lubac's argument is to show that the same logic applies *mutatis mutandis* in our consideration of human finality. For just as I did not precede my being, so my being did not precede its supernatural finality. Thus, according to de Lubac, "from the time I say 'I' exist, I have my being; and from the time I exist, from the time I have my being, I am finalized. It is impossible actually to dissociate these three elements in order to divide them into three times between which one would have to conceive of a twofold hiatus."[50]

To presume that the gratuity of the supernatural is strictly dependent on the possibility (whether actual or merely hypothetical) of a purely immanent teleology is therefore, according to de Lubac, to misunderstand the sheer contingency of created being and, correlatively, the absolute freedom of God in relation to God's creatures. For just as God could never have been constrained by anything to give me being, "neither could he be constrained by anything to imprint in my being a supernatural finality."[51] To insist otherwise, or to posit man as an absolute over and against God, is to collapse the radical distinction between created and uncreated being, thereby reducing the first cause to the realm of natural agency.[52] For, as Thomas Aquinas argues, whereas "the action of a natural agent does not produce being absolutely, but determines pre-existing being to this or that," God produces "the whole subsistent being, without anything pre-existing, since he is the principle of all being."[53] God does not therefore act externally or competitively with human beings, granting them a supernatural finality *from without*, as it were. Rather, as John Webster succinctly states, "in establishing another thing in being, God bestows finality, a tendency or active bent and movement towards the completion of that thing's nature."[54] The gift of a supernatural finality, though logically distinct from the gift of created human existence, is nevertheless included within the latter.

Whereas the first error of imagination was thus an unintended consequence of an otherwise noble concern for the gratuity of the supernatural, the second error (thinking of man in the same way as a "natural being") was more foundational to neo-Scholastic accounts of human nature, functioning as a metaphysical a priori for any and all theological treatments of the relation between nature and the supernatural. According to de Lubac, this makes the second error of imagination all the more pernicious. Common to the Neoplatonism of Denys the Carthusian and the neo-Thomism(s) of such thinkers as Cajetan and Suárez was the general assumption that "all being must have its connatural end, proportioned to its nature and of the same order as it."[55] This unassailable principle, applied uncritically by the advocates of pure nature to the ontological status of human being, owes its inspiration, not to any particular strand of Christian anthropology, but to the general cosmology of Aristotle. For it was Aristotle's conviction that, "if nature had given the heavens an inclination toward progressive motion, it would also have given the means for that motion."[56] As with every other creature, therefore, human beings have (1) an end within the limits of their nature, (2) an absolute desire for this connatural end, and (3) an innate capacity for satiating the desire of their nature and attaining their final end. It is hardly surprising, therefore, that the advocates of pure nature would reject as contradictory a finality "natural with respect to appetite, [but] supernatural with respect to attainment."[57] For as Suárez argues, "All other natures are able to pursue their natural ends by means suitable to their nature: why then is human nature of a worse condition in this?"[58]

De Lubac readily concedes that, given such an a priori commitment to an Aristotelian account of nature, it is indeed absurd to imagine a natural being with a supernatural finality. However, it is precisely the premise that human being *ought* to be so subsumed under a univocal account of created nature that de Lubac refuses to grant. According to de Lubac, the laws that obtain within the cosmos to natural beings cannot be applied without serious qualification to human nature, for it is precisely "the property of this spiritual creature not to have its destiny circumscribed within the cosmos."[59] In mitigating the radical difference that pertains between human being and natural beings (between *this* particular nature and nature *as such*), the advocates of pure nature thus betray the unique ontological status of spiritual being. In so doing, these thinkers set themselves in contradiction to an overwhelming consensus in patristic and medieval anthropology, a consensus neatly summarized in the words of St. Thomas: "The rational creature in this surpasses all creation, because he has the capacity for the highest good through divine vision and enjoyment, although for this he needs the divine help of grace."[60] This admittedly paradoxical condition—whereby human beings are created for an end that infinitely surpasses their nature—is not, as Suárez would have us think, a deficiency of human being in relation to all other created natures. It is rather this paradox that constitutes precisely the dignity of human being. To return to an earlier quotation from St. Thomas: "The nature that can attain perfect good, although it needs help from without in order to attain it, is of more noble condition than a nature which cannot attain perfect good, but attains some imperfect good, although it need no help from without in order to attain it."[61] It is this "noble condition" that de Lubac seeks to explicate in his positive consideration of the drama of human existence.

THE PARADOX OF HUMAN NATURE

Being and Finality

In the previous section we noted de Lubac's dismissal of neo-Scholastic attempts to circumscribe human being within a univocal account of created nature. Conceding too much ground to the principles of Aristotelian cosmology, the advocates of pure nature insist that *all* natural beings are ordered to an end within the capacities of their nature to attain. For de Lubac, however, the laws that obtain within the cosmos cannot be applied univocally to the nature of human beings without serious ontological violence. For "it is the property of this spiritual creature not to have its destiny circumscribed within the cosmos. The spiritual creature has a direct relation to God that comes to it from its origin."[62] We will return shortly (and again in subsequent chapters) to discuss de Lubac's understanding of the nature of created *spirit*. For now, it is worth unpacking his insistence on the essential relation between *protology* and *teleology*. De Lubac is of course under no illusion that human beings are somehow unique in their ontological derivation from God. He takes it as a given that "God's first effect in things is existence itself. . . . And everything that exists in any way is necessarily from God."[63] In what sense then is humanity's "direct relation to God" consequent upon its divine origin?

For de Lubac (as indeed for most theologians throughout the church's history), human beings transcend the beings of nature, not by virtue of their mere status as creatures, but by virtue of their creation *according to the image of God.* De Lubac insists at a number of points that human beings have "certain prerogatives that, making them in the image of God, make them at the same stroke higher than any order of the cosmos."[64] The precise nature of these prerogatives, however, remains conspicuously undeveloped. On occasion, de Lubac treats them as faculties or creaturely capacities, such as "reason, freedom, immortality and dominion by right over nature." But de Lubac makes little effort to qualify or elaborate on these capacities, moving swiftly instead to a consideration of the image's relation to human *finality*. According to de Lubac, "man, created in the image of God, . . . was made in view of his resemblance to God, who is the perfection of this image, which is to say, that he was destined to live eternally in God, to enter into the inner movement of the trinitarian Life and to bring all creation along with him."[65] For de Lubac, the image of God in humanity betokens less a creaturely analogue to the Creator than an innate vocation to supernatural fellowship with God. Following a host of patristic authors,[66] de Lubac thus interprets the Genesis passages concerning the *imago Dei* in the light of the Johannine assurance that, though we do not yet know what we will be, we know that when the Lord appears, "we will be *like* him [ὅμοιοι αὐτῷ], for we will see him as he is."[67] The image of God in humanity finds its ultimate telos in the eschatological vision of God. Humanity's creation is for the purpose of deification—the elevation and transformation of human nature by the indwelling of the Spirit and in union with Christ.

Returning then to de Lubac's critique of the theory of pure nature, it is clear that for de Lubac the crux of the disagreement centers on one's construal of the relation between being and finality. For without denying that God has determined to elevate human beings to the beatific vision, the advocates of pure nature remain unconvinced that such a divine determination entails a corresponding alteration in a nature otherwise ordered to a strictly connatural end. We have already seen that the proponents of pure nature are convinced that an end without which a nature is inconceivable cannot be gratuitous. In order for the vision of God to remain unexacted, human nature must be intelligible in terms applicable to every other created nature. We may know by faith, therefore, that God has ordained for human beings a supernatural end, but a purely natural (that is, philosophical) investigation of human nature reveals a purely natural end. For de Lubac, however, this line of reasoning is problematic in at least two respects. First, it assumes a wholly extrinsic relation between human being and finality. That is to say, for the advocates of pure nature, finality is treated, not as "a destiny inscribed in the very structure of the being and which, ontologically, he cannot avoid," but rather as "a destination received more or less from outside and after the fact."[68] Humanity's supernatural end is therefore "superadded" to an already immanently self-sufficient nature. For de Lubac, meanwhile, finality is something ontological, something intrinsic to the creature that cannot be altered without altering in turn the very nature of that being itself. To insist therefore that human beings alone (at least among corporeal beings) are ordered to a supernatural end is to insist likewise on a radical disproportionality between human being and the beings of nature, one that can only be accounted for under a properly analogical construal of created nature.

Second, given his commitment to the intrinsic relation between being and finality, de Lubac's confidence in the exercise of "pure reason" to arrive at an immanently comprehensive understanding of human being is far more chastened than that of his neo-Scholastic interlocutors. For if, as de Lubac insists, finality affects the depths of one's being, and if the destiny of human being infinitely surpasses the capacities of human nature, then a purely natural/philosophical investigation of human nature will terminate, not at the discovery of a purely natural telos, but at that ontological enigma that constitutes the human condition (what Ricoeur refers to as the "irreducible opacity" of human being[69]). The paradox of human nature is such that the splendor of our end entails the *insufficiency* of our nature. "One of our differences from other creatures," notes de Lubac, quoting the seventeenth-century mystic Pierre Bérulle, "is that they were created perfect in their state and without the expectation of a further new degree which they lack; but man's nature was not created to remain in the limitations of nature; it was made for grace, and destined for a state raised above its power."[70] Because human nature was created with the expectation of a "new degree which it lacks," a purely natural/philosophical investigation of human existence results in the discovery of an inexplicable deficiency in its object of inquiry. In applying itself to the question of human finality, therefore, a philosophy attentive to the insufficiency of human being can only arrive at the supposition of a principle at once *necessary* and *inaccessible* for the attainment of human perfection.

The Influence of Maurice Blondel

This latter conviction, concerning the nature and scope of a strictly rational investigation of human existence, demonstrates the profound influence of the Catholic lay philosopher Maurice Blondel (1861–1949) on de Lubac's thinking.[71] According to de Lubac, it was Blondel who provided the main impulse for Latin theology's return to a more authentic understanding of the relation between nature and the supernatural. It was Blondel who "launched the decisive attack on the dualist theory which was destroying Christian thought," and it was largely because of his influence that "we have consciously ceased to conceive of the natural and the supernatural orders as though they were two superposed storeys without any inner connections."[72] In his widely celebrated (and fiercely contested) thesis, *L'Action* (1893), Blondel comes to the problem of the supernatural by way of a rigorously developed phenomenology of human action. After demonstrating the insufficiency of the "natural order" to satisfy the spontaneous movement of the will, Blondel attempts to show that "in every human consciousness, inevitably there arises the sense that the will is not its principle, nor its rule, nor its own end."[73] There resides in each of us an inexplicable and disconcerting disproportion between what we *believe* we will (what Blondel terms *la volonté voulue*) and what we *actually* will (*la volonté voulante*). Blondel's phenomenology thus leads him to unavoidable aporia: "Not only do we have to undergo what we do not will; in addition, we do not truly will what we will. . . . What [the will] lacks is the thought of willing and doing what it willed to do and think."[74] Faced with both the insufficiency of every object offered to the will and the contradiction implicit in the human condition, human consciousness thus arrives at the idea of a "unique necessary" (*l'unique nécessaire*). That is, in the recognition of the deficiency of our own action, we become aware of a *something* to which our will and our actions fall short. Conversely, it is the idea of this something that makes possible the very consciousness of this disproportion. In order for human beings to overcome their infirmity, in order for "the will to will itself freely" without contradiction, human beings must therefore avail themselves of that which ultimately escapes their grasp. Confronted with the insufficiency of the natural order, human beings must have recourse to the *supernatural.* As Blondel argues, both in *L'Action* and again in his "Letter on Apologetics," it is not within the competence of philosophy to indicate the reality or the content of this supernatural.[75] Following the dynamism of the will and the logic of human action, philosophy can only arrive at the postulate of the supernatural as that which is both absolutely *necessary* and absolutely *inaccessible.*[76]

During his years as a student of philosophy in Jersey, de Lubac read with great enthusiasm Blondel's *L'Action* and his "Letter on Apologetics," and a trip to Aix in 1922—in order to care for an injury sustained during the war—afforded him his first opportunity to meet with the philosopher in person. The tremendous influence of Blondel on de Lubac's thinking is evident in a series of missives exchanged between the two in April 1932.[77] Writing in reference to Blondel's *Le Problème de la philosophie catholique,*[78] de Lubac expresses his frustration that certain theologians sought to prove the orthodoxy of Blondel's work by appealing to the system of pure nature.[79] According to de Lubac, no ecclesiastical document imposes belief in such a system.[80] Moreover, even if one were to deny the possibility of a state of pure nature, one would not for all that be obliged to deny the gratuity of the supernatural. According to de Lubac, "this concept of a pure nature runs into great difficulties, the principal one of which seems to me to be the following: How can a conscious spirit be anything other than an absolute desire [for] God?"[81]

In his response to de Lubac, Blondel insists that, in his own investigations of the supernatural, it was never his intent to play the part of a theologian. "Even if in fact one were to imagine that the supernatural were unconscious," notes Blondel, "I could in no way observe it and speculate as a philosopher. . . . My role, my goal does not involve an observation from above of what is below, I could only observe the above from below without piercing the cloud where the God to be revealed is enveloped."[82] De Lubac responds by confessing that, in gesturing toward a theology of the supernatural in his previous letter, "it was with the idea, not at all that you should do it, but that it could now be done because your philosophical work had paved the way."[83] De Lubac is not, of course, suggesting that a theology of the supernatural requires, as a foundation or methodological prerequisite, a correlative phenomenology of human existence. Such a foundationalist construal of the relation between nature and the supernatural (and the corresponding disciplines of philosophy and theology) would only reinforce the "two-storied" thinking decried by both Blondel and de Lubac. The real insight of Blondel's project, according to de Lubac, is in giving the lie to those advocates (both philosophical *and* theological) of a purely immanent teleology, of an order of nature closed in on itself. Blondel's philosophy moreover provides de Lubac with a means of articulating the intrinsic relation between nature and humanity's supernatural finality *without* thereby falling into intrinsicism. For it is the burden of much of Blondel's phenomenology to demonstrate the extent to which the dynamism of human existence gestures in the direction of nature's "supernatural insufficiency."[84] What Blondel therefore sought to show by way of a phenomenology of action—namely, that the problem of human destiny cannot be resolved without recourse to some form of transcendence—de Lubac would attempt to demonstrate at the level of positive theology. Whereas Blondel could only observe the above "from below," de Lubac's investigations of the supernatural would entail a hermeneutics of the below "from above," presupposing, that is, the *finis ultimus* toward which nature is teleologically ordered. The spontaneous movement of Blondel's philosophy, like the exigencies of the will to which it is devoted, terminates at the absolute necessity of the supernatural. As we will see in what follows, de Lubac insists that this élan betrays the existence of a deeper spiritual dynamism. For according to de Lubac, there is in every human being *a natural desire for the supernatural.*

The Desire for God

Just as he had confided to Blondel more than a decade earlier, de Lubac insists in the concluding chapter of *Surnaturel* that human spirit simply *is* the desire for God.[85] This desire is an unconditional desire of human nature, "the most absolute of all desires."[86] In thus refusing to speak of the desire for God as a mere "velleity" (a wish or volition in its weakest form), de Lubac nonetheless maintains that the desire is in itself wholly inefficacious. "The spirit," notes de Lubac, "does not desire God as an animal desires its prey. It desires him as a gift. . . . [I]t wills the free and gratuitous communication of a personal Being. If therefore, *per impossibile*, it were able on this occasion to capture its supreme good, it would no longer be its good."[87] According to de Lubac, to designate the desire for God as an *exigence* of human nature is therefore to misconstrue both the desiring subject and its supernatural "object." The created spirit longs for God as a lover for his or her beloved. Far from exercising any claim over its object, the natural desire for the supernatural demands only that its object be, as it were, *incapable of being demanded.* The spirit thus desires God precisely as God has determined to give himself to the creature—according to God's own sovereign initiative. Moreover, according to de Lubac, "if there is in our nature a desire to see God, this can only be because God wills for us this supernatural end which consists in seeing him. It is because, willing it and never ceasing to will it, he therefore sets up and never ceases to set up this desire in our nature. So that this desire is nothing other than his call."[88]

Such, in summary, is the argument put forward by de Lubac in the concluding chapter of *Surnaturel.* The end of human nature is the vision of God. Human spirit, in turn, is the desire for this end, a desire at once absolute and inefficacious. We have already seen how, for the advocates of pure nature, only the supposition of a purely natural finality secures the gratuity of humanity's supernatural end. De Lubac's critics were thus convinced that, however noble his intentions, his insistence on a natural desire for God is ultimately irreconcilable with the gratuity of the supernatural. The main point of contention thus revolves around de Lubac's assertion that the spirit's desire for God is both *absolute* and *inefficacious.* Concerning the latter, all parties are in agreement that human beings are incapable of procuring their supernatural destiny without the assistance of divine grace. But in what sense then can human beings be said to enjoy an *absolute* desire for such a strictly gratuitous end? As Philip J. Donnelly, one of de Lubac's earliest critics, puts it, "either God was free to elevate or not to elevate our actually existing human nature, or in the existing human race there is an exigency for the supernatural; for, an absolute and infrustrable desire of the beatific vision . . . is completely unintelligible except in terms of strict exigency."[89] The force of Donnelly's critique, however, is predicated on a somewhat facile reading of de Lubac on the *absolute* character of the desire for God. For according to Donnelly, when de Lubac speaks of the spirit's desire to see God as absolute, what he means is that "God cannot refuse to fulfil this supernatural destiny which is inscribed in the very nature of finite spirits."[90] For de Lubac, however, the desire for God is absolute, not because it places any obligation on God to satisfy it, but rather because it imposes itself necessarily on human nature. The desire for God is absolute because *we cannot not desire it.*[91] For de Lubac, therefore, exigency runs in the exact opposite direction. The desire of our nature is not an exigency for the supernatural, but rather a *divine exigency*, an innate expression of the divine right over spiritual creatures.[92] To construe the matter otherwise is to fall once more into the error of imagining God in the same way as a human being, overlooking, that is, the sheer contingency of created being.

While we may therefore go some way toward resolving the contradiction of a desire at once absolute and inefficacious by requisite attention to the contingency of created being, there nevertheless remains a certain ontological ambiguity in de Lubac's articulation of the natural desire. For coupled with the ambiguity of referring to the natural desire for the beatific vision as "nothing other than [God's] call,"[93] the concluding chapter of *Surnaturel* would seem to indicate at a number of points that the desire for God is actually supernatural. Thus, according to de Lubac, "whatever were the good reasons for calling it 'natural' (since it is essentially in nature and expresses the heart of it), one must add that it is already, in a sense, something from God."[94] The natural desire for the supernatural is the "permanent action in us of the God who creates our nature."[95] This desire for God is *in us*, but it is not therefore *of us*, "since it is satisfied only in mortifying us."[96] Such comments, among others, make it difficult to distinguish analytically between the "natural" and "supernatural" elements of humanity's desire for God. According to de Lubac's critics, "this creates an unresolved (and . . . unresolvable) tension in de Lubac's thought as to whether the natural desire to see God should be conceived as purely natural, or as also somehow divine."[97] For others, such as John Milbank, the mediating status of the natural desire for the supernatural typifies precisely the theological revolution inaugurated in *Surnaturel.* For according to Milbank, the natural desire of the supernatural implies "the dynamic link" between the orders of nature and the supernatural.[98] De Lubac explicitly denies in subsequent treatments of the supernatural any such mediating relation between nature and grace, locating the desire for God strictly within the order of created nature. It remains to be seen, however, whether such a denial marks a shift in de Lubac's thinking or merely a clarification of his original project.

THE QUESTION OF INTRINSICISM

By Milbank's estimation, de Lubac's *Surnaturel* was "almost as important an event of cultural revision as *Being and Time* or the *Philosophical Investigations*."[99] Under the guise of a somewhat esoteric collection of predominantly historical inquiries, de Lubac inaugurated nothing less than a bold new ontology "between the field of pure immanent being proper to philosophy on the one hand, and the field of the revelatory event proper to theology on the other." This new ontological discourse, which Milbank describes as de Lubac's *non-ontology*, consists in an account of human nature as "intrinsically raised above itself to the 'supernature' of divinity."[100] That is to say, for de Lubac, human nature is always already *superadded nature*, "pulling us naturally beyond our nature in an *ecstasis* at the outset";[101] the supernatural is in turn always already immanent in our nature by virtue of an absolute desire of/for the supernatural. Thus, according to Milbank, whereas some Catholic conservatives today seek to mitigate de Lubac's revolutionary ontology by claiming "only the fulfillment is granted by grace, while the impulse to the beatific vision is purely natural,"[102] for de Lubac the longing for grace is itself already graced. The natural desire for the supernatural is the dynamic link between the orders of nature and grace, which, without constituting a *tertium quid* alongside the gifts of created and deified existence, are nevertheless "at once entirely an aspect of the Creation and entirely also the work, in advance of itself, of grace which unites human creatures to the Creator."[103]

Such at least is Milbank's reading of *Surnaturel*. By the time that de Lubac returns to the subject of the *desiderium naturae* in *Augustinianism and Modern Theology* and *The Mystery of the Supernatural* (1965), a different picture begins to emerge. Whereas de Lubac had earlier insisted that the desire for God is "already, in a certain sense, something from

God,"[104] he now insists that the longing for the supernatural is "a longing 'born of a lack,' and not arising from 'the beginnings of possession.'"[105] Thus, whatever the ambiguity surrounding the ontological status of the natural desire in *Surnaturel*, de Lubac goes to great lengths in *The Mystery of the Supernatural* to ward off precisely the reading of his work offered by Milbank above. For according to de Lubac, "The fact that the nature of spiritual being . . . is not conceived as an order destined to close in finally upon itself, but [is] in a sense open to an inevitably supernatural end, *does not mean that it already has in itself, or as part of its basis, the smallest positively supernatural element.* It does not mean that this nature, 'as nature, and by nature,' is elevated."[106] This passage is scarcely idiosyncratic among de Lubac's later writings in denying the least supernatural element in human being. As de Lubac goes on to argue, though human nature may contain a certain *capacity* for the supernatural, this does not mean that it participates in any way in the latter.[107] For between our nature and our supernatural finality, "the distance is as great, the difference is as radical, as that between non-being and being."[108] Similarly, in his 1980 publication *A Brief Catechesis on Nature and Grace* (a text entirely ignored in the first edition of Milbank's *The Suspended Middle* and only briefly treated in the second),[109] de Lubac insists that the supernatural (here defined as "that divine element which man's effort cannot reach . . . which unites itself to man, . . . penetrating him in order to divinize him") is strictly an attribute of the "new man" described by St. Paul.[110] *A Brief Catechesis* is likewise remarkable among de Lubac's publications on the supernatural in treating not only the relation between nature (somewhat abstractly considered) and the supernatural but more concretely that of *sinful* nature and the present economy of grace. De Lubac writes: "Between sinful human nature and divine grace we have not only a dissimilarity, a heterogeneity between two orders of being, an infinite distance that man alone cannot bridge. There is an antagonism, violent conflict." In the present, sinful condition of human existence, "the call of grace is no longer an invitation to a simple 'elevation,' . . . in a more radical fashion it is a summons to a 'total upheaval,' to a 'conversion' (of the 'heart,' i.e., of all one's being)."[111] Considered historically, therefore, the drama of human existence is doubly disproportionate to the end that fulfills it. On account of humanity's finitude and fallenness, human beings must undergo a kind of mortification *prior* to partaking in the gift of the supernatural.

Why the sudden shift in de Lubac's thinking? According to Milbank, the revisions introduced in *The Mystery of the Supernatural*, and maintained throughout his later writings, were primarily the result of the promulgation of Pius XII's encyclical *Humani generis* in 1950. For despite de Lubac's protestations to the contrary,[112] this encyclical "concerning some false opinions threatening to undermine the foundations of Catholic doctrine"[113] was believed by many to have implicated his thinking on the supernatural. Of particular consequence to de Lubac's theology of nature and the supernatural is a line in the encyclical concerning certain theologians who "destroy the gratuity of the supernatural order, since God, they say, cannot create intellectual beings without ordering and calling them to the beatific vision."[114] According to Milbank, the consequences of this exhortation for de Lubac's subsequent theological development were monumental: "After *Humani generis*, outside his historical work, de Lubac comes across as a stuttering, somewhat traumatized theologian, only able to articulate his convictions in somewhat oblique fragments."[115] The encyclical provoked in de Lubac "severe theoretical incoherence," forcing him to rework some of the more radical aspects of his project in an attempt to assuage the official misgivings of a conservative church hierarchy. The natural desire for the supernatural was therefore bereaved of its mediating status, dissolving de Lubac's non-ontology into the familiar dichotomy of grace and immanent being, revelation and secular reason.

There is much to commend Milbank's reading, and any attempt to displace his corruption narrative must take seriously the conceptual/ontological ambiguity surrounding de Lubac's earliest accounts of the *desiderium naturae* and the significance of the debates surrounding *Humani generis* for de Lubac's mature theology. Moreover, despite the rhetorical excess of Milbank's psychological account of de Lubac as a stammering and traumatized theologian, there is no denying that de Lubac was profoundly affected by the sanctions and accusations leveled against him around the time of *Humani generis*. Thus, in a letter addressed to his father provincial on July 1, 1950 (a month before the promulgation of Pius XII's encyclical), de Lubac confessed his distress at the accusations brought against him by Father Janssens, the father general of the Jesuit Order. "I am wounded to the depths of my soul," writes de Lubac, "by the one we call our Father."[116] As we will see shortly, however, de Lubac's situation had improved dramatically by the time that he returned to the subject of the supernatural in 1965, and it is far from self-evident that his prolific theological output over the next two and a half decades suffered under the trauma of these original controversies. Thus, despite the *prima facie* plausibility of Milbank's narrative, there are serious grounds for denying the revisionary status of de Lubac's later writings on the supernatural.

The first difficulty with positing a shift in de Lubac's thinking as a *response* to *Humani generis* is that such a change (if indeed we are to think of it as a change) is already evident in de Lubac's work *prior* to the promulgation of Pius XII's encyclical. It was in "The Mystery of the Supernatural" of 1949, *not* the expanded edition of the same title in 1965, that de Lubac initially (at least explicitly) denied any advance manifestation of the supernatural prior to the gift of sanctifying grace. Originally intended as the second part of a book responding to various objections made to *Surnaturel*,[117] "The Mystery of the Supernatural" offers a constructive complement to the argument set forth in the concluding chapter of *Surnaturel*. Whereas the latter sought to show how the gratuity of the supernatural could be affirmed *without* the hypothesis of pure nature, "The Mystery of the Supernatural" considers the extent to which the pure nature hypothesis fails in its own right to protect the gratuity of the supernatural. Among the various contributions and clarifications made to de Lubac's ongoing treatment of the supernatural, the 1949 article takes a first step toward resolving the ontological ambiguity surrounding the status of the natural desire in *Surnaturel*. As he would eventually repeat in *The Mystery of the Supernatural* of 1965, de Lubac here insists that nature does not have "the least positively supernatural element in itself or as part of its property."[118] The natural desire for the supernatural cannot possibly constitute a bond or link between the two orders of nature and the supernatural, for between these two orders, "the distance is as great, the abyss is as profound, the heterogeneity is as radical as between nonbeing and being."[119] Thus, though it is possible that de Lubac revised his original thesis in deference to *Surnaturel*'s earliest critics, Milbank's insistence that this revision was a response to *Humani generis* is an error in historical judgment.

The second difficulty with Milbank's thesis is that *Humani generis* calls for no such concession. We've noted that the only line in the encyclical directly pertaining to the question of the supernatural concerns those theologians who "destroy the gratuity of the supernatural" by denying that God could create intellectual beings "without ordering . . . them to the beatific vision."[120] The encyclical thus leaves entirely unaddressed the problem surrounding the ontological status of the desire for the supernatural. This is not to say, however, that de Lubac's work was in no way implicated in the encyclical's remarks. For the burden of *Surnaturel* was, at least according to its earliest readers, precisely to disprove the possibility of an order of pure nature. When, for instance, *Surnaturel* was subjected to the scrutiny of four anonymous censors in 1947, two of the book's reviewers delineated "the concrete impossibility of an order of pure nature" as the work's central thesis.[121] If therefore we are to look for a concession in de Lubac's thinking with respect to *Humani generis*, it must be in terms of this concrete (im)possibility and *not* in terms of the ontological status of the desire for God. As it turns out, this is precisely what we find. Already in "The Mystery of the Supernatural" of 1949, de Lubac insists "that if God had wanted, he could have not given us being, and that he could have not called this being that he gave us to see him."[122] This caveat eventually allows de Lubac to deny any conflict between his work and the words of *Humani generis*, even insisting at one point that the encyclical "reproduces exactly" what he wrote in 1949.[123] But even though it is certainly true that the clarification introduced by de Lubac in "The Mystery of the Supernatural" left him well protected against the line of criticism eventually taken in *Humani generis*, it is likely that such a clarification was already a deliberate concession to *Surnaturel*'s earliest critics. This is evident, for instance, in a number of subtle revisions introduced in *Augustinianism and Modern Theology* (1965). In *Surnaturel*, for example, de Lubac had insisted that such thinkers as Dominic Soto, Augustine, Aquinas, Bonaventure, and Duns Scotus "never considered *as possible* for man or for any created spirit an end at once transcendent and natural, consisting in a knowledge of God other than the beatific vision."[124] De Lubac reproduces this sentence almost verbatim in

Augustinianism and Modern Theology with one notable exception: he now drops the language of possibility altogether. De Lubac now simply notes that none of the above-mentioned thinkers had ever envisaged for any created spirit "an end which would be both transcendent and 'purely natural.'"[125] The fact that "*comme possible*" failed to make it into the reworked 1965 volume was hardly an editorial mistake.

As Milbank rightly notes, however, it is unlikely that de Lubac's sudden admission of the *possibility* of an order of pure nature betokens any real shift in his thinking on the subject of the supernatural.[126] For though it is true that de Lubac now grants that God *could* have created intellectual beings without ordering them to the beatific vision, he is quick to add that such an allowance in no way guarantees the gratuity of the supernatural. De Lubac's argument runs as follows: According to the advocates of pure nature, an order *might* have existed in which man, "without prejudice perhaps to another desire, had restricted his reasonable ambitions to some inferior beatitude. But that being said, one is, indeed, obliged to concede that in our world, in fact, the ambitions of man cannot be so limited."[127] In the concrete order of human existence, there is in each of us a natural desire to see God: an innate expression of our supernatural finality. It therefore remains to be shown how the supernatural is gratuitous precisely in relation to *this* nature. According to de Lubac, any attempt at securing the gratuity of the supernatural must take into account the ontological implications of humanity's actual supernatural end. For in positing another finality, the advocates of pure nature have ultimately posited *another humanity*, a nature teleologically (and thus ontologically) distinct from the humanity to which we in fact belong.

The third difficulty with Milbank's narrative concerns his claim that de Lubac's later writings on the supernatural bear the psychological trauma induced by the promulgation of *Humani generis*. Without attempting to read behind de Lubac's writings the emotional well-being of their author, we may at least call Milbank's reading into question by noting the remarkable shift in de Lubac's intellectual fortunes from the time of the encyclical's promulgation to the publication of de Lubac's "twins" in 1965. The 1950s were no doubt unfavorable to de Lubac. In the early months of 1950, de Lubac was forced to resign as editor of *Recherches de science religieuse* and to cease all teaching. Shortly thereafter, "lightning struck Fourvière." In June 1950, the order was given to remove de Lubac (as well as Emile Delaye, Henri Bouillard, Alexandre Durand, and Pierre Ganne) from his religious duties in Lyon. The order was also given to withdraw from Jesuit libraries three of de Lubac's books (*Surnaturel*, *Corpus mysticum*, and *Connaisance de Dieu*) and the volume of *Recherches* containing his article "The Mystery of the Supernatural." De Lubac was swiftly "exiled" to Paris, at which time (on the very day of his arrival), the encyclical *Humani generis* appeared in the French Roman Catholic newspaper *La Croix*. For nearly a decade thereafter, de Lubac remained a largely marginalized figure. Numerous ministries were refused to him, and for most of the 1950s he was prevented from teaching and from publishing in the field of constructive theology.

By the time de Lubac returned to the subject of the supernatural in 1965, however, his situation had improved dramatically. In 1956, de Lubac returned to Lyon, where he was permitted to give instruction at the Catholic Faculties on the subjects of Hinduism and Buddhism.[128] That same year, de Lubac published *Sur le chemins de Dieu* (later translated as *The Discovery of God*), an enlarged edition of the heretofore censured *Connaisance de Dieu*. In 1958, de Lubac received letters from Pius XII and Father Janssens indicating (in the former) a renewed confidence in de Lubac's work and (in the latter) the acknowledgment of a certain complicity in the "misunderstandings" surrounding de Lubac's professional and ecclesial misfortunes throughout the 1950s.[129] With the accession of John XXIII later that year, de Lubac's rehabilitation took an enormous leap forward. The new pope made known his displeasure with the events surrounding *Humani generis*, and in August 1960 he confirmed his confidence in de Lubac by selecting him as a consulter to the Preparatory Theological Commission for the Second Vatican Council. De Lubac then went on to serve in an official capacity as a *peritus* to the council. He was involved in revising the famous Schema 13, which served as the foundation for the *Pastoral Constitution on the Church in the Modern World* (*Gaudium et spes*), and he played a significant role in the formation of *Dei verbum*.

Along with his personal and professional rehabilitation, there is much to suggest that de Lubac's work on the supernatural had been, if not cleared of *all* suspicion, at least considerably vindicated by the mid-1960s. In his review of *Augustinisme et théologie moderne* and *Le Mystère du surnaturel*, for instance, the French historian and philosopher Xavier Tilliette notes that in the nearly twenty years since the publication of *Surnaturel*, "the discussions and clarifications, indeed the polemics, have confirmed the soundness, the validity of this celebrated book. The theological sky having cleared, Father de Lubac . . . has been able to pick up once again and considerably develop several chapters of *Surnaturel*."[130] As further confirmation that the debate surrounding the supernatural had all but settled by the time of the publication of "the twins," de Lubac notes the justification of the *Surnaturel* thesis in Father S. Dockx's 1964 contribution to the *Archives de philosophie*, "Du désir naturel de voir l'essence divine d'après saint Thomas" (On the natural desire to see the divine essence according to Saint Thomas), and a number of favorable reviews of his work by such leading interpreters of Thomas Aquinas as Étienne Gilson and Jean-Pierre Torrell.[131] Writing with respect to the "twins" of 1965, Gilson notes, "Here . . . are two austere titles to introduce an impassioned work that includes all of the substance of *Surnaturel*, but enriched, matured, brought right up to the minute, and topped off with a refreshing fillip of that quiet satisfaction that characterizes every brilliant man when he finds, at last, that he was the one who had it right all along!"[132] Gilson's characterization of de Lubac in 1965 clearly bears little resemblance to the "stuttering, somewhat traumatized theologian" derided by Milbank. Without denying therefore that de Lubac's work on the supernatural still faced some concerted opposition in the mid-1960s (as indeed it does still today), Milbank's account of a trauma-induced victim of hierarchical censure is difficult to square with de Lubac's own return to favor and to a theological milieu marked increasingly by the conciliar principles of *ressourcement* and *aggiornamento.*

The objections raised thus far against Milbank's narrative have been primarily historical. We have seen how de Lubac's "concession" to *Humani generis* actually antedates the encyclical, how the encyclical itself remains notably silent with respect to the nature of the desire for God, and how the controversy surrounding de Lubac had largely dissipated by the time that he returned to the subject of the supernatural. Whatever the reasons for excluding from the later writings the idea that nature enjoys a dynamic link with the supernatural prior to the gift of sanctifying grace, there is no reason to presume that such a move was made in deference to the encyclical. None of this, however, finally disproves Milbank's insistence on a shift in de Lubac's thinking with respect to the ontological status of the natural desire. It is still possible that de Lubac revised his original thesis for reasons other than the encyclical's provocation—perhaps in deference to *Surnaturel*'s earliest critics. Such a suggestion, though possible, is still highly unlikely. For far from nullifying the divergence between him and his critics, de Lubac's insistence that the desire for the supernatural is a longing "born of a lack" actually places his thinking at *greater* variance with his theological detractors. As we have seen, the advocates of pure nature deny that human beings have an innate desire for a supernatural end, insisting instead that the desire for the beatific vision is strictly consequent upon the activating presence of grace. Milbank's reading of the natural desire as already in some sense the work of grace thus pushes de Lubac *closer* to the direction of his theological opponents, undermining what he insists to be the uniquely paradoxical status of spiritual nature. Milbank's "suspended middle" thus shares more in common with Karl Rahner's "supernatural existential" than it does with de Lubac's own articulation of the natural desire for the supernatural. For despite Milbank's insistence that his own reading of de Lubac "supernaturalizes the natural," while Rahner's construal of nature and grace "naturalizes the supernatural," the material differences between these two positions are negligible.[133] In his formulation of the supernatural existential, Rahner attempts to offer a *via media* between de Lubac and his neo-Scholastic opponents, seeking to avoid both extrinsicism and a natural exigency for the supernatural.[134] Like de Lubac, Rahner decries the "two-storied" thinking represented by the advocates of pure nature, insisting with de Lubac that every human being has an unconditional desire for God. However, Rahner likewise takes issue with de Lubac's insistence that this desire for God is a constituent of human *nature*, arguing instead that the desire is already itself a gift of *grace*.[135] The desire for God, according to Rahner, belongs to humanity's *supernatural existential*, the supernatural (and thus wholly gratuitous) gift of humanity's absolute ordination to a supernatural end. What Milbank takes to be a "radicalization" of de Lubac's thesis was actually, in the work of Rahner, an attempt to synthesize de Lubac's insistence on a natural desire for the supernatural with the theory of pure nature.[136]

If therefore there is little *historical* warrant for suggesting that de Lubac revised his original thesis, and if the postencyclical writings only serve to strengthen the theological distinctiveness of de Lubac's project over and against the position of his neo-Scholastic opponents, then it would seem that we have sufficient warrant for taking de Lubac at his word that the later writings were in no way an attempt to correct what he wrote in *Surnaturel.*[137] Presupposing a fundamental continuity between *Surnaturel* and subsequent treatments of the ontological status of the natural desire, it is worth inquiring to what extent the later writings may serve as a hermeneutical key for unlocking some of the more ambiguous claims in *Surnaturel.* For if, as we have suggested, the later writings make explicit the otherwise implicit ontological commitments of *Surnaturel,* then continuity will be demonstrated by the ability of the former to illumine the latter.

We begin with the ambiguity surrounding the relation between the desire for God and "God's call." What sense does de Lubac's claim that the longing for God is "a longing born of a lack" make of his original assertion that the natural desire is "nothing other than God's call"? According to Milbank, the divine call entails an advance manifestation of the supernatural that invokes on the side of nature the natural desire for the supernatural. The fact that de Lubac continues to refer to the divine call would thus seem to indicate that, despite the explicit denial of an inchoate participation in the supernatural in his later writings, de Lubac remains committed (however covertly) to the ontological radicalism of his original project.[138] Considering de Lubac's corpus "the other way around," however—that is, presupposing the radical heterogeneity between humanity's natural desire and supernatural finality—one comes to a different conclusion. For as early as "The Mystery of the Supernatural" of 1949, de Lubac denies that this call entails an advance communication of the supernatural. "The call to union," notes de Lubac, "is not yet union. In other words, the priority of the supernatural in the order of intention . . . does not mean that created nature is to the slightest degree in continuity with the supernatural in the order of execution."[139] God's call is not the introduction of a supernatural quality or principle in our nature, but rather the inscription of a supernatural *finality*.[140] This call is constitutive, insofar as the end determines the nature of a being, but the end corresponding to this call is only ever procured by means of sanctifying grace.[141] Rather than collapsing the supernatural into the order of nature, the "call of God" names precisely the paradox of humanity's supernatural *vocation*.[142] To be *called* by God is to be created for the purpose of deification, to be created, that is, for an end that infinitely surpasses the capacities of our nature.

But what of de Lubac's statements in *Surnaturel* suggesting that the natural desire for the supernatural is something always already exceeding the order of nature? What sense do the later writings make of his insistence that "whatever were the good reasons for calling it 'natural' . . . one must add that it is already, in a sense, something from God"?[143] The argument to which this statement belongs is concerned primarily with the gratuity of the beatific vision. The advocates of pure nature, we have seen, maintain that an absolute desire for the supernatural places a demand on God to fulfill it. For in refusing to satisfy this desire God would ultimately be responsible for the frustration of our nature. However, for de Lubac, the desire for God entails no such exigence on the side of the creature. In fulfilling our desire, God simply responds to his own call. Seen in this light, it becomes clear that de Lubac's insistence that the desire for God is already "something from God" is not an indication of the supernaturally elevated status of human nature, but rather an appeal to the nature of humanity's desire as itself *created*. De Lubac confirms this reading in the paragraph that follows, insisting that the natural desire for the supernatural is "the permanent action in us of the God who creates our nature, as grace is the permanent action in us of the God who creates the moral order."[144] Two things are of particular importance in this assertion for our understanding of the natural desire. First, de Lubac clearly distinguishes between two modes of humanity's relatedness to God, that of nature and that of grace, locating the desire of the supernatural strictly within the former. Second, in affirming "the permanent action in us of the God who creates our nature," de Lubac denies any account of created nature in abstraction from the claim of divine governance. It is a false dichotomy, in other words, to imagine that nature (and the desire of our nature in particular) entails either the presence of grace or the complete absence of divine causality.[145] For as Thomas Aquinas reminds us, the will is always moved by God, even if it is not always moved by grace.[146] God is the cause of our desire, the one from whom we receive not only this longing to see him but the very power of willing itself. Moreover, God is the object of our desire, summoning the will as its ultimate end. Finally, God preserves this desire by his providential governance, moving the will interiorly according to its own proper inclination. God is all of these things—the origin, object, and sustainer of our will—precisely because he is the one who creates our nature. And it is because of our created status as spiritual beings, not by virtue of some prior manifestation of grace, that there resides in our nature a longing to see him. The gift of deification presupposes the gift of creaturely being, but the latter is no less contingent on the sustaining love of God than the former. Indeed, for de Lubac, it is precisely the gift of the supernatural that reveals to us the original giftedness of our being and its ultimate ordination to the self-giving of God.

CONCLUSION

What is gained or lost in affirming or denying that human nature is always already graced? Having distinguished de Lubac's position from the intrinsicism of his later interpreters, what is the theological justification for insisting on the supernatural insufficiency of human nature? According to de Lubac, the answer centers on the biblical call to *metanoia*, to the evangelical summons to mortification as the necessary condition for humanity's vivification: "I have been crucified with Christ; and it is no longer I who live, but it is Christ who lives in me."[147] For de Lubac, the gift of deification—that creaturely participation in the supernatural fellowship of intra-Trinitarian love—entails nothing less than a new creation. "So if anyone is in Christ, there is a new creation: everything old has passed away; see, everything has become new!"[148] The danger of intrinsicism is therefore the mitigation of what de Lubac refers to as the "truly revolutionary newness" of the Christian gospel.[149] As we will see in the chapters that follow, for de Lubac this newness entails both an ontic and a noetic *novum*. The former refers to the new creation brought about by humanity's incorporation into the mystery of Christ, the radical transfiguration of human being into the divine likeness. The latter names the inability of the dynamism of human reason to arrive at the supernatural truths of revelation. Both aspects are of course closely allied. An intrinsicist account of nature and the supernatural betokens an intrinsicist construal of reason and revelation. For de Lubac, therefore, it is necessary to affirm an intrinsic relation between nature and the supernatural *without* thereby sliding into intrinsicism. Nature is teleologically ordered to the supernatural without in any way (however inchoately or implicitly) possessing the latter. The desire for this end is a longing born entirely from lack.

In the introduction, I noted that for de Lubac the drama of human existence is a "mystery" in two senses: first, human beings enjoy a privileged relation among the "beings of nature" to the source of all being; second, by virtue of this relation, there is an "irreducible opacity" to human being that resists all attempts at schematization. In this chapter, we have begun to see how this twofold mystery converges on de Lubac's articulation of the paradox of humanity's vocation. Human beings are called to the supernatural enjoyment of the beatific vision of God. This call is constitutive, determining the very nature of human being and manifesting itself in a natural desire for the supernatural. However, because human nature finds its fulfillment only in its graced elevation to fellowship with God, human beings remain an enigma unto themselves. The apophatic implications of humanity's paradoxical finality are evident in the Johannine assurance: *we do not yet know* what we will be.[150] This is true, as the passage from 1 John makes clear, for those who have already encountered by faith the revelation of humanity's telos in the person and works of Jesus Christ. It is all the more the case, therefore, for those who restrict their gaze to the order of immanence. Echoing the insights of Maurice Blondel, de Lubac thus insists that a purely "natural" investigation of human existence can only reveal the "supernatural insufficiency of human nature."[151] The dynamism of human existence cries out for that which is absolutely necessary and wholly inaccessible.

In terms of a theological hermeneutics of human existence, the theologian must therefore seek to convey both the explanatory power of the gospel's claim on human existence and the unintelligibility of human being in abstraction from the revelation of humanity's supernatural finality. According to de Lubac, "This should not, however, be confused with that type of apologetics which is intended to convince the man who as yet does not believe, that first tried to get him to recognize a 'natural desire' in himself and then to believe that this natural desire should lead him to the 'supernatural word' revealed in Jesus Christ."[152] In terms of mere intellectual persuasiveness, such an apologetic assumes an idea of "nature" that is no longer commonly shared. An argument for the credibility of Christianity predicated on an account of natural ends and desires will have a difficult time securing an audience in an intellectual milieu increasingly suspicious of the tyranny of metaphysics. At a more fundamental level, however, de Lubac insists that an analysis of this desire itself presupposes the content of revelation. In itself, the desire for God remains "hidden 'in the ontological depths,' and only the Christian revelation makes it possible to interpret either its indications or its meaning correctly."[153] For de Lubac, therefore, the hermeneutical circle moves in the opposite direction. Revelation encounters a nature inherently open to the call of grace, but the latter receives its intelligibility—the implicit desire of our nature becomes explicit—only in the light of this revelation: "Certain depths of our nature can be opened only by the shock of revelation." Thus, according to de Lubac, "it is by the promise given us of seeing God face to face that we really learn to recognize our 'desire.'"[154]

THREE

The Knowledge of God

INTRODUCTION

Having considered the paradox of humanity's vocation in terms of *desire*, we turn in this chapter to an investigation of the dynamism of human *reason*. What relation does the *intellect* bear to humanity's supernatural finality? It is worth noting at the outset that de Lubac generally resists a neat metaphysical demarcation between the will and the intellect in his explorations of the knowing and willing subject. Eager to avoid what he believes to be the false dichotomy of intellectualism and voluntarism, de Lubac is content to consider the intelligence and the will not as two hermetically contained faculties but rather as "two functions equally relative to our condition as *viatores*."[1] It is the destiny of created *spirit*—neither the will nor the intellect in isolation—to enjoy what William of St.-Thierry refers to as "the knowledge of love."[2] Thus, in an obvious play on the intellectualist mantra of Pierre Rousselot that "intelligence is the faculty of being because it is the sense of the divine," de Lubac insists that "intelligence is the faculty of being, because *spirit* is the capacity for God."[3] The unity of spiritual being attained in the eschatological vision of God consists in the final integration of will and intellect. Although these two faculties remain in a certain state of discord (both with one another and with their common *telos*) throughout the spirit's journey *in via*, they are nevertheless united by virtue of their shared finality. Part of the burden of what follows is to demonstrate this intimate relation between the knowledge and the desire of God in de Lubac's hermeneutics of human existence.

We will begin our investigation of reason's relation to God with one of de Lubac's earliest publications, "On Christian Philosophy" (1936). In this brief contribution to the Christian philosophy debates of the 1930s, de Lubac provides an initial sketch of what he takes to be the intellectual implications of humanity's supernatural vocation. As we will see, "On Christian Philosophy" contains one of de Lubac's earliest appeals to the natural desire for the supernatural, one that anticipates precisely the theology of nature and the supernatural we articulated in chapter 2. Greatly indebted to the philosophy of Blondel, de Lubac advances in this essay "a truly intrinsic relationship between rational speculation and supernatural revelation" in terms of the radical insufficiency of the former.[4] According to de Lubac, the dynamism of human reason cannot find its place of completion except in revelation. Reason is therefore teleologically ordered to revelation without in any way anticipating the claims of the latter.

After treating de Lubac's articulation of the supernatural insufficiency of the intellect in terms of the relationship between reason and revelation, we will turn our attention to de Lubac's most sustained attempt at a metaphysical elucidation of reason itself. In *The Discovery of God* (1945), a text originally published nearly a decade after his "On Christian Philosophy," de Lubac portrays the dynamism of human reason, no longer strictly in terms of the intellect's insufficiency, but in terms of an innate apprehension of the one to whom the intellect is teleologically ordered. By virtue of their creation in the *imago Dei* and the continual operation of God upon the intellect, human beings enjoy what de Lubac refers to as a "transcendental affirmation of God." Drawing once more on the philosophy of Blondel, and on the transcendental Thomism of Joseph Maréchal, de Lubac insists that the affirmation of God is the necessary a priori condition for every act of the intellect. This allows de Lubac to affirm not only the intrinsic relation between reason and revelation but also the deleterious noetic consequences of humanity's rejection of God.

There is therefore, at the very least, an obvious change in emphasis between the two texts analyzed in this chapter. But whereas the account of human reason provided by de Lubac in the 1936 essay maps neatly onto the theology of nature and the supernatural presented in chapter 2, the transcendental affirmation of God defended in *The Discovery of God* would seem to compromise de Lubac's fundamental commitment to the supernatural insufficiency of human nature, pushing his thought in a more intrinsicist direction. For how are we to reconcile de Lubac's conviction in "On Christian Philosophy" that reason in no way anticipates revelation with his insistence in *The Discovery of God* that "all knowers know God implicitly in all they know"?[5] What does reason discover in revelation that it does not already possess as an a priori of every act of cognition? Without denying a certain tension between these two accounts and the risks (both theological and philosophical) attending the kind of transcendental analysis performed in *The Discovery of God*, I will argue that these two accounts converge precisely on de Lubac's formulation of the *desiderium naturae.* The reason for this is twofold. First, according to de Lubac, a certain inchoate knowledge of God is a necessary correlate to humanity's natural desire for the supernatural. Second, there is for de Lubac an infinite qualitative difference between the supernatural knowledge of God attainable by grace and the natural knowledge of God arising from the transcendental affirmation of the Absolute. Only the former satiates the *desiderium naturae.* The spirit's search for God does not therefore terminate at the mere objectification of humanity's prereflective experience of the Absolute. This knowledge may constitute the culmination of philosophical reasoning, but it ultimately fails to satisfy the spirit's longing for God. As de Lubac insists, the dynamism of human reason finds its place of completion and rest only in the spirit's graced participation in God.

ON CHRISTIAN PHILOSOPHY

The Christian Philosophy Debates

The occasion for de Lubac's earliest investigation of the nature and limits of human reason was a series of widely publicized debates among Francophone historians, philosophers, and theologians in the early 1930s on the relation between Christianity and philosophy.[6] It was the Sorbonne philosopher and historian of philosophy Emile Bréhier who fired the first shot of what would come to be known as "the Christian philosophy debates." Beginning in 1927 with an essay on the relation between Hellenistic philosophy and early Christianity, Bréhier "claimed to demonstrate that the advent of Christianity had exercised hardly any influence on the development of philosophical thought."[7] Bréhier expanded this argument in the first volume of his influential *Histoire de la philosophie* and in a series of lectures delivered at the Institut des Études in Brussels in 1928 under the title "Y a-t-il une philosophie chrétienne?" ("Is There a Christian Philosophy?"). According to Bréhier, there is an irresolvable contradiction between Christianity and the task of philosophy. Whereas philosophy seeks to discover the eternal order of things, the intrinsic rationality of the cosmos, Christianity commends belief in a worldless deity, one who capriciously creates the order of nature and subsequently interrupts this order to incarnate himself in human history. Moreover, whereas philosophy pursues its object under the strictures of reason alone, Christianity imposes a number of dogmas on the minds of its adherents, thus depriving philosophy of its own proper autonomy. Bréhier provocatively concludes his lectures by insisting that "one can no more speak of a Christian philosophy than of a Christian mathematics or a Christian physics."[8] Those systems of thought that commonly go under the name "Christian philosophy" are either parasitic on other forms of philosophy (e.g., Augustinian Neoplatonism and Thomist Aristotelianism) or entirely independent of the claims of Christian revelation (e.g., the philosophy of Descartes), in which case they are scarcely "Christian" in any meaningful sense.

Not surprisingly, Bréhier's thesis provoked a strong reaction from a number of historians and philosophers. In March 1931, the Société française de Philosophie (S.f. P.) held a public debate on the question of Christian philosophy, chaired by the society's secretary and founder, Xavier Léon. The S.f. P. meeting included papers delivered by Étienne Gilson, Jacques Maritain, Léon Brunschvicg, Edouard Le Roy, Raymond Lenoir, and Bréhier, and included letters delivered in absentia from Maurice Blondel and Jacques Chevalier. The meeting (and the corresponding *Bulletin de la Société française de Philosophie*)[9] served as the catalyst for the ensuing debates, and a number of the meeting's participants continued to publish on the topic of Christian philosophy throughout the 1930s. Among the various contributors to the 1931 session, the most influential proponents of "Christian philosophy" were arguably Gilson, Maritain, and Blondel.[10] It was the contribution of these three respondents to Bréhier's thesis that provided the point of departure for de Lubac's own 1936 essay "Sur la philosophie chrétienne."

The Contributions of Gilson, Maritain, and Blondel

As de Lubac recounts in his memoir, his article on Christian philosophy was "a kind of review" of the positions of Gilson, Maritain, and Blondel in response to Bréhier: "In it, I tried to show, without 'concordism,' that these three positions did not contradict each other but were responding to three different situations engendering three different problems."[11] As is often the case, de Lubac's own position thus emerges somewhat tacitly by way of an analysis of other key figures. As the above quotation indicates, "On Christian Philosophy" offers something like a synthesis of these three positions, albeit with a clear preference for the position set forth by Blondel. For without denying the utility of each of these accounts of Christian philosophy for refuting the rationalist critiques of Bréhier, de Lubac is convinced that only Blondel succeeds in articulating a truly intrinsic relation between philosophy and Christianity. Only Blondel, that is, accounts for the spiritual dynamism that animates the task of philosophy itself. Before proceeding to an analysis of de Lubac's own position, a few words are in order on the positions set forth by Gilson, Maritain, and Blondel.

The Position of Étienne Gilson

According to Gilson, who originally suggested to Xavier Léon the topic of the famous 1931 debate, the problem of "Christian philosophy" is resolvable primarily at the level of history. Gilson notes in his contribution to the S.f. P. session, "If there have been philosophies, that is, systems of rational truths, whose existence cannot be explained historically without taking account of Christianity's existence, those philosophies should bear the name of Christian philosophies."[12] While Gilson's S.f. P presentation indicates the theoretical *possibility* of such a philosophy, his Gifford Lectures delivered at the University of Aberdeen around the same time (May 29–June 2, 1931, February 8–12, May 30–June 3, 1932) sought to demonstrate precisely the extent to which a great deal of medieval thought met the above criteria for an authentically Christian philosophy. Gilson argues at length in these lectures that the content of this philosophy is "that body of rational truths discovered, explored or simply safeguarded, thanks to the help that reason receives from revelation."[13] Rather than impeding the exercise of the philosopher's reason, revelation thus serves these philosophers as "an indispensable auxiliary to reason."[14] The Christian philosopher discovers a number of truths that, though revealed to him by God, are nevertheless accessible to natural reason and reducible to the first principles of philosophy. Gilson makes a similar argument in his magnum opus, *Le Thomisme*, a book that went through six editions between 1919 and 1965, and that Gilson called "l'oeuvre d'une vie entière."[15] Here Gilson makes an important distinction between *the revealed* (*revelatum*) and *the revealable* (*revalabile*). Whereas the former includes "that whose very essence it is to be revealed because we can only come to know it by revelation," the latter consists of knowledge that, albeit revealed by God, is also naturally accessible to human reason.[16] Whereas theology concerns itself with both the revealed and the revealable, the latter alone falls within the purview of Christian philosophy.

The Position of Jacques Maritain

In *An Essay on Christian Philosophy* (an expanded edition of Maritain's contribution to the S.f. P. meeting), Maritain aligns his own position closely with that of Gilson. However, whereas Gilson provides a largely historical defense of the notion of Christian philosophy, Maritain offers a more theoretical account. For Maritain, the solution to the question of Christian philosophy resides in the classical distinction between the *nature* of philosophy and the *state* of philosophy, between what Maritain refers to as *the order of specification* and *the order of exercise*. According to Maritain, the nature of philosophy is determined by the object toward which it tends by virtue of itself. The order of specification thus consists of "a whole class of objects which are *of their nature attainable* through the natural faculties of the human mind."[17] The designation "Christian" does not therefore apply to philosophy's nature, for the latter is essentially "independent of the Christian faith as to its object, its principles, and its methods."[18] In the order of exercise, however, which pertains to the contingent historical conditions of a given philosophy, the philosopher receives a number of objective and subjective benefits from her Christian faith. Objectively, as Gilson pointed out, the Christian philosopher profits from those truths that, though belonging by nature within the field of philosophy, are discovered in fact by means of revelation. Subjectively, the philosopher receives enormous assistance from her faith: "The virtue of faith, for example, enables the philosopher, who knows of the existence of God by purely natural means to adhere rationally to this truth with a sturdier grasp."[19] The sanctifying presence of grace, moreover, aids in liberating the philosopher's reason from the "manifold futilities and opacities" that result from the intellect's bondage to sin.[20] For these reasons, one may indeed speak of a "Christian philosophy," so long as one means by this a philosophy operating under the historical/contingent conditions of Christianity.

The Position of Maurice Blondel

In a letter submitted to the S.f.P. session, and included in the society's *Bulletin*, Blondel challenges Gilson's claim that the problem of Christian philosophy can only be resolved at the level of history. "It seems to me," remarks Blondel, "that on a purely historical ground the question can receive only an equivocal and doubly regrettable solution."[21] Moreover, whereas Maritain insists that the designation "Christian" applies only to a possible *state* of philosophy, Blondel argues that philosophy is related to Christianity by its very *nature*. The burden of Blondel's philosophy is to demonstrate the extent to which the dynamism of thought and action leads *necessarily* to the idea of the supernatural. Already in *L'Action* (1899), Blondel insists, "The fullness of philosophy consists not in a presumptuous self-sufficiency, but in the study of its own powerlessness and of the means which are offered from elsewhere to supply for its powerlessness."[22] Philosophy raises inevitable problems that it is incapable of resolving on its own, problems that find their resolution only in the supernatural claims of Christianity.

OF THESE THREE POSITIONS, DE LUBAC PLACES THE LEAST amount of value in the argument of Maritain. "The affirmations of Maritain's thesis come out to very little," remarks de Lubac, reducing Maritain's position to the mere "subjective comfort" that some Christian philosophers receive from their faith.[23] Though generally more sympathetic to Gilson's argument, de Lubac insists that Gilson likewise fails to provide an *intrinsic* relation between Christianity and philosophy. For according to Gilson, "where reason is able to understand, faith has no further role to play. In other words, we cannot both know and believe the same thing at the same time and under the same aspect."[24] Revelation is therefore "an indispensible auxiliary to reason," in the sense that certain truths accessible to reason are nevertheless discovered by means of revelation, but once these truths are properly *understood*—that is, resolved into first principles—they may be abstracted from their location among the data of Christian revelation. Thus, as de Lubac summarizes Gilson's position elsewhere, although a philosophy may draw its origins from Christianity, it "[ceases] to be Christian in order to become rational at the moment it [becomes] truly a philosophy."[25] By de Lubac's estimation, therefore, only Blondel "establishes a truly intrinsic relationship between rational speculation and supernatural revelation, without, for all that, opening to philosophy the mysterious content of this revelation."[26] We will see in the next section that this endorsement of Blondel's position—and the particular way in which de Lubac articulates that position—is of tremendous importance for our understanding of the development of de Lubac's theology of nature and the supernatural. For what de Lubac claims to discover here in the "Christian philosophy" of Blondel is precisely what he discerns elsewhere in the writings of Augustine and Thomas Aquinas: the doctrine of the natural desire to see God.[27] Philosophy, following the dynamism of human reason and the paradox of humanity's spiritual vocation, terminates at the acknowledgment of its own insufficiency. Something further is therefore required for the satisfaction of speculative reason, something that can only be received in the form of a divine gift.

Three Modes of Christian Philosophy

Having considered the principal responses to Bréhier in support of the viability of Christian philosophy, de Lubac devotes the remainder of his essay to articulating his own understanding of the relation between reason and revelation, doing so under the continued purview of the question of Christian philosophy. Drawing on his earlier remarks on the positions of Gilson, Maritain, and Blondel, and on the insights of such philosophers as Pierre Rousselot and Gabriel Marcel, de Lubac advances three "modes" of Christian philosophy, corresponding in turn to three ways in which the intellect relates to the claims of Christian revelation. First, following Gilson and Maritain, de Lubac maintains that philosophy may be *historically/contingently* Christian. Second, in keeping with the thesis advanced by Blondel, de Lubac insists that *all* philosophy is—whether knowingly or unknowingly—*naturally* Christian. Finally, taking his inspiration from Marcel and "the Fathers of the Church," de Lubac argues that philosophy must eventually become *operatively* Christian.

Philosophy as Historically/Contingently Christian

In contradistinction to the idealist hubris that seeks to ground philosophy in a pure presuppositionless foundation, de Lubac contends that philosophy always sets out from a presupposed theoretical given. "Descartes's wet-nurse is more responsible than he himself believed for all that he drew from his *cogito*," de Lubac quips. "This is not to question the value of philosophical reason but to refuse to see it as a sort of absolute beginning."[28] Philosophy, which de Lubac here rather vaguely defines as "reason reflected in its exercise," is incapable of inventing its own object. Rather, it always performs a critical function in relation to the prereflective patterns of thought from which it emerges. Philosophy transforms "the givens furnished it by its extrarational sources" into rational truths, cleansing them of impurities, rejecting them if/when necessary, and finally integrating them into a system of logical relations.[29] Philosophy is contingently Christian, therefore, if/when it exercises its critique in some relation to the practical and theoretical givens of the Christian faith. To speak of philosophy as Christian in this sense is to say nothing of the nature of philosophy itself, other than to appeal to the necessarily contextual nature of all philosophy.[30] Moreover, to speak of a philosophy as historically/contingently Christian is to say nothing of that philosophy's faithfulness to the articles of Christian belief. As history attests, there are more and less faithful expressions of contingently Christian philosophy. For, as we saw in chapter 1, Christian philosophy in this mode is always susceptible to what de Lubac refers to as *dépassement*—the reduction of the Christian mystery into the immanentist categories of "secular" philosophy.

Philosophy as Naturally Christian

In the order of exercise, only those philosophies that develop in some form of dependence on the beliefs and practices of Christianity merit the title "Christian philosophy" (Christian philosophy in the first mode, as historically/contingently Christian), but there is a sense in which, according to de Lubac, philosophy itself is *naturally/essentially/metaphysically* Christian. Here it is no longer a question of *a* philosophy, but of *all* philosophy. As de Lubac explains:

> This is not to say that philosophy, left to itself, could find the Christian truths or their rational 'equivalent'. . . . This, in fact, is to say exactly the contrary, to know that philosophy, unable to give the total response to the problem of man and yet unable to disinterest itself in this response, cannot find its place of completion and rest—a rest always active—except in revelation, which is nothing other, in fact, than Christian revelation. This is to say that philosophy, by its own movement and without exterior prompting, tends toward revelation.[31]

Here we have, in no uncertain terms, the paradox of humanity's supernatural vocation as considered under the aspect of the dynamism of human reason. For de Lubac remarks in an important footnote to the above passage that the conception of philosophy here employed is not that of a "pure technique," but is rather "coextensive to all concrete effort of the reason."[32] As we indicated earlier with respect to de Lubac's treatment of the "Christian philosophy" of Blondel, the rational need to which such a philosophy corresponds is the spirit's desire to know God. To say that philosophy is naturally Christian is therefore to insist that human reason is teleologically ordered to the gift of God in revelation. Reason does not anticipate this gift, except by way of acknowledging its own radical insufficiency. Philosophy can only ever attain its end, therefore, by relinquishing its own autonomy. For de Lubac it is only by the "shock of revelation" that human beings come to identify their own natural desire for the supernatural, so philosophy only recognizes itself as open by its very essence to the claims of Christianity when it is already informed by the content of Christian revelation. Only a philosophy that is Christian in the first mode, therefore, knows itself to be Christian in the second mode.

Philosophy as Operatively Christian

In response to a criticism of his work by Bréhier, who suggests that Blondel's phenomenology of action proceeds somewhat duplicitously under the presupposition of conclusions already drawn from Christian doctrine,[33] Blondel insists, "I introduce nothing, I enter nowhere into the least content of the Catholic religion. I stop at the threshold, and as a philosopher I forbid myself finally to pronounce a single little word that I would have to say as a believer."[34] For Blondel, as we have seen, this reticence belongs to the very nature of philosophy. For according to Blondel, the philosophical endeavor terminates with the natural dynamism of reason at the profession of its own inadequacy. But does one thereby cease to speak as a philosopher the moment one begins to speak as a believer? Is such compartmentalization necessary? Or even possible? What becomes of the philosopher who is led by grace *beyond* the limitations of pure reason? Is there not a sense in which, having abdicated its autonomy at the threshold of revelation, the life of the intellect is subsequently reborn under the aegis of the supernatural? According to de Lubac, one must move with and beyond Blondel to speak of "Christian philosophy" in a third sense, one that he defines as "the synthesis of all knowledge, operating in the light of faith."[35] Christian philosophy in this sense is not simply the understanding *of* faith, the interpretation of a number of revealed truths. It is also an understanding *by* faith, an interpretation of all things by the power of, and in relation to, the Christian mystery. Following Marcel, de Lubac defines this mystery, as he does elsewhere,[36] primarily in terms of the Incarnation: "A Christian philosophy seems to me to define itself by the fact that it finds its point of ontological beginning in a *unique* fact . . . which is the Incarnation." The essence of such a philosophy is thus "a meditation on the implications and consequences of all orders coming from this basic principle, which is not only unforeseeable but contrary to the superficial demands of reason which *pose themselves erroneously as unsurpassable*."[37] The basic principle of this hermeneutic (the Incarnation) remains wholly unanticipated by the natural exercise of human reason, but de Lubac nevertheless insists that the light shed by this principle on the problem of human existence is, to a certain extent, directly intelligible to the unbeliever. For according to de Lubac, "If someone explains myself better to me than I have succeeded in doing myself, why should I spurn this explanation, whose value I directly perceive?"[38] What de Lubac here describes as the third mode of Christian philosophy is therefore the necessary precondition for that compenetration of apologetics and theology set forth in his inaugural lecture at the Université Catholique de Lyon. It is, in other words, that mode of theological and philosophical reasoning within which a theological hermeneutics of human existence is properly located.

The Contribution of "On Christian Philosophy"

As a review of the Christian philosophy debates, "On Christian Philosophy" is admittedly one-sided. De Lubac's intellectual allegiance to Blondel often leads him to a somewhat injudicious handling of the other contributors. This is especially true of his treatment of Maritain. Not only does de Lubac exaggerate the differences between the positions of Gilson and Maritain,[39] but he likewise fails to acknowledge the extent to which Maritain's position anticipates his own articulation of the third mode of "Christian philosophy" (philosophy operating in the light of faith). Maritain insists that "the state of philosophy has been changed and lifted up by Christianity, not only with respect to the objective material proposed but also with respect to the vitality and deepest dynamism of the intellect."[40] To reduce, as de Lubac does, Maritain's position to the mere "subjective comfort" that Christian philosophers receive from their faith is to significantly misrepresent the important role that Maritain allots to grace and the theological virtues in his articulation of the state of Christian philosophy.[41]

As a contribution to the debates in its own right, "On Christian Philosophy" also suffers from a rather conspicuous oversight. That is, in an essay devoted specifically to the question of "Christian philosophy," de Lubac fails to provide a sufficient account of the nature and ends of philosophy. This lacuna is evident, for instance, in de Lubac's discussion of the first mode of Christian philosophy (philosophy as historically/contingently Christian). Here de Lubac defines philosophy as "reason reflected in its exercise."[42] By de Lubac's account, the task of such an enterprise is to "rationalize," by which he means "to criticize and reject, as much as to welcome and integrate." Philosophy is therefore "a work of purification," the transformation of prereflective beliefs into rational truths.[43] By what criteria does the intellect perform such a critical function? And what relation do such truths in the order of knowing bear to the order of *being*, that (presumably) extramental world of objects and essences and other Christian philosophers? De Lubac fails to say. His primary concern at this stage in the argument is simply to remind his readers that the task of philosophy (Christian or otherwise) always presupposes a nexus of prephilosophical beliefs and behaviors.

This semantic and methodological ambiguity with respect to the nature and ends of philosophy extends also to de Lubac's treatment of the second mode of Christian philosophy. Following Blondel, de Lubac insists that philosophy tends by its very nature toward revelation. But whereas Blondel arrives at this conclusion at the end of a rigorously developed phenomenology of action, de Lubac offers no such methodological specificity with respect to the means by which philosophy discovers itself as ordered to an end beyond its competence. Rather, de Lubac simply asserts that philosophy, "unable to give the total response to the problem of man and yet unable to disinterest itself in this response, cannot find its place of completion and rest . . . except in revelation."[44] But surely this raises a host of important questions concerning the nature of philosophy itself. Is "the problem of man," for instance, the only, or even the primary, concern of philosophy? How does philosophy go about seeking to resolve this problem? In what respect does the problem of man transcend the scope of philosophical inquiry? For all its rhetorical force, de Lubac's insistence that philosophy is teleologically Christian is, at least in this essay, an assertion in need of further argumentation.

Finally, de Lubac's failure to provide a sufficient account of the nature and ends of philosophy leads to a certain formal ambiguity in his articulation of the third mode of Christian philosophy. For if, as de Lubac insists, Christian philosophy in the operative mode is the "synthesis of all knowledge, operating in the light of faith," how are we to distinguish between the task of philosophy and the task of theology? What space does Christian philosophy leave for the science of *sacra doctrina*, that speculative enterprise whose object is God and all things in relation to God?[45] As Hans Urs von Balthasar suggests, de Lubac's position occupied a "suspended middle in which he could not practice any philosophy without its transcendence into theology, but also no theology without its essential inner substructure of philosophy."[46] De Lubac himself readily acknowledges this ambiguity. However, whereas his earliest critics saw this "suspended middle" as a troublesome equivocation in de Lubac's argument,[47] de Lubac retains such ambiguity precisely for the purpose of problematizing extrinsicist construals of the relation between philosophy and theology. The reason that de Lubac thus avoids referring to the third mode of Christian philosophy as "theology" is because, in the then regnant terminology of the manualist tradition, theology was no longer "the science of all things in their final reasons under the light of faith." Rather, theology named the science of strictly supernatural truths, a body of knowledge increasingly shut off from the order of nature and the world of lived experience.[48] De Lubac does not yet explicitly associate this construal of theology with the neo-Scholastic theory of "pure nature," but it is clear that his principal target in "On Christian Philosophy" is an overly extrinsic account of nature and the supernatural (and the problematic relation between reason and revelation that such an account engenders).

Considered in this light—as an exploration of the intrinsic relation between nature and the supernatural—the ambiguity we've just seen becomes less problematic. We noted in our consideration of the second mode of Christian philosophy that de Lubac employs the term "philosophy," not as a "pure technique," but as a shorthand for "all concrete effort of the reason."[49] De Lubac may therefore fail to provide us with a *technical* definition of the nature and ends of philosophy, but he nevertheless lays the groundwork for an understanding of the paradox of humanity's supernatural vocation in terms of the nature and ends of human reason. Philosophy is naturally Christian, because reason is intrinsically related to the revelation that fulfills it. Philosophy becomes operatively Christian when the intellect begins to consider all things in relation to and under the inspiration of this supernatural given. Thus, whatever we are to make of "Sur la philosophie chrétienne" as a contribution to the Christian philosophy debates, in it de Lubac marks a crucial stage in the development of his theology of nature and the supernatural, one that anticipates the supernatural insufficiency of human nature that we explored in chapter 2.

"On Christian Philosophy" introduces us to the noetic implications of de Lubac's theology of nature and the supernatural, but the essay also sets the stage for what we have referred to as the twin aspects of de Lubac's hermeneutics of human existence: an account of the intelligibility of human being in terms of the revelation of humanity's supernatural vocation and a corresponding account of the meaninglessness of human existence on strictly immanentist grounds. As de Lubac's treatment of Blondel shows, the latter judgment—concerning the inadequacy of immanentist accounts of human being—is itself immanently demonstrable. Following its own autonomous movement, philosophy comes to recognize itself as incapable of resolving the problem of human existence, a problem that it is meanwhile incapable of disregarding. In Blondelian terms, the "method of immanence" occludes the "doctrine of immanence."[50] De Lubac's insistence on the meaningfulness of human existence in terms of humanity's supernatural vocation is, of course, contingent on a prior knowledge of the content of Christian revelation. However, as we saw in de Lubac's treatment of the third mode of Christian philosophy, the revelation of the supernatural entails an interpretation of human nature that is intelligible even to the unbeliever. This allows for what de Lubac describes in his inaugural lecture as the necessary task of "fundamental theology": the point of contact between the *fides quaerens intellectum* and the *intellectus quaerens fidem.*[51] For the content of faith is not "a block of revealed truth with no relationship whatsoever to natural man."[52] It is rather the disclosure of God's creative purposes for humankind and the assurance that such purposes have been achieved in the life, death, and resurrection of Jesus Christ. The intrinsic relation between created nature and humanity's supernatural destiny means that only the latter is capable of unlocking the mysteries of the former. De Lubac suggests as much in "On Christian Philosophy" with respect to the dynamism of human reason, but it is in *The Discovery of God* that he brings this hermeneutic to bear on the nature of the intellect.

THE DISCOVERY OF GOD

Introduction

In "On Christian Philosophy," de Lubac suggests that a philosophy operating under the inspiration of faith (the third mode of Christian philosophy) will entail "a metaphysical elucidation of reason itself or of the rational content which puts its radically mysterious character in relief."[53] For de Lubac, Christian revelation is not simply an inert body of truths awaiting interpretation. The interpreter is herself interpreted in the event of encountering God's self-revelation. Likewise, the reason that understands is itself understood only in the light of this mystery. In *The Discovery of God*, de Lubac returns to the self-illuminating aspect of Christian philosophy, developing at length his own metaphysical elucidation of reason in the light of humanity's supernatural vocation. What results is one of de Lubac's most idiosyncratic publications. Whereas "On Christian Philosophy" was written for a largely specialist, academic audience,[54] *The Discovery of God* is more difficult to place in terms of genre and intended readership. The text alternates between technical prose and doxological aphorisms. It is at once an exercise in natural theology and an assault on rationalist attempts to "prove" the existence of God. In the years following its publication, *The Discovery of God* was charged both with fideism and with ignoring the knowledge of God revealed in Jesus Christ. It was perceived as both too modern and too archaically indebted to the theology of the church fathers.[55] The obscurity of the book's genre (and in many places the book's argument) is due in part to its complicated publication history. Originally published as *De la connaissance de Dieu* in 1945, the book was removed from Jesuit libraries in 1950 when de Lubac was implicated in the Fourvière affair. When, in the mid-1950s, "a certain relaxation in official severity began to manifest itself," de Lubac was permitted to publish an enlarged edition under the title *Sur les chemins de Dieu* (1956). De Lubac notes that the latter "was furnished with a few new explanations, numerous documentary texts as well as with a postface that responded to the principal complaints recently formulated, passing at times into a discreet counterattack."[56] While these additions did much to insulate de Lubac's text from (predominantly neo-Scholastic) critiques, they ended up cluttering and occasionally distracting from the argument originally set forth in *De la connaissance de Dieu.*

De Lubac recounts in his memoirs that the first edition of *The Discovery of God* arose from the convergence of three motivating occasions/concerns. First, *De la connaissance de Dieu* was inspired by a number of conversations that he had with an unbelieving comrade during World War I. De Lubac writes: "In 1915–1917, during the war, I had among my companions a future primary-school teacher, a student in a teacher's college. He was not a Christian, and, without being a militant atheist, he did not believe in God. We talked. We debated. . . . It was from our conversations that my first slightly serious personal reflections date. This was the source of the plan, which had not yet taken shape, of what would later be this little book."[57] As this indicates, *The Discovery of God*—perhaps more so than any of de Lubac's other works—was written with an eye to the unbeliever. "My first intention had simply been to lend a helping hand to a few people in their search for God," reflects de Lubac in the postscript to *Sur les chemins de Dieu.*[58] As an attempt at fundamental theology, *The Discovery of God* ventures often into the terrain of "natural theology," witnessing both to the self-disclosure of God in creation (what de Lubac terms "objective revelation") and more directly to the revelation of God at the heart of human consciousness (what de Lubac terms "subjective revelation").[59] In addition to providing a defense of the rationality of belief in God, *The Discovery of God* also extends de Lubac's confrontation with atheist humanism. Like *The Drama of Atheist Humanism* and the concluding chapter of *Catholicism*, *The Discovery of God* appeals often to the dehumanizing effects of purely immanentist (and ultimately nihilistic) accounts of human being.[60] As we will see, *The Discovery of God* applies this critique in particular to the noetic consequences of the denial of God.

According to de Lubac, the second impetus for *The Discovery of God* was his brief stint as a student of philosophy in Jersey (1920–23). It was at this time that de Lubac came across the writings of Blondel. As in "On Christian Philosophy," the philosopher from Aix looms large in *The Discovery of God*, particularly his insistence on an immanent affirmation of the transcendent. According to Blondel, the very notions of immanence and autonomy are realized in human consciousness only by the effective presence of the corresponding notions of transcendence and heteronomy.[61] The idea of perfection, moreover, imposes itself on the intellect in the inevitable apprehension of a disproportion between the "willed will" (what we believe that we will) and the "willing will" (what we will most profoundly). "To admit the insufficiency of every object offered to the will," Blondel insists, is "to betray a higher pretension" of that which alone can satisfy the desire of our nature.[62] This "higher pretension" comes to play a crucial regulative function in de Lubac's account of the intellect. However, as significant as the philosophy of Blondel was for the development of the argument set forth in *The Discovery of God*, it was his encounter with another philosopher during his time as a student in Jersey that provided the main stimulus for what de Lubac comes to refer to as the "transcendental affirmation of God." It was the transcendental Thomism of Joseph Maréchal that ultimately equipped de Lubac with the philosophical categories for articulating the relation between humanity's intellectual vocation and the affirmation of the Absolute that serves as a necessary "a priori condition of the possibility of every object in consciousness."[63]

The final motivation for the argument advanced by de Lubac in *The Discovery of God* was a course that he taught at the Theology Faculty of Lyon on the origins of religion. It was in the spring of 1930, just six months after he had begun teaching as the chair in fundamental theology, that de Lubac was approached about the possibility of lecturing on the history of religions. As de Lubac recounts, the subject had by that time become something of a staple in French universities and teachers' colleges, and the dean of the Theology Faculty was adamant that young priests in training be introduced to the subject from a Christian perspective. Given the Faculty's lack of resources to found a new chair, it was decided that de Lubac's area of specialty (fundamental theology) was the discipline closest to the history of religions. De Lubac "had the weakness to accept" the dean's proposal, and in October of that year, he began lecturing on the origins of religion.[64] As we can see in a published summary of these lectures,[65] de Lubac devoted himself throughout this course to dispelling a number of common "illusions" in nineteenth-century attempts to locate the genesis of the idea of God. In addition to calling into question the very possibility of discovering by means of ethnology, sociology, or psychology the "primitive" state of religion, de Lubac contends that the vast majority of such attempts are determined in advance by some form of atheistic ideology, whether that be Durkheimian sociologism, Comtean positivism, or the materialism of Leninist Marxism. De Lubac remarks in the conclusion to these lectures that all such attempts to pinpoint the origin of religion are doomed to failure, for the idea of God "appeared in humanity as something spontaneous and specific."[66] According to de Lubac, the spontaneity and universality of this idea receives its greatest intelligibility from the vantage of Christian revelation: "In a humanity made in the *image of God* but nevertheless sinful and compelled to make a long and groping ascent since, from its awakening, it has been obsessed by a call from above, it is normal that the *idea of God* is, simultaneously, always ready to spring up and always threatened with suffocation."[67] This relation between the *image* and the *idea* of God comes to play a crucial role in de Lubac's account of the intellect's supernatural vocation in *The Discovery of God.*

Taken together, these three occasions provide us with the principal aims and audience of *The Discovery of God.* The intended reader is the (learned) unbeliever. This explains why the book largely refrains from "crossing the threshold" of the Christian mystery.[68] The knowledge of God considered is not primarily the knowledge revealed in the person and works of Jesus Christ. It is rather the knowledge attainable (and presupposed) by the natural dynamism of human reason. Yet, *The Discovery of God* nevertheless remains an exercise in fundamental theology. As such, de Lubac is committed throughout to demonstrating the intelligibility of all things (and the intellect in particular) in the light of the revelation of humanity's supernatural vocation. De Lubac here interprets the origin of the idea of God in terms of humanity's transcendental affirmation of the Absolute. According to de Lubac, this a priori condition of all human cognition is a constitutive element of humanity's creation in the *imago Dei* and a sign of humanity's intellectual vocation to the vision of God.

The Transcendental Affirmation of God

Following de Lubac's 1930 lectures on the history of religions, *The Discovery of God* takes as its point of departure the question concerning the origin of the idea of God. "It is said that man deifies the heavens," de Lubac remarks. "Let it be granted. But where, exactly, did he find the idea of the divine which he applies to the heavens?"[69] According to de Lubac, there are two fundamental ways of answering this question: the way of Xenophanes or the way of "Moses" (by which he means the protological discourse contained in the earliest chapters of the book of Genesis). Either God was made in the image of humankind or human beings were created in the image of God. If the former, then the idea of transcendence is itself contingent on the data of finite experience. The divine being is, as Feuerbach so persuasively argued, the human being projected into infinite objectivity. If the latter, however, then the origin of the idea of God is ultimately inaccessible to historical, psychological, or sociological inquiry. For such an idea germinates spontaneously on account of the intellect's own dependence on the creative and sustaining activity of God. Thus, according to de Lubac, if Moses is right, then the very impulse to deify, which Xenophanes and Feuerbach rightly discern, itself presupposes a more basic affirmation of divinity: an affirmation that is not consequent upon the cognition of finite objects but is rather the precondition for all such knowledge. This basic idea of divinity is what de

Lubac refers to throughout *The Discovery of God* as the transcendental affirmation of God.

According to de Lubac, whereas an objective affirmation entails *an assertion expressed in words* (a judgment made by way of concepts and belonging to a larger network of semantic relations), a transcendental affirmation denotes *an assertion lived by thought* (a basic preconceptual experience of the Absolute that conditions all finite acts of knowing and willing).[70] It is an affirmation, therefore, only in an analogical sense. De Lubac explains:

> The affirmation of God rises up from the very roots of being and thought, before all conscious acts, before the formation of concepts, conferring upon consciousness its guarantee and upon the concept its universal validity. Shrouded and secret, though necessary and permanent, it lies at the basis of all our judgments about being. It is one with the life of thinking being. It is the affirmation of God which gives the thinking being, at all levels, coherence and consistency—without which it would vanish into dust, just as without God the world itself would vanish.[71]

According to de Lubac, the transcendental affirmation of God is a necessary a priori for all acts of knowing without being itself an immediate object of cognition. Every act of knowledge and volition presupposes this transcendental affirmation: "For God is the Absolute; and nothing can be thought without positing the Absolute in relating it to that Absolute; nothing can be willed without tending towards the Absolute, nor valued unless weighed in terms of the Absolute."[72] Becoming has meaning only in relation to absolute being. The affirmation of immanence is intelligible only in the light of the immanent affirmation of transcendence. But however necessary the idea of God may be, "it does not immediately shine forth in all its brilliance."[73] It is possible, in other words, for one to know God without knowing that one knows him. For as Joseph Maréchal insists, the transcendental affirmation of God is "purely implicit and 'exercised' in the apperception of finite objects." It is made explicit, therefore, "only dialectically, by reflection and analysis."[74]

At the conclusion of his "Notes on Chapter Three" in *Sur les chemins de Dieu*, de Lubac acknowledges his indebtedness to the work of Maréchal in his own formulation of the transcendental affirmation.[75] In his five-volume *Le point de départ de la recherché métaphysique* (particularly "Cahier Five: Thomism Confronting Critical Philosophy"), Maréchal sought to demonstrate the extent to which metaphysical realism is capable of satisfying the critical demands of modern (i.e., Kantian) philosophy. Kant's transcendental analysis, in other words, need not eventuate in Kant's metaphysical agnosticism. Crucial to Maréchal's argument is his twin emphases on the mind's dynamism toward the Absolute and the affirmation of the Infinite as "a *constitutive* condition of our apperception of particular objects."[76] Both assertions are, in the philosophy of Maréchal, mutually conditioning. For according to Maréchal, "since the total objective capacity of our intelligence rejects every limit but nonbeing, it extends as far as being pure and simple. To such a formal capacity there can only correspond one absolutely last and saturating end: the *infinite* Being."[77] Anthony Matteo helpfully summarizes the position of Maréchal on this score: the intellect strives for a comprehensive understanding of being in its totality, and this dynamism serves in turn as "a necessary a priori condition for the possibility of cognition as such."[78] Every act of knowing occurs along the intellect's pursuit of its final end. The perception of finitude in every act of cognition therefore presupposes an inchoate awareness of the unlimited absolute toward which the intellect necessarily strives.

De Lubac is less invested in responding to the critical demands of Kant's transcendental project, but he nevertheless discovers in Maréchal an account of the intellect's vocation that closely corresponds to his own convictions concerning the paradox of created spirit. De Lubac thus employs the results of Maréchal's philosophy for wholly theological ends, insisting that what Maréchal discovers in the exercise of his transcendental analysis is simply the noetic implication of humanity's supernatural finality. The mind's dynamism toward infinite Being attests to the spirit's desire for God. For, as de Lubac already insists in "On Christian Philosophy," the intellect finds its place of completion and rest only in the supernatural vision of God. De Lubac's *articulation* of a preconceptual apprehension of God is thus heavily indebted to the "transcendental

Thomism" of Maréchal, but his *motivation* for positing such a transcendental affirmation is primarily theological. For de Lubac, human beings enjoy a basic knowledge of God by virtue of their creation in the divine image and their intellectual vocation to the beatific vision. De Lubac insists that "God reveals himself continuously to man by imprinting his image upon him. That divine operation constitutes the very center of man. That is what makes him spirit and constitutes his reasonableness."[79] The language of "revelation" is of vital importance for de Lubac's account of the transcendental affirmation, for de Lubac is emphatic that *all* knowledge of God is strictly dependent upon divine action: "God himself is our authority about God; otherwise he is not known. . . . No one can have any knowledge of God unless God teaches him."[80] Humanity's basic apprehension of God is not therefore a purely autonomous acquisition of human reasoning. It is rather a creaturely effect of divine agency, a result of the continual operation of God on the intellect. Human beings know God, because God gives himself to be known. The operation of the intellect that results in the affirmation of God is always a *moved* movement. De Lubac insists, "Our intelligence does not grasp the Absolute . . . without first of all having been grasped by it."[81]

BEFORE PROCEEDING TO AN INVESTIGATION OF THE MEANS by which this transcendental affirmation becomes an object of conceptual knowledge, and the relation that this knowledge bears to the knowledge of God attainable by grace, it is worth considering a number of possible philosophical and theological criticisms of de Lubac's construal of the transcendental affirmation. As Fergus Kerr notes, the philosophical difficulties with de Lubac's position are considerable.[82] For just as "On Christian Philosophy" argues *from* the results of Blondel's phenomenology without providing sufficient warrant of its own for the methodology employed or the conclusions drawn by Blondel, so *The Discovery of God* uncritically presupposes the data of Maréchal's transcendental analysis. De Lubac thus inherits the contested status of Maréchal's philosophy without providing anything like an apologia for his own employment of Maréchal's argument. This leaves *The Discovery of God* vulnerable to a number of misgivings and misunderstandings.

To begin with, the very attempt to provide a transcendental deduction—whereby one seeks to determine the necessary conditions for the possibility of all experience—has come under increasing scrutiny by a number of philosophers. As Stephan Körner argues with respect to Kant's transcendental argument, and as Karen Kilby repeats with regard to Rahner's articulation of the "pre-apprehension of being," we can never be in a position to know for sure that a particular categorial schema or transcendental affirmation is the only possible means for intelligibly organizing our experiences.[83] Kilby notes, "In order to identify our conceptual scheme, or some part of it, as a condition of the possibility of experience we would have to be able to consider all possible alternatives to it—but . . . how could we ever know that we had thought up all the alternatives?"[84] There is, in other words, no vantage outside our particular conceptual scheme from which we can determine its necessity or contingency. Although de Lubac may therefore be able to argue on theological grounds that, given humanity's creation in the *imago Dei* and the intellect's vocation to the knowledge of God, every act of cognition presupposes a basic affirmation of the divine, his assertion that "nothing can be thought without positing the Absolute in relating it to that Absolute" requires further philosophical justification.

The tenuousness of all transcendental deductions aside, what are we to make of de Lubac's insistence on an affirmation that somehow *precedes* the use of all concepts? Kerr inquires, "How does one 'affirm' God—even secretly—prior to one's thinking about God in some way that is in principle communicable to others? What affirming God can there be prior to being able to say something intelligible?"[85] To put the question in a more Lindbeckian/Wittgensteinian register, to what extent is our basic experience of the Absolute already conditioned by prior practices of communication?[86] Not only does de Lubac's account of the transcendental affirmation push him in the direction of the very foundationalist idealism that he sought to avoid in "On Christian Philosophy,"[87] but it risks abstracting the knowing subject altogether from the network of creaturely conditions that attend her being in the world. In this sense, de Lubac's insistence on a basic knowledge of God that conditions all other acts of knowing would appear to lead him in the direction of "ontologism," an epistemological doctrine dating back to Nicholas Malebranche

(1638–1715), which asserts that "only the intuitive knowledge of God makes all other forms of real knowledge possible, for only God truly is."[88] In 1861, seven propositions pertaining to ontologism were condemned by the Holy Office as "unsafe for teaching" (*tuto tradi non posse*). Although the precise reasons for the condemnation were unspecified in the Holy Office's decree, the general anxiety was that such an intuitive knowledge seemed to render grace superfluous. According to one critic, "If by nature, without reference to supernature, man is granted a direct, even if obscure, glimpse of God's reality, it is difficult to see how any grace given to him can differ in kind from the light of reason he receives in his natural creation."[89] Moreover, in terms of de Lubac's own rendering of the *desiderium naturae*, it is unclear why such a basic apprehension of God would fail to satisfy the desire of nature. In a footnote citing the Dominican cardinal Tommaso Zigliara (1833–93), de Lubac grants a certain "element of truth" in ontologism, though he insists in the book's postscript that he is "in opposition to all the doctrines which tend to 'ontologism.'"[90] Following Maréchal, de Lubac presumes to avoid the errors of ontologism by distinguishing sharply between an "*intuitive* knowledge" of God and a "*transcendental* affirmation." Whereas the former consists in an immediate vision of the Infinite—an innate *conceptual* knowledge of God given directly to the intellect by way of divine illumination—the latter is, as we have seen, a nonconceptual assertion lived by thought. Thus, according to Maréchal, the transcendental affirmation "has nothing in common with a 'vision of objects in God' nor with an 'innate idea.'"[91] Such qualifications may go some way in distancing de Lubac's position from a form of ontological intuitionism, but the philosophical problems with de Lubac's articulation of a transcendental affirmation are scarcely dispensed. For what sense does it finally make to speak of a "knowledge" that is both prior to experience and yet nonintuitive, an implicit affirmation and yet not an innate idea? At the very least, de Lubac's articulation of a transcendental affirmation remains severely underdeveloped.

Theologically, de Lubac's account of the transcendental affirmation of God is susceptible to charges of projectionism, the unwitting ascription to God of exclusively anthropomorphic idealizations. For if, as de Lubac insists, the affirmation of God is an a priori condition of every act of knowledge and volition, how do we know that the referent of the word "God" is not simply the projection onto extramental reality of a mere postulate of practical and theoretical reason? How do we know, in other words, whether the necessity of the Absolute is more than noetic?

A related theological critique of de Lubac's position concerns the epistemic consequences of humanity's sinful condition. As with much of de Lubac's theology, hamartiology plays a less-than-crucial role in his articulation of the transcendental affirmation. For even if human beings enjoy a basic experience of the Absolute by virtue of their creation according to the divine image, what becomes of this experience under the debilitating effects of sin? As we will see in the next section, de Lubac's response to the first concern (the worry about projectionism) entails a judgment concerning the latter (the epistemic consequences of sin). According to de Lubac's treatment of Moses and Xenophanes, humanity's tendency to deify presupposes humanity's basic affirmation of divinity. God created human beings in his image, instilling them with a preconceptual knowledge of him. Human beings, limited in their finitude and marred by sin, create in turn an image of God after their own likeness, objectifying the transcendental affirmation in the form of an idol. Thus, rather than succumbing idly to the temptation of projectionism, de Lubac subsumes this very temptation into his own account of the dialectic of the knowledge of God and the epistemic implications of sin.

Finally, and most significantly for our own articulation of de Lubac's hermeneutics of human existence, de Lubac's account of the transcendental affirmation of God risks compromising his insistence on the supernatural insufficiency of nature. For what need is there for the intrusion of a supernatural revelation if human beings always already enjoy a certain "habitual knowledge" of God by nature? What do human beings discover in the former that they are incapable of discerning by way of transcendental reflection upon the dynamism of human reason? To apply a common critique of Rahner's "experiential-expressivism" to de Lubac's argument in *The Discovery of God*: to what extent does de Lubac's "heuristic strategy of returning us always to the self's experience of transcending finitude" divert our attention from "allowing God's unique self-revelation historically in Jesus Christ to shape Christian self-understanding"?[92] In chapter 2, we argued that de Lubac's construal of the *desiderium naturae* was intended to maintain both the intrinsic relation between nature and the supernatural (against extrinsicism) and the sheer unforeseeable novelty of the supernatural (against intrinsicism). De Lubac's articulation of the transcendental affirmation of God succeeds in upholding the former, but it remains to be seen to what extent it can be reconciled with the latter. It remains to be seen, in other words, how de Lubac might continue to affirm that Christ brought all *newness* by bringing himself.

The Dialectic of the Idea of God

As significant as the transcendental affirmation is for de Lubac's account of the spirit's intellectual vocation, it is only the first stage of what de Lubac refers to as "the dialectic of the idea of God."[93] According to de Lubac, in order for the intellect to attain its final end, the object of humanity's transcendental affirmation must first be made explicit. That is to say, the basic experience of the Absolute that conditions every objective affirmation must itself rise to the level of consciousness, objectifying itself in the definite form of a concept. The "assertion lived by thought" must become an "assertion expressed in words."[94] According to de Lubac, the idea of God undergoes such objectivization through both a process of "introversion" and reflection upon God's created effects. By introversion, de Lubac means something like the transcendental analysis of Maréchal whereby the idea of the Absolute is rendered intelligible as the condition for the possibility of cognition. Reflective inquiry reveals the prereflective affirmation of infinity, thus bringing the latter to explicit conceptual awareness. It is this task of objectivization by way of introversion that de Lubac devotes himself to throughout *The Discovery of God* in his treatment of the transcendental affirmation. The objectivization of the idea of God likewise occurs through the intellect's reflection on created being. "In principle," notes de Lubac, "as well as for the straightforward, honest mind, 'the merest glance reveals the hand that has made everything.' "[95] The traditional "proofs" for the existence of God based on movement, causality, contingency, and so forth thus provide the occasion for the objectivization of humanity's transcendental affirmation. Without providing anything like rational certainty, these proofs facilitate the "closest attention" to the object of humanity's basic affirmation.[96] In both cases, through introversion and reflection on contingent being, "reason rises to the Absolute from the relative."[97] There is therefore a certain circularity with respect to the intellect's cognition of immanence and transcendence: every objective affirmation of the finite rests secretly on the transcendental affirmation of the infinite. Every objective affirmation of the infinite, meanwhile, presupposes a nexus of prior judgments pertaining to the world of experience.

Although the objectivization of the transcendental affirmation is thus a necessary stage in the intellect's pursuit of its final end, it is nevertheless fraught with difficulties that retard the intellect's movement toward God on account of both reason's finitude and the spirit's moral deviation. For it is precisely at this stage in the dialectic of the idea of God that the risk of projectionism rears its head. According to de Lubac, the moment the transcendental affirmation expresses itself in the form of a judgment, "there is the tendency to confuse the Author of Nature with the Nature through which he reveals himself obscurely, whose characteristics we cannot help employing in order to think of him; and there is the tendency to forsake an exacting and incorruptible God in favor of something inferior or fictitious."[98] The influence of sin has not completely destroyed the intellect's basic affirmation of divinity—such an affirmation remains a constitutive element of humanity's being in the image of God—but it seriously disorders the intellect's reference to God. Like the seed sown in the gospel, therefore, the idea of God "fell among thorns and thistles and was quickly stifled by the incredible proliferation of myths."[99] Idolatry emerges as the perverse objectification of humanity's transcendental affirmation. The gods-of-our-own-making are thus parasitic upon the idea of God implanted in us by nature.

Even excluding the risk of idolatry, however, the dialectic of the idea of God requires a further stage in order for the intellect to attain its final end. For however necessary the use of concepts may be in the objectivization of the transcendental affirmation, they are nevertheless inadequate to the task of describing the wholly transcendent reality of God. As de Lubac insists, our concepts are only suited to the world of experience. As such, any element that can be grasped by means of our concepts "will always be too gross to express the Being whose essence is Being, pure

Being, pure 'Existence,' pure Act undefiled and simple, a Subject which cannot be a predicate, which must be posited 'absolutely,' and in respect of whom a 'qualification' is a sacrilegious 'restriction.'"[100] In order for our concepts to be adapted to divine reality, they must therefore by subjected to a process of purification. The objective affirmation of God must be submitted to a negative dialectic, "which is turned against all the gross elements from which it seems to take its substance."[101] The *via affirmationis* must eventuate in the *via negativa*.[102] Only then is God affirmed as the One beyond all affirmation. Only then is God known in the knowledge of what God is not.

However necessary this stage of the dialectic may be, de Lubac's treatment of the means by which our language attains such purification is largely underdeveloped. Aside from gesturing occasionally in the direction of analogy,[103] de Lubac largely neglects to provide an account of the semantic implications of the relation between created and uncreated being. Instead, de Lubac is more concerned to distance his own articulation of the *via negativa*—as a necessary stage in the intellect's movement toward a more *positive* apprehension of God—from what he perceives to be the common conflation of apophaticism with some form of agnosticism.[104] De Lubac insists, "When we say that God is ineffable, it does not mean that we cannot say anything about him! It does not mean that there is nothing to say on the subject, or that there is nothing to be done but keep silence."[105] How is it then that we can say anything meaningful about God? What prevents the process of semantic purification from leading us into the quagmire of sheer negation? According to de Lubac, the negative dialectic is sustained and directed throughout by the transcendental affirmation of God: "It is that affirmation which obliges us, when the moment comes, to deny everything: and so it cannot be denied. . . . That affirmation is always the soul of our negations, and if we come to deny it the process of negation would come to a halt." It is the transcendental affirmation, therefore, that allows for the *via negativa* without landing us in nihilism. It is the preconceptual experience of the one who transcends all of our concepts that "obliges us always to affirm God without ever allowing us to stop at anything unworthy of him."[106]

Like the second stage in the dialectic of the idea of God, the third stage is also susceptible to the disordering effects of sin. For whereas idolatry arises as the perverse objectification of the transcendental affirmation, so the process of negation easily gives way to atheism or agnosticism. To a certain extent, de Lubac acknowledges the service rendered to theological speech by the critiques of atheism. "Unbeknown to and in spite of himself," de Lubac insists, "the atheist is often the greatest help the believer can have. . . . He cooperates, unintentionally, in the 'purification of faith,' which consists in 'freeing it more and more from the senses and human reasonings.'"[107] In liberating human beings from the bondage of superstition, however, the atheist ultimately subjects the intellect to a new form of captivity. For rather than employing the dialectic of negation for the purpose of affirming divine transcendence, the atheist negates the order of transcendence altogether. In so doing, the atheist places himself in a position of supreme contradiction. For, as we have argued at length, de Lubac is convinced that a basic affirmation of God is the necessary condition for every objective affirmation. In denying the infinite, therefore, the atheist negates the very ground upon which he is capable of affirming anything. The atheist "leans upon God in the very act of denying him."[108] To deny God in this way is not simply to subject the intellect to contradiction. It is also, and more importantly, to place oneself in violent opposition to the image of God in humanity and the spirit's vocation to the beatific vision.

At this stage in the dialectic, reason is therefore still a long way off from the repose that it seeks in God. The dialectic of the idea of God is not a straightforward ascent, but a perpetually tumultuous enterprise. What begins as an abiding affirmation of the Absolute quickly descends into idolatry. Efforts to free the intellect from idolatry give rise in turn to atheism. De Lubac's attempt at a natural theology does not therefore produce the results that one might have initially expected from his confident exposition of the transcendental affirmation. In principle, reason may be sufficient to a natural knowledge of God, but in practice—that is, under the conditions of human finitude and depravity—"the world conceals God more than it reveals him."[109] In order for the intellect to attain its final end, it must therefore have recourse to a principle that transcends it. Amidst the constant oscillation between objectivization and negation, the Spirit of God must intervene. Quoting at length a passage by Louis Bouyer, De Lubac insists:

> The Spirit enables us to know [God] in a certain measure, because it assimilates us to him. . . . The Spirit alone can plumb the depths of God. The Spirit alone grants us a knowledge of God which is more than radically inadequate or purely negative knowledge. The Spirit makes new men of us, men participating in the divine nature, as the Second Epistle of St. Peter makes bold to say, and gives us the only knowledge of God which is on his own level, because it is a connatural knowledge.[110]

According to de Lubac, therefore, it is the gift of the Spirit of God—"in fact the 'Spirit of Jesus' "—that elevates the dialectic of the idea of God to its place of final rest.[111] For without suspending the natural laws of the intelligence—the necessary interplay of affirmation and negation—the Spirit comes to assure the intellect of "the tranquil enjoyment of its object." St. Paul declares in Romans (5:5), "God's love has been poured into our hearts through the Holy Spirit that has been given to us." And according to the author of 1 John (4:7), "everyone who loves is born of God and knows God." To return therefore to the words of William of St.-Thierry, the Spirit of God is the means by which the spirit comes to enjoy "the knowledge of love." And though this knowledge constitutes the end of our nature, it is only ever procured by means of the gift of the supernatural.

The Desire of Nature and the Knowledge of God

Without therefore denying the constancy of the transcendental affirmation or disparaging the importance of the dialectic of the idea of God, the metaphysical elucidation of reason undertaken in *The Discovery of God* arrives at the same conclusion as de Lubac's "On Christian Philosophy": the dynamism of human reason finds its place of completion only in the gift of the supernatural. This concurrence lends itself rather nicely to the theology of nature and the supernatural we advanced in chapter 2, but it would appear to undermine the constant refrain throughout *The Discovery of God* that the intellect always already enjoys a basic knowledge of the one to whom it is teleologically ordered. For what sense does it make to insist on an implicit knowledge of God if reason is ultimately incapable of anticipating the grace that fulfills it? What relation does the idea of God at the heart of human consciousness bear to the "knowledge of love" revealed in Christ and received by means of the Holy Spirit? As we suggested at the outset of this chapter, the answer resides in de Lubac's treatment of the *desiderium naturae.*

"God is naturally known to all," remarks de Lubac in the first edition of *De la connaissance de Dieu*, "but he is not always recognized. Not everyone knows that they know him: as when I see Peter coming toward me, without yet knowing that it is he, as St. Thomas says."[112] De Lubac returns to this saying of St. Thomas in *Sur les chemins de Dieu*, and it is this passage in the *Summa theologiae* (*ST* Ia, q. 2, a. 1, ad 2) that provides de Lubac with the occasion for reflecting on the precise relation between the desire of nature, the transcendental affirmation of God, and the knowledge of God received by grace. According to Thomas, "To know that God exists in a general and confused way is implanted in us by nature, inasmuch as God is man's beatitude. For man naturally desires happiness, and what is naturally desired by man must be naturally known to him."[113] The basic knowledge of God implanted in us by nature (which de Lubac equates with the transcendental affirmation) is therefore the necessary correlate to humanity's desire for the supernatural. This desire is not elicited by a prior object of cognition, but rather precedes every explicit act of knowing, inasmuch as the affirmation to which it corresponds "comes before the operation of will and intellect."[114] The spirit desires to know by grace the one whom it already knows (however imperfectly) by nature. Conversely, the spirit always already knows God implicitly as the object of its natural desire for beatitude. This allows de Lubac to affirm both the intrinsic relation between reason and revelation and the supernatural insufficiency of the former. De Lubac insists:

> When I reach an explicit knowledge of God, I certainly do not recognize him as someone whom I had already known with the same sort of knowledge, and had since forgotten or lost to view. . . . Nevertheless, the extraordinary thing is that knowing God for the first time I do, in fact, *recognize him.* For . . . when I come to know God as the one who will make me happy, I realize at the same time that God is identified with the beatitude which I knew by desiring it, but which I

> placed, at first, among objects which deceived me; or rather I can now identify my beatitude with him.[115]

In giving himself to be known, God reveals himself as the object of our deepest desire. Humanity's supernatural vocation is therefore revealed as it is realized by grace.

But what about the *natural* knowledge of God attainable by means of the dialectic of the idea of God? What relation does this objectivization and purification of the transcendental affirmation bear to the desire of our nature and the supernatural object of this desire? De Lubac acknowledges that the process whereby the intellect arrives at such a natural knowledge is fraught with difficulties. The twin dangers of idolatry and atheistic negation continually reassert themselves. But this is not to say that the intellect is wholly incapable of acquiring such knowledge. Sin has not completely eradicated reason's capacity to discover, by means of introversion and reflection on created being, the revelation of God in nature. In the penultimate chapter of *The Discovery of God*, de Lubac distinguishes between the "philosopher" and the "mystic" in an attempt to both distinguish and unite the knowledge of God attainable by means of the dialectic of the idea of God and the knowledge of God attainable by grace.[116] The philosopher, notes de Lubac, is driven by the desire to comprehend the universe, to provide a total explanation of the relation that pertains between all things. The knowledge of God that the philosopher pursues is not therefore the knowledge of God as he is in himself. It is rather the knowledge of the relation that God bears to everything that is not God. Even though this knowledge may satisfy the philosopher's reason, it is incapable of satiating the mystical aspiration. For according to de Lubac, "the mystic reaches out beyond the supreme Cause and the unifying One . . . and pursues the One itself. He seeks the One in its being and unity. And the least knowledge of that One is worth more in his eyes than the profoundest and most comprehensive knowledge of all else."[117] Without denying the importance of this distinction between the "philosopher" and the "mystic," de Lubac nevertheless insists that there is something artificial in their dissociation. For according to de Lubac, the "philosopher" and the "mystic" do not exist in abstraction. They rather name two corresponding aspirations of the intellect, aspirations fundamentally united in the spirit's vocation to the knowledge of God. The philosophical endeavor terminates at the knowledge of God attainable by natural reason, but the mystical aspiration terminates only at the knowledge of God attainable by grace. And although the former consists in the knowledge of God's existence, the latter is satisfied only in the supernatural vision of God's essence. Thus, the philosopher may succeed in arriving at a knowledge of God as "the explanatory principle of all things," but the spirit remains ever restless until it rests in the mystical contemplation of God alone. With Thomas (and the proponents of pure nature), de Lubac thus distinguishes between a twofold beatitude corresponding to humanity's twofold knowledge of God: "One is proportionate to human nature, a happiness, to wit, which man can obtain by means of his natural principles. The other is a happiness surpassing man's nature, and which man can obtain by the power of God alone, by a kind of participation of the Godhead."[118] However, whereas the advocates of pure nature understand the former to be the final end of a purely natural order, de Lubac insists with St. Thomas that the beatitude proportionate to our nature is an *imperfect* beatitude that fails to fully satisfy the desire of nature.[119] The *desiderium naturae*, in other words, extends beyond the reach of the intellect's natural capacities. The mystical aspiration *sets the philosophical enterprise in motion*, but the latter is finally incapable of satisfying the former.

In a lecture delivered before the International Anselm Congress in 1959, de Lubac returns to a consideration of the "mystic" and the "philosopher" as a means of considering the relation between the desire of nature and the limits of natural reason.[120] In "Seigneur, je cherche ton visage" (Lord, I seek your face), de Lubac devotes himself in particular to the famous *argumentum* of Anselm's *Proslogion*. According to de Lubac, having succeeded in providing "a single argument" sufficient to demonstrate the existence of God, Anselm nevertheless acknowledges a feeling of failure in his search for God. Having found God to be "that than which nothing greater can be conceived," Anselm confesses his disappointment: "If you have found [Him], why is it that you do not experience what you have found? Why, O Lord God, does my soul not experience You if it has found You?"[121] According to de Lubac, the Anselmian anxiety does not arise from a failure of discursive reasoning. On the contrary, Anselm's *reason* is satisfied, "but not the initial *desire* that had set it in place."[122] The crisis that Anselm undergoes in chapter 14 of his *Proslogion* is the result of that inevitable disproportion between the philosophical task and the mystical impulse, between the dialectic of the idea of God and the natural desire for the supernatural. "The more God is 'proved' or 'understood,'" de Lubac insists, "the less he is 'found,' because the understanding obtained . . . results in a more vivid awareness, if not of the desire for the divine presence, at least of *the absence that wounds this desire*."[123] When, in chapter 23, the *Proslogion* eventually culminates in joy, it is not because Anselm is led there "by degrees of the understanding." He comes there instead "through the data of Scripture. He listens to God who has revealed himself as Father, Son and Holy Spirit."[124] Anselm's reason achieves its telos, therefore, only in its encounter with the supernatural revelation of God. Moreover, just as de Lubac insists in *The Discovery of God* that the intellect comes to enjoy the object of its desire through the infusion of love, so he concludes his reflections on Anselm's *Proslogion* with "a hymn to hope."[125] It is by the supernatural virtue of hope, notes de Lubac, not by an effort of the understanding, that Anselm begins to participate in that joy that ultimately awaits him in the beatific vision.[126] Thus, just as the intellect requires a supernatural *object* in order to attain its final end, so the intellect itself must undergo a supernatural transformation—a participation in the divine life and the infusion of the supernatural virtues—in order to rest in the knowledge of this object. As de Lubac argues elsewhere, the dynamism of human reason must undergo a movement of conversion in order to give way to the dynamism of faith.[127]

CONCLUSION

In both "On Christian Philosophy" and his "metaphysical elucidation of reason itself" in *The Discovery of God*, de Lubac attempts to narrate the dynamism of human existence in terms of reason's paradoxical relation to humanity's supernatural vocation. As in his inaugural lecture on "Apologetics and Theology," de Lubac sets himself firmly against extrinsicist construals of the relationship between the supernatural content of

Christian revelation and the concrete effort of human reason. The end of the rational creature is the knowledge of love, the final integration of will and intellect in the beatific vision of the divine essence. It is by means of this knowledge, this graced participation in the knowledge and love of God, that human beings come to share in the divine beatitude, thus attaining their supernatural end. It is axiomatic for de Lubac that there is an intrinsic relation between being and finality. Reason is therefore "ontologically other" than it would be were human beings ordered to a strictly natural end. In his contribution to the Christian philosophy debates, de Lubac follows Blondel in articulating this intrinsic relationship in terms of reason's natural inclination toward revelation. Philosophy is "naturally Christian" because reason is teleologically ordered to the intellect's repose in God. In *The Discovery of God*, de Lubac supplements his earlier reflections on the dynamism of reason with an ambitious (if not always convincing) investigation of what he refers to as the "transcendental affirmation of God" and the "dialectic of the idea of God" in humanity. In this text, the intrinsic relation between reason and revelation is portrayed in terms of a preconceptual apprehension of God that functions as an a priori condition for all finite acts of cognition and that becomes itself an object of conceptual knowledge only at the end of a long and arduous process of objectivization and negation. Though rhetorically persuasive and theologically inventive, de Lubac's argument in *The Discovery of God* suffers from a number of serious philosophical difficulties. Where it succeeds, however, is in its vigilance to uphold the *creaturely* status of the created intellect. Human reason is created and upheld by God in order to actualize itself in the knowledge of truth. To rely on such divine assistance (*auxilio divino*) in the very act of denying God is therefore to place the intellect in a perilous state of self-contradiction.

In both of the writings discussed in this chapter, and also in his 1959 lecture on Anselm and his inaugural lecture on "Apologetics and Theology," de Lubac thus refuses modernity's bifurcation of faith and reason. Bréhier is mistaken to oppose Christianity and philosophy, just as the fideist is wrong to "deny knowledge in order to make room for faith." Rationalist appeals to "pure reason" and fideist disavowals of all natural knowledge of God err alike in restricting the dynamism of reason to a strictly natural finality. And yet it would be a mistake to thereby read de

Lubac as denying an essential distinction between faith and reason.[128] A more thoroughgoing treatment of the nature of faith will have to wait until chapter 5, but we might note here that for de Lubac, faith is "a movement which begins by 'conversion.'"[129] It is the dynamism of human existence *taken up and transformed under the vivifying conditions of grace.*[130] Faith is not *opposed* to reason, insofar as the God "toward whom faith rushes" is "already the One toward whom the mind and spirit of man naturally tend, without knowing it, as toward their end."[131] Nevertheless, faith is a uniquely *supernatural* act, a movement animated by the corresponding virtues of hope and charity in response to a personal encounter with the self-revelation of God in Jesus Christ.[132] This essential distinction between faith and reason is already evident in the works we've discussed in this chapter. In "On Christian Philosophy," without denying "a truly intrinsic relationship between rational speculation and supernatural revelation," de Lubac nevertheless insists that reason is incapable of anticipating the content of revelation. The dynamism of human reason terminates at the acknowledgment of its own insufficiency. Likewise, in *The Discovery of God*, de Lubac maintains that the dialectic of the idea of God is incapable of satisfying the desire of nature. The mystical élan outpaces the limits of discursive reasoning. The desire that motivates Anselm's *argumentum* is only satiated through the biblical mediation of the supernatural revelation of Father, Son, and Holy Spirit. A theological hermeneutics of human existence must encompass both aspects of this paradoxical relation between reason and the supernatural that fulfills it.

FOUR

Being in History

INTRODUCTION

Thus far we have spoken of the drama of human existence in largely *un*dramatic terms. The picture of human being that emerges from the previous two chapters is one of a knowing and willing subject ordered by nature to, that is, created for the purpose of, the supernatural enjoyment of God. However illuminating such an investigation of faculties and finality may be for an understanding of human *nature*, we are still some way from an adequate account of human *existence*. For if the former is concerned primarily with the constitutive features of a particular kind of agent, the latter requires especial attention to the contingencies of that agent's being in history. To speak of human existence is to speak of human beings, not simply as individual instantiations of a common nature, but as *persons*. And as de Lubac insists, "The summons to personal life is a *vocation*," a divine invitation to play a particular role within the broader narrative of God's creative and redemptive purposes.[1] The drama of human existence finds its meaning only in relation to the drama of history taken as a whole. Conversely, "It is because the world is a history, a single history, that each individual life is a drama."[2]

For de Lubac, to speak of human existence in terms of personality and historicity is to attend to the irreducibly *social* nature of human beings and their common destiny. De Lubac insists in a 1941 lecture to the École des cadres d'Uriage, "Beings do not exist independently from each other. They neither live nor develop alone. Spiritual beings, persons, even less. Ontological solitude would be their annihilation. If we exist through God, then we exist as well through one another."[3] We will see that the social and historical dimensions of human existence are closely allied in de Lubac's thought. For de Lubac, the *telos* of history is the recovery of lost unity, the supernatural restoration of the original fellowship of human persons with one another and with God. The Christian understanding of salvation is not therefore an individualist doctrine of escape, the soul's anagogical ascent to a disembodied contemplation of God in heaven. It is rather the perfection of human society in union with Christ. For de Lubac, it is precisely because salvation is social that the drama of human existence is historically intelligible: "For if the salvation offered by God is in fact the salvation of the human race, since this human race lives and develops in time, any account of this salvation will naturally take a historical form—it will be the history of the penetration of humanity by Christ."[4] To be human is therefore to stand in a particular historical relation to the life, death, and resurrection of Jesus Christ. It is also to stand in a particular relation to Christ's body, the church.

In this chapter, we will investigate the social and historical dimensions of human existence by way of reflection on de Lubac's theology of history. That is, we will attempt to shed some light on the vocation of human persons—the unique role and destiny prescribed to human agents—by locating them within the larger drama of God's purposes for creation. On this account, the intelligibility of human existence presupposes an essentially *meaningful* history. That such a theology of history is possible or theologically permissible, however, is scarcely self-evident. According to a growing number of theologians, "the question of meaning in history has become meaningless."[5] To ascribe meaning to historical processes is either to confuse the accidental for the necessary (the latter alone being of real philosophical/theological interest) or to implicate God in the atrocities of human history. The former is a category mistake; the latter is a morally disastrous attempt at theodicy. For de Lubac, however, history is meaningful, and thus theologically interesting, for a number of reasons. First, *being in history is a necessary dimension of human existence*: "Man is made in history and by history."[6] Historicity is a created constituent of human being and must therefore stand in some kind of meaningful relation to its creator. As Ben Quash notes, "Christian theology is obliged to think about history because in believing that heaven and earth and everything in them are God's creation, it therefore believes that the irreducibly historical dimension of being is also something created by God: its temporal extension, its successiveness, its narratability."[7] Second, and correlatively, precisely as created, *history is subject to the providential governance of God.* History is contingent, not simply on the spontaneous interplay of created agents, but upon the creative and sustaining activity of God. God has not abandoned historical processes to the caprice of strictly immanent causes. Rather, God lovingly directs his creatures to the perfection of their appointed ends (a point that we shall come to shortly). Third, *theology attends to history as the appointed locus of God's revelatory activity*: "God acts in history and reveals himself through history. Or rather, God inserts himself in history and so bestows on it a 'religious consecration' which compels us to treat it with due respect."[8] History speaks of God because God acts and speaks in and through history. For de Lubac, the interpretation of sacred scripture is first and foremost the interpretation of sacred *history*, that series of events through which the divine purposes for creation become uniquely (though never exhaustively) transparent to the eyes of faith. In the gathering of a people to himself, in the manifestations of God's theophanic glory, and most definitively in the life, death, and resurrection of Jesus Christ, God reveals the meaning of history precisely in revealing himself. Finally, according to de Lubac, *history has meaning because it is ordered to a divinely appointed end.* The divine will, "controlling all things," brings the world infallibly into port: "For there is a port, a definite terminus. The whole universe cries out for its delivery and it is sure to obtain it. Its groaning is begotten by hope."[9] As Karl Löwith argues, the language of "meaning" implies "purpose" and is therefore necessarily teleological. History is meaningful "only by indicating some transcendent purpose beyond the actual facts. But, since history is a movement in time, the purpose is a goal. . . . To venture a statement about the meaning of historical events is possible only when their *telos* becomes apparent."[10] For de Lubac, the meaning of history is therefore *eschatology*: "The liberation of all creation, the consummation of all things in the unity of the Body of Christ now fully perfected."[11]

It is worth mentioning at the outset that de Lubac nowhere develops a discrete "theology of history" in the manner of, for example, his confrères Jean Daniélou or Hans Urs von Balthasar.[12] De Lubac's theology of history is distributed across a number of theological and historical inquiries, from his writings on ecclesiology and spiritual exegesis to his genealogical foray into modern and medieval apocalypticism. The investigation of de Lubac's theology of history that follows will take as its point of departure his decades-long confrontation with the philosophy of Marx, which extends de Lubac's critique of atheist humanism to immanentist construals of history. In contradistinction to the "absolute temporalism" of Marx's philosophy of history, de Lubac insists that the dialectic of immanently historical processes is incapable of procuring the "end of history" as envisioned by Marx. Only Christian eschatology secures the liberation of humanity from its captivity to social antagonism. The drama of history is thus analogous to the drama of human existence: history itself is teleologically ordered to the gratuitous disposal of a wholly supernatural end. As such, history is only intelligible to the eyes of faith. In the second part of this chapter, we turn our attention to de Lubac's meticulous and far-reaching genealogy of the "spiritual posterity" of the twelfth-century abbot and apocalypticist Joachim of Fiore. Just as de Lubac noted a certain complicity between the neo-Scholastic theory of pure nature and the anthropology of secular humanism, so he traces the evolution of deviant forms of Christian apocalypticism into secular narrations of history. Finally, having treated the theological motivations for de Lubac's dismissal of immanentist accounts of history (both theological and atheological), we will turn in the remainder of the chapter to de Lubac's positive account of the meaning of history. By locating de Lubac's theology of history within a particular hermeneutics of scripture we will see that, for de Lubac, the meaning of history resides in the supernatural restoration of humanity's abrogated unity in the person of Jesus Christ and in his body, the church. It is this history of the reunification of humanity in the *totus Christus* that constitutes the narrative within which each individual drama finds its ultimate meaning.

THE MARXIST IDEA OF MAN AND HIS DESTINY

De Lubac's confrontation with Marxism began as early as *Catholicism* (1938) and continued, to greater and lesser degrees, until the early 1980s.[13] An invitation to deliver a lecture to the Semaine sociale de Paris in 1947 on "The Christian Conception of Man" afforded de Lubac the opportunity to respond in particular to Marx's materialist interpretation of history. During the period of liberation following the collapse of the Vichy regime, Marxist ideology exercised a tremendous influence on the French imagination, and the initial postwar success of the French Communist Party (PCF) suggested at least the possibility of a communist future for France.[14] Despite the expulsion of the PCF from government in May 1947, Marxism continued to enjoy a privileged, albeit contested, status among French intelligentsia, including a growing number of Roman Catholics. As de Lubac laments in a letter to a friend on February 3, 1949, "these 'progressive Christians' . . . play into the hands of the worst of totalitarianisms. The leading ones among them, who have fought against totalitarians of the nazi party and the nazi state, fail to perceive that they are fighting today for the totalitarians of the communist party and the communist state."[15] In addition to offering a Christian response to the Marxist conception of man and the meaning of history, de Lubac's 1947 lecture was thus intended to disabuse these "progressive Christians" of their uncritical allegiance to Marx. In contrast to those who discerned in Marxism a strictly temporal program capable of being integrated into the spiritual domain of faith, de Lubac sought to demonstrate the absolutism of the former. According to de Lubac, one cannot adopt the Marxist critique without also adopting the Marxist metaphysic. The immanent ideals of Marxism are predicated on the absolute negation of transcendence.[16]

Even before the start of the Semaine sociale, de Lubac's lecture was mired in controversy. Less than a month before he was scheduled to present, de Lubac received word that authorities in Rome had vetoed his participation in the event, likely on account of the bourgeoning controversy surrounding his work on the supernatural.[17] The event's organizers, Charles Flory and Alfred Michelin, were able to convince the authorities to permit de Lubac's lecture, but only under the condition that he first submit his paper to the censorship of the archbishop of Paris. Once it was delivered (and subsequently published),[18] the reaction to de Lubac's paper was no less controversial. Several readers thought that they discerned in de Lubac's argument the doctrinal inspiration for "Christian communism." Others reproached de Lubac for criticizing Marxism from a Christian perspective, rather than refuting it "solely through the resources of natural philosophy."[19] The former could only have arisen from a superficial understanding of de Lubac's argument (as we will see, de Lubac's lecture was anything but an apologia for Christian communism!),[20] but the latter names precisely the methodological discrepancies among divergent construals of the relation between nature and the supernatural. For the advocates of pure nature, human nature is intrinsically intelligible without recourse to the revealed content of the Christian faith. The Marxist conception of man is thus refutable on strictly immanent (that is, purely natural) grounds. For de Lubac, however, the drama of human existence is intelligible only in the light of humanity's supernatural finality. As such, de Lubac challenges the "absolute temporalism" of Marxist humanism by appealing precisely to the necessity of transcendence for the accomplishment of the "end of history" as envisioned by Marx. Only Christian eschatology provides the conditions for the fulfillment of Marxist teleology.

De Lubac's lecture takes as its point of departure Marxist appeals to *un homme nouveau* ("a new man"). In France, particularly during the interwar period, the search for a new man represented the overcoming of the "bourgeois humanism" of the Third Republic and an attempt on the part of communists, Catholics, and noncomformists (and, by the mid-1940s, existentialists) to forge a new humanism in its wake as a viable alternative.[21] In its distinctly Marxist key, the new man—what the popular Marxist philosopher and sociologist Henri Lefebvre terms *l'homme total* ("the total man")[22]—designates the return of man to full possession of himself through the elimination of all forms of alienation. The new man names both the *liberator* and the *liberated subject* of a human society no longer in the throes of social antagonism, an association "in which the free development of each is the condition for the free development of all."[23]

According to de Lubac, there is a superficial likeness between this Marxist teleology and the hope of Christian eschatology. The Christian scriptures support "the ideal of a liberated, unified humanity that has recovered full possession of its essence, reconciled with itself as with the universe, living in fullness until the consummation of History."[24] There is an analogy then between the Marxist "eschaton" and the Christian understanding of the Kingdom of God. Both envision a future devoid of struggle and exclusion, in which the individual attains unity with his or her own nature and the greater human totality. However, according to de Lubac, in seeking to arrive at this reality without any recourse to a dimension of transcendence, the Marxist ultimately denies to himself the very conditions for achieving such an end. De Lubac insists that

> what the Christian hopes for in another world, at the end of time, the Marxist dreams of for this present world, within our time. What the Christian awaits from a supernatural intervention, the Marxist anticipates as the natural end of a wholly immanent process. A transfiguration of the here and now without the presence of a Beyond! An end of history in the midst of a time that continues to unfold! . . . A perfect peace, a perfect harmony, a total reciprocity of consciousness, without the insertion of any new principle in this humanity, which will not have ceased until then to misunderstand and to tear itself to pieces![25]

It is this reduction to immanence that de Lubac finds so contradictory in the Marxist ideal of a new man. For where does the Marxist derive such knowledge of the end toward which history is moving? If, as Marx insists, "it is not the consciousness of men that determines their essence, but, on the contrary, their social existence [that] determines their consciousness,"[26] from where does the Marxist prophet obtain the prescience by which to stand in judgment over the history of all hitherto existing society? Surely not from the very social conditions upon which he exercises his critique![27] Correlatively, if, as the Marxist contends, history progresses dialectically on the basis of socioeconomic antagonism—the constant jockeying of the oppressor and the oppressed—how is a definitive stasis ever attainable? As de Lubac insists, the clashes of dialectic are incapable of procuring a final end: "The pendulum always reverses itself anew. Any solution is thus provisional, one extreme calls for the other extreme, and there is no reason for this movement in a broken line to stop. . . . Definitive harmony cannot emerge from the midst of contradiction."[28] According to de Lubac, the Marxist hermeneutics of history thus requires a more concerted abdication of reason than the demands of Christian faith, for the latter at least posits the necessary conditions for achieving its final end. Moreover, even supposing the possibility of the "end of history" as envisioned by Marx, the Marxist ideal of a new man entails an insufficient liberation for humanity. For if nothing transcends the dialectic of immanently historical processes—if humanity is simply the totality of beings relegated to particular moments in time—then it is not *humanity* that is freed from alienation, but rather a conglomerate of future individuals.[29] It is therefore necessary, as de Lubac insists already in *Catholicism*, "that humanity should have a meeting place in which, in every generation, it can be gathered together, a centre to which it can converge, an Eternal to make it complete, an Absolute which, in the strongest and most real sense of the word, will make it *exist*."[30]

Having considered the insufficiency of the Marxist search for a new man, de Lubac concludes his lecture with an appeal to Christian anthropology, gesturing as he does so in the direction of a distinctly Christian theology of history. With Marx, de Lubac readily grants that human exchange is, and will continue to be, marred (and, in important respects, constituted) by violent antagonism until the "end of history." However, according to de Lubac, such antagonism is the result of *sin* and is not therefore reducible to the contingencies of social organization. Belief in sin, moreover, deters de Lubac from thinking "that an equitable and peaceful order can ever be established by a simple interplay of freedoms."[31] The evils of human history reveal the evil of human beings, an evil that can only be eradicated from without. The drama of history is therefore coterminous with the drama of each individual. For just as our perfection "is not simply the straightforward and normal completion" of strictly immanent tendencies,[32] so humanity cannot reach a state of completion without the interruption of a wholly different principle. This principle is not the outworking of humanity's *natural* capacities or the teleological march of history's immanent dialectic. It is rather a "new creation," the eschatological transfiguration of human society by the inbreaking of God's grace. De Lubac's theology of history thus bears the familiar features of his theology of human existence. History is teleologically ordered to the gratuitous disposal of a wholly supernatural finality.

From de Lubac's response to the Marxist ideal of a "new man," a number of conclusions can be drawn with respect to his overall theology of history. First, *the meaning of history is revealed.* That is, it belongs to what Étienne Gilson describes as *revelatum*, "that whose very essence it is to be revealed because we can only come to know it by revelation."[33] De Lubac's confrontation with historical materialism takes the shape of an appeal to Christian eschatology because, as Löwith insists, only the latter "gives orientation in time by pointing to the Kingdom of God as the ultimate end and purpose."[34] The drama of history, like the drama of human existence, is unintelligible on its own terms. Second, *the meaning of history is social.* Though de Lubac disagrees with Marx with respect to the means by which history arrives at the inauguration of a new, or rather renewed, humanity, he nevertheless agrees that the end of history will consist in the perfection of social relations. Correlatively, third, *the end of history entails the resolution of social antagonism.* Again, de Lubac believes that Marx misdiagnoses the cause of such antagonism, thus depriving himself of its essential remedy, but he is in full agreement with Marx that social discord is one of the last enemies to be overcome. Christianity, like Marxism, acknowledges the necessity of transcending all philosophy.[35] "It [Christianity] does not appeal to principles: it brings us the power of Christ. Come to attack evil, Christ did not come to resolve a problem or dissipate a mirage: he came to destroy an adversary."[36] Finally, *the end of history is supernatural*:

> Now this passage is not within man's reach. It is not, in fact, a question of any dialectical reversal, even the most incredible of all. . . . It is not a question of passing over into a new degree in the same order. The *supernatural* is not a higher, more beautiful or more fruitful nature. . . . It is *the irruption of a wholly different principle*. . . . Nature evolves and advances all through time: through the supernatural, we pass endlessly from time to eternity. The first builds the earthly city: the second introduces us to the kingdom of God.[37]

This paragraph, written well before the promulgation of *Humani generis*, is unequivocal in its avowal of what I have referred to throughout as the key to understanding de Lubac's theology of nature and the supernatural—that is, the supernatural insufficiency of nature.[38] History, like every individual person, has no positive claim on the supernatural principle that fulfills it. The end of history resides only on the other side of death and resurrection.

THE APOCALYPTIC LEGACY OF JOACHIM DE FIORE

In chapter 2, we noted de Lubac's insistence that the neo-Scholastic theory of pure nature was complicit in the hegemony of secular humanism insofar as it provided a theological warrant for strictly immanentist construals of human being. This critique remains a constant refrain throughout de Lubac's writings on nature and the supernatural, but his hermeneutics of secular modernity receives a more genealogically ambitious inflection in his later treatment of the "spiritual posterity" of the twelfth-century abbot Joachim of Fiore. According to de Lubac, the immanentism evinced in Marx's philosophy of history, which is indebted in important respects to the dogmatic structure that he inherits from Hegel, belongs within a trajectory of secular and Christian "apocalypticism" dating back to the writings of Joachim. By de Lubac's estimation, the legacy of Joachimite apocalyptic "has constituted one of the principal conduits on the path leading to secularization, that is to say, to the denaturation of Christian faith, thought and action."[39] Thus, although developments in late Scholastic theology left the Roman Catholic Church ill-equipped to counter the reduction to immanence in philosophical modernity, earlier developments in medieval apocalypticism—developments originally set *against* the rationalist excesses of Scholasticism[40]—helped to pave the way for the reduction to immanence in modern philosophies of history. It is important to note that, in countering such apocalyptic strands in Christian theology and modern philosophy, de Lubac is not advocating for a strictly *nonapocalyptic* theology of history. As Cyril O'Regan notes with respect to de Lubac's (and Balthasar's) resistance to certain forms of apocalyptic, "it is possible that theological discourses can be or even should be more rather than less apocalyptic in order to function adequately as a diagnostic and refutation of apocalyptic forms of thought."[41] Our treatment of de Lubac's confrontation with Marx's philosophy of history in the previous section would seem to confirm O'Regan's suspicion. De Lubac's conviction that the "end of history" designates "the irruption of a wholly different principle" and the destruction of a present order marred by antagonism bears obvious apocalyptic overtones. As we will see, it is not apocalyptic qua apocalyptic that de Lubac seeks to refute, but rather the immanentizing of eschatology by means of an expectation of a future *temporal* epoch in the divine economy. As de Lubac attempts to demonstrate, it is this hope in a new age *within history*—what Joachim terms the "age of the Spirit"—that helps pave the way for the loss of transcendence in secular narrations of history. It is also, according to de Lubac, one of the principal factors leading to the eclipse of Christology and ecclesiology in a great deal of modern Christian thought.

Arguably the most important apocalyptic thinker of the Middle Ages, Joachim of Fiore (ca. 1135–1202) has aroused controversy since the time of his life and ministry. Invited by Pope Lucius III in 1184 to interpret a prophecy attributed to the Sibyl[42] and commissioned by the pope to write two of his major works, the *Liber Concordie* and the *Expositio in Apocalypsim*, Joachim's views on the Trinity were later condemned at the Fourth Lateran Council in 1215.[43] Hugely influential among the Franciscans after his death, Joachim was denounced during his lifetime by the Cistercians as a runaway.[44] An essentially conservative religious thinker, Joachim became "the chief impetus for a radical movement in the later Middle Ages."[45] The inspiration for Joachim's vision of history occurred on the morning of Easter around 1183 when, according to Joachim, he received an epiphany from God. Meditating on the book of Revelation during "the hour when it is thought that our lion of the tribe of Judah rose from the dead," Joachim suddenly perceived "something of the fullness of this book and of the entire agreement [*concordie*] of the Old and New Testaments."[46] Whatever we are to make of Joachim's narration of that Easter unveiling, the intervening centuries of apocalyptic discourse attest the fruitfulness of Joachim's vision.

Of particular consequence to the history of Christian apocalypticism is the Joachimite division of history into three overlapping dispensations corresponding to the three persons of the Trinity. Joachim was scarcely the first to occupy himself with the "ages" of salvation history or to discern a tripartite structure in the divine economy,[47] but his relocation of the typical caesuras between the various dispensations and the archetypal role allotted to the Trinity in his theology of history constitute a uniquely Joachimite innovation.[48] The basic contours of Joachim's Trinitarian theology of history may be gleaned from the following paragraph in his *Expositio in Apocalypsim*:

> The first of the three *status* of which we speak was in the time of the Law when the people of the Lord served like a little child for a time under the elements of the world. They were not yet able to attain the freedom of the Spirit until he came who said: "If the Son liberates you, you will be free indeed" (John 8:66). The second *status* was under the Gospel and remains until the present *with freedom in comparison to the past but not with freedom in comparison to the future.* For the Apostle says: "Now we know in part and prophesy in part, but when that which is perfect has come that which is in part shall be done away with" (1 Cor. 13:12). And in another place: "Where the Spirit of the Lord is, there is liberty" (2 Cor. 3:17). Therefore the third *status* will come toward the End of the world, no longer under the veil of the letter, but in the full freedom of the Spirit when, after the destruction and cancellation of the false gospel of the Son of Perdition and his prophets, those who will teach many about justice will be like the splendor of the firmament.[49]

Joachim's three states correspond to the progressive actualization of freedom in human history. The first *status* began with Adam and "seems by a certain property of likeness to pertain to the Father."[50] This "age of the Father" corresponds especially with a literal reading of the Old Testament. The second *status* was inaugurated with the reign of King Uzziah, though it finds its definitive hypostatization in the person of Jesus Christ.[51] This "age of the Son" spans throughout the present history of the institutional/hierarchical church and corresponds especially with a literal reading of the New Testament. The final age, "the age of the Spirit," was inaugurated by St. Benedict, but, as the excerpt from Joachim's *Expositio* makes clear, its definitive manifestation is yet to come (Joachim anticipated the beginning of this third age sometime around the year 1260).[52] Whereas the first two states correspond to a literal reading of the Old and New Testaments, respectively, the third *status* will consist in a spiritual understanding of the entire biblical corpus. For just as the Spirit proceeds from both the Father and the Son, so the spiritual understanding proceeds from both testaments. The immanent expectation of Joachim's third age thus consists in the fullness of revelation, the culmination of the divine self-disclosure and the perfection of human knowledge. It is likewise "the coming into being of perfected relationship with God, a relationship that has the character of equality."[53] To the recipients of this charismatic fellowship—the "spiritual men" (*viri spirituales*) of Joachim's third *status*—belong the promises of both Old and New Testaments, "the celebration of the Sabbath for the people of God."[54] Only, according to de Lubac, what the majority of Christians prior to Joachim looked forward to *at the end of history* (that is, after the final judgment), Joachim expects to come to fruition *within history*, in a concluding epoch situated between the present age and the "end of the world."

De Lubac's dialogue with Joachim began as early as *Histoire et esprit* (1950), where he contrasts Joachimite and Origenian interpretations of the "eternal gospel" (Rev. 14:6).[55] Whereas for Origen this gospel denotes the perfect enjoyment of the vision of God in heaven, for Joachim it consists in the spiritual gnosis granted to the *viri spirituales* of the third age. Thus, in contradistinction to those such as Xavier Rousselot who argue for an Origenian inspiration to Joachim's eternal gospel, de Lubac insists that there is nothing more in common between these two thinkers "than this name, eternal gospel . . . and the idea that this eternal gospel consists in the thorough spiritual interpretation of the Gospel—but they completely disagree on the nature and time of this interpretation."[56] In *Méditation sur l'Église* (1953), de Lubac devotes a brief, though highly significant, portion of his chapter on the sacramentality of the church to confronting the penultimacy of the church and the New Testament in Joachimite appeals to a third age.[57] We will return shortly to a more detailed account of this particular line of critique. At this point it will suffice to note that, for de Lubac, any such appeal to a third age risks relativizing the church's present relation to Christ and the disclosive capacity of the Christian scriptures. De Lubac's most substantial engagement with the theology of Joachim occurs in the final two volumes of his *Exégèse medieval* (1961, 1964)[58] and in his two-volume *La Postérité spirituelle de Joachim de Flore* (1978, 1981). According to de Lubac, while he was devoting a lengthy chapter to Joachim in volume 3 of *Exégèse medieval*, he became struck "by the powerful originality of [Joachim's] exegesis and methods as well as by the fullness of his dream."[59] De Lubac likewise became fixated on the extent of the Joachimite influence. Thus, what was originally intended as an additional chapter in volume 4 quickly took on a life of its own, culminating in nearly a thousand pages and roughly two decades of work.

According to de Lubac, the Joachimite legacy is twofold:

> On the one hand, a properly exegetic line, that is, the immense forest of commentaries interpreting the Apocalypse "literally" as a prophecy of the history of the Church, and, on the other, a spiritual line with numerous ramifications, that of the thinkers or men of action who (whether or not quoting him as their authority but all more or less betraying his dream) tend, like him, to conceive of a third age, an age of the Spirit, succeeding that of Christ of which the Church was the guardian.[60]

This twofold legacy—which de Lubac refers to respectively as the posterity of "apocalyptic historiosophy" (*historiosophie apocalyptique*) and the "spiritual posterity" of Joachim of Fiore[61]—constitutes the basic Joachimite "tradition" and serves as one of the primary theological foils for de Lubac's own theology of history. The spiritual posterity occupies the majority of de Lubac's genealogical attention,[62] but both of these trajectories are closely united at their source. That is, for Joachim, a Trinitarian construal of world history—culminating in a future age of the Spirit—arises from a reading of the biblical canon that grants a certain hermeneutical primacy to a "literal" interpretation of the book of Revelation. Joachim's reading of history is thus first and foremost a reading of scripture. That Joachim's "spiritual posterity" should capitalize on the former without due attention to the latter would have been unconscionable to the Calabrian monk.

In his genealogy of Joachim's spiritual posterity, de Lubac demonstrates a number of deleterious theological and philosophical consequences arising from Joachim's theology of history. De Lubac's genealogy places especial emphasis on the immanentizing of eschatology in Joachimite apocalyptic. With his announcement of a coming age of the Spirit, Joachim introduced "the idea of a sudden, inevitable, irreversible progress caused by the passage from one era to another within the interior of time itself—that is to say, the equivalent of what would be, in the modern sense of the word, 'a revolution.'"[63] In thus shifting the locus of Christian hope from the consummation of all things at the eschaton to the immanent expectation of an age of social and spiritual utopia, Joachim was, according to de Lubac, tilling the ground for the seeds of secularization.[64] It is hardly surprising, therefore, that Joachimite ideas were explicitly assimilated in Lessing's famous *Education of the Human Race* as a means of heralding the coming age of reason. Nearly two centuries after Lessing, the Marxist philosopher Ernst Bloch goes so far as to portray Joachim as a communist *avant la lettre*. According to Bloch, Joachim's third age consists of "the illumination of all, in mystical democracy, without masters and Church." In this great society of the third epoch, "there are no classes any more; there will be an 'age of monks,' that is universalized monastic and consumer communism, an 'age of the free spirit,' that is spiritual illumination."[65] Bloch's reading of Joachim is more ascriptive than descriptive, but it makes a strong case nonetheless for the ease by which Joachimite ideals are drafted into the service of wholly secular narrations of history. For Joachim, the age of the Spirit is realized only by the progressive revelation of God, but this ideal was inevitably—perhaps all too easily—taken over "five centuries later, by a philosophical priesthood, which interpreted the process of secularization in terms of a 'spiritual' realization of the Kingdom of God on earth."[66]

Alongside the immanentizing of eschatology, de Lubac discerns in Joachim's spiritual posterity a tendency to divorce pneumatology from Christology, essentially evacuating the former of its biblically prescribed content. For de Lubac, this unmooring of pneumatology from Christology is reflected in a number of historiosophical, ecclesiological, and gnoseological missteps. At the level of history, Christ is no longer seen as the *fulfillment* of history, but rather as the apex of a penultimate epoch. In the historical construction inaugurated by Joachim, "Jesus merely fosters the development of a seed deposited in Israel at the time of King Ozias [= Uzziah], and, on the other side, the fruit of that seed must be exhausted shortly before the consummation of the age."[67] In distinguishing successively between the age of the Son and the age of the Spirit, Joachim thereby denigrates the former in anticipation of the latter. This denigration of the age of the Son bears significant ecclesiological and Christological consequences. For if the church in its present form belongs to the penultimate reign of Christ, then it will have to undergo a radical transfiguration at the inauguration of the age of the Spirit. And although there is much disagreement about the fate of the church in Joachim's theology of history, de Lubac insists that Joachim's vision lends itself all too easily to the dissolution of the church's hierarchy. The spiritual men of the third age will enjoy perfect fellowship with God and one another. There will therefore be no need for institutional and sacramental forms of mediation in the age of the Spirit.[68] The radical nature of this rupture between the church of the present and the church of the third age is largely inchoate in the writings of Joachim,[69] but it was exploited to great effect by Joachim's spiritual posterity. In the "concluding" chapter to *La Postérité spirituelle de Joachim de Flore*, de Lubac canvasses an array of contemporary neo-Joachimites—from José Comblin's *theology of revolution* to Jürgen Moltmann's *theology of hope*—who insist on a radical discontinuity between the church of the past and the church of the future. Since Vatican II, de Lubac insists, there has been a whole crop of "apostles of the Spirit" heralding the birth of a new church.[70] However divergent these eschatological programs may be, they are in agreement that the society inaugurated in the age of the Spirit will bear little resemblance to the present institutional church.

Finally, according to de Lubac, the unmooring of pneumatology from Christology in Joachim's theology of history results in the denigration of the knowledge of God revealed in Jesus Christ. Joachim heralds the coming of an eternal gospel (*evangelium aeternum*), the fullness of God's revelation to humanity and the perfection of human knowledge. Joachim is scarcely alone in his insistence that faith will one day give way to a more perfect knowledge. "For now we see in a mirror, dimly," declares the Apostle Paul, "but then we will see face to face. Now I know only in part; then I will know fully, even as I have been fully known."[71] The novelty of the Joachimite ideal is in locating the perfection of such knowledge *within* history. Not only does this result in the historicization of the eschatological promises—locating *within time* that which is properly reserved for the "new heavens and the new earth" *at the end of time*[72]—but it also relativizes the Spirit's present witness to the revelatory work of Christ. According to de Lubac, when the Lord promises to his disciples, "When the Spirit of truth comes, he will guide you into all the truth,"[73] he is not, as Joachim believed, speaking of a distant future epoch in the divine economy. Thomas argues that "these foolish notions are refuted by the statement (John 7:39) that 'as yet the Spirit was not given, because Jesus was not yet glorified'; from which we gather that the Holy Ghost was given as soon as Christ was glorified in His Resurrection and Ascension."[74] The Lord's promises were fulfilled with the outpouring of the Holy Spirit at Pentecost. The spiritual understanding of scripture is not, therefore, something reserved for the spiritual men of the third age. It is rather, as de Lubac insists, the understanding that the Spirit currently gives to the church, that is to say, the interpretation of the entirety of scripture (and thus the entirety of history) in the light of Jesus Christ. In positing another, more perfect knowledge, Joachimism risks subordinating the concrete objectivity of "faith in Christ" to a more general and ultimately subjective spiritual gnosis. In the Joachimism of Hegel, for instance, faith in the "not-yet transfigured shape of Christ" is only a "conditional foundation" for the "spiritual expansion" that Christ promises to his disciples. However necessary, the object of faith must be passed through, transcended, in order that one might "receive the spirit [that is] the truth itself."[75] For de Lubac, such a "passing through" risks a "leaving behind," and as the secular posterity of Joachim everywhere attests, the spirit of the third age quickly becomes something other than the Spirit of Christ.

Anticipating the positive treatment of de Lubac's theology of history that follows, and bearing in mind the conclusions previously drawn from his confrontation with Marx, a number of observations are in order with respect to de Lubac's survey of the spiritual posterity of Joachim of Fiore. First, perhaps surprisingly, de Lubac is not wholly unsympathetic to Joachim's apocalypticism. Like Joachim, de Lubac is committed to the essentially *historical* nature of Christian soteriology. De Lubac thus opposes the suppression of eschatology in certain "Dionysian" accounts of anagogy whereby the horizontal/temporal element of salvation is supplanted by a strictly vertical/mystical account of the soul's ascent to God.[76] From the very beginning, de Lubac insists, Christianity confronted the Hellenic image "of the ascent of the individual from sphere to sphere" with "that of a collective progress from one age to another."[77] Second, de Lubac affirms with Joachim that a hermeneutics of history entails, and in important respects *corresponds* to, a hermeneutics of scripture. "The Bible," de Lubac insists, "which contains the revelation of salvation, contains too, in its own way, the history of the world."[78] Finally, as we saw in his treatment of Marx, de Lubac agrees with Joachim that the culmination of history entails the perfection of human society, the reconciliation of human beings with one another and with God.

For each of these similarities, however, there are even greater dissimilarities. First, though de Lubac concurs that salvation history consists in "a collective progress from one age to another," he refuses to speak of the present age as a penultimate epoch in the divine economy. For de Lubac, there are, strictly speaking, two "Dispensations," two "Testaments,"

> which have given birth to two peoples, to two orders, established by God one after the other in order to regulate man's relationship with him. The goal of the one that is prior in time is to prepare the way for the second. But this is not what merits them those respective terms of "old" and "new." The New Testament does not take its name solely from the fact that it comes second in time. It is not merely "modern." It is the last word, in an absolute sense.[79]

We will return in the following section to investigate further this relation between the Old and New Testaments. For now, it is worth simply noting that, according to de Lubac, the "New Testament" inaugurated in the person and works of Jesus Christ designates the "last word" in the history of God's dealings with humanity—the final age before "the passing of time into eternity."[80] Second, insofar as "the fullness of time" has already come to pass in the Christ event, the meaning of scripture—and hence the meaning of history—has already been revealed. "All of biblical history and all of biblical reality had Christ for its unique end."[81] Whereas for Joachim the gospel of Christ (the "literal" reading of the New Testament) must eventually give way to the gospel of the Spirit (the "spiritual" reading of both Old and New Testaments), for de Lubac, the two are in fact identical. That is to say, the Spirit reveals the meaning of scripture by leading us precisely to Christ: "The Spirit teaches us 'all truth' but neither speaks of himself nor seeks his own glory. . . . Faithful to the mission he received from him in whose name he was sent to us, he makes us understand his message—'brings it to mind'—but adds nothing to it."[82] Finally, with respect to the perfection of human society, de Lubac challenges both the utopianism of Joachim's third age and the historical penultimacy of the institutional/hierarchical church in Joachim's theology of history. With Joachim, de Lubac readily grants that the church of the "second age" is a mixed society: wheat and tare, Babylon and Jerusalem, whore and faithful bride. But de Lubac is less optimistic than Joachim with respect to the church's temporal future. So long as the church is *in via*, she will remain a *corpus mixtum*. Only upon her entrance into eternal beatitude will the church enjoy "definitive repose in the 'bridal chamber of glory.'"[83] In thus tempering the Joachimite optimism with respect to the church of the future, de Lubac is no less insistent on countering the Joachimite pessimism with respect to the church of the present. "Being adapted to our temporal condition," de Lubac argues, the visible/institutional church is indeed "destined to disappear in the face of the definitive reality it effectively signifies."[84] However, as long as our temporal condition endures, the church remains, according to de Lubac, a necessary means of salvation.

HENRI DE LUBAC'S THEOLOGY OF HISTORY

Having treated de Lubac's confrontation with immanentist construals of history and deviant forms of Christian apocalypticism, we turn now to de Lubac's positive account of the meaning of history. Like Karl Löwith, de Lubac insists that a *philosophy* of history—the interpretation of historical phenomena by means of a universal teleology—presupposes a *theology* of history.[85] Theology alone "makes sense" of the contingencies of historicized being. In a passage of tremendous importance for his theology of history, de Lubac insists:

> To explicate the facts [of history] . . . one thus applies a principle of discernment which can itself be inserted within the facts, but which, as such, pertains to a different sphere and overflows into the observation of the facts. One has recourse to the final causes that the facts would be unable to furnish and which give a retrospective clarification to the whole unfolding of these facts. This is why, if any not merely partial and relative but total, comprehensive, and absolutely valid explication of history is truly possible, this explication can only be theological. Only faith anticipates the future with security.[86]

At one level, this passage evokes the metaphysical axiom presented by de Lubac in his treatment of theological epistemology: "Becoming can only be thought by Being."[87] The accidental phenomena of history are universally contingent upon the necessary being of God. As *created*, history thus bears a meaningful relation to its *Creator*. Without denying the importance of this metaphysical substratum—indeed, the language of "final cause" is in important respects a synecdoche for this larger metaphysics of created being—de Lubac's primary interest here is the intelligibility of historical *events* rather than *essences*. The events of history, in other words, are to be interpreted by means of their relation to a specific event that ultimately transcends the contingencies of history itself. We've seen that for de Lubac it is the Christ event in particular that constitutes the definitive occurrence from which the facts of history derive their inner significance. The "Mystery of Christ" is "the absolutely ultimate final cause" of history that provides both a retrospective and a prospective hermeneutic of historical reality.[88] In the incarnate life and ministry of Jesus Christ, God reveals himself in history, thereby revealing the meaning of history in relation to himself. According to de Lubac, Christ is therefore the "essential Object" of a theological interpretation of history.[89] In terms of cognitive principles, however, de Lubac argues that it is only by means of *a spiritual understanding of scripture* that believers are granted epistemic access to the meaning of history as revealed in Jesus Christ. Scripture is the divinely appointed witness to God's saving acts in history, and the Spirit is the means by which the "singular facts" of history are interpreted in the light of the "singular Fact" of Jesus Christ.[90] If Christ is therefore the "essential Object" of a theological understanding of history, the Spirit is its "interior principle." "Christ cannot be recognized except through the Spirit," and this Spirit is always "the Spirit of Christ."[91]

Christ and the Meaning of Scripture

De Lubac's theology of history is thoroughly Christocentric, but it nevertheless presupposes an understanding of history inherited from and dependent on the Jewish scriptures and the history of God's covenants with Israel. In terms of salvation history, the New Covenant established in the life, death, and resurrection of Jesus Christ stands in a relation of both continuity and discontinuity with the Old. De Lubac insists that "the novelty of Christianity consists in its being a transfiguration rather than a fresh creation. . . . The Old Covenant is entirely oriented toward the preparation of the New—and it is in this that it achieves again its full meaning at the very moment when, as such, it ceases to be."[92] From Judaism, Christianity inherits a view of salvation that is both social and historical. The object of Jewish hope was never "an individual reward beyond the grave." Rather, in placing their hope in the promises of God to Abraham (Gen. 12:1–3; 15), the Jews looked forward to "their common destiny as a race . . . in the glory of their earthly Jerusalem."[93] Israel's common expectation was thus conditioned by the knowledge of Israel's common election, the divine assurance that through Abraham's offspring "all the families of the earth shall be blessed." According to de Lubac, however, this twofold insistence upon the particularity of Israel's election and the universality of the divine blessing presented something of a challenge for Jewish eschatology. For if God is the particular God of Israel, if "his worship remains linked to the observations of the Torah and to the service of the Temple in Jerusalem," what relation do foreign nations bear to the Abrahamic promises? According to de Lubac, the Hebrew scriptures suggest two possible solutions. The first solution entails either the extermination or the subjugation of the pagans: the triumph of Israel over her enemies by means of destruction or domination.[94] "Your gates shall always be open," declares the Lord through the prophet Isaiah, "so that nations shall bring you their wealth, with their kings led in procession. For the nation and kingdom that will not serve you shall perish; those nations shall be utterly laid to waste."[95] According to this solution, the conversion of the nations to Yahweh is coextensive with the gathering of all people in the service of Israel. Elsewhere in the book of Isaiah, however, the blessings of Israel are turned outward. In the enigmatic figure of the "Servant of Yahweh," for instance, Jewish universalism is expressed in terms of Israel's *missionary* vocation: "It is too little that you should be my Servant to reestablish the tribes of Jacob and restore the preserved of Israel," declares the Lord. "I will make you a Light of the nations to carry my salvation to the ends of the world!"[96] According to this second solution, the salvation of Yahweh will extend out to all peoples, rather than the nations having to converge upon a common subjection to the nation of Israel. Yet even here a conflict remains. For how is Israel to reconcile the particularities of its national cultus with its universal mission? How might the people of Israel devote themselves to the latter without thereby abdicating the former?

According to de Lubac, the whole history of Israel thus ends in an essential impasse: "No means for Israel to be faithful both to its vocation and to its being, no means of surviving without losing its reason for living—unless through a transformation of its whole self, through an extraordinary and unforeseeable change, through a death according to the letter for a rebirth according to the spirit."[97] The consummation of Israel's mission must therefore consist in a radical transfiguration. Without denying the continuity of God's saving acts in history, de Lubac nevertheless insists that "the history of revelation also offers the spectacle of a discontinuity that has no equal."[98] The advent of Christ is not simply the prolongation of a trajectory inaugurated in the history of God's covenant(s) with Israel. As Israel's long-awaited messiah, Christ does indeed fulfill Israel's missionary vocation. However, in so doing, Christ establishes a *new* covenant.[99] "The people of God would no longer be an ethnic group. The Divine Presence would no longer be located in one spot, in a material tabernacle. From now on God would be in Jesus

Christ and everywhere."[100] The newness of this covenant is not simply a matter of chronological sequence. It is not merely relative, in other words, to that which came before it. The transcendence of the Christ event "is not only something original, something superior, a provisional novelty, clearing the way for some ulterior invention destined to go beyond it. It is an absolute transcendence. 'Omnem novitatem attulit' ['He brought something entirely new']."[101] The Christ event is a "critical instant" that becomes the "eternal instant."[102]

De Lubac's exposition of this "critical instant" and its relation to the biblical history that precedes it (and a theology of history more generally) is developed at length in his treatment of the history of spiritual exegesis. Beginning with his work on Origen and culminating in his four-volume *Medieval Exegesis*, de Lubac canvasses a vast exegetical tradition in patristic and medieval theology. According to this tradition, scripture contains a plurality of meanings. The precise number and sequence of these multiple senses vary,[103] but the tradition is nearly unanimous in affirming a basic dialectic between the *literal* and *spiritual* meanings of scripture. According to de Lubac, "these two meanings have the same kind of relationship to each other as do the Old and New Testaments to each other. More exactly, and in all strictness, they constitute, they *are* the Old and New Testaments."[104] The literal meaning of scripture thus refers primarily to the history of events as recorded in the Hebrew Bible.[105] The spiritual meaning refers both to the history of events as recorded in the New Testament (most notably the Christ event) *and* to the subsequent interpretation of the Old Testament in the light of the New. The spiritual understanding of scripture is an interpretation of the entirety of biblical history in the light of the incarnation, crucifixion, and resurrection of Jesus Christ. For de Lubac, moreover, this dialectic of letter and spirit is not a strictly *textual* phenomenon: "Scripture first delivers us facts. . . . It recounts a series of events which have really transpired and concerning which it is essential that they should really have transpired."[106] It is therefore the *events* to which the Old Testament refers—the saving acts of God *in history*—that prefigure the coming of Christ and the establishment of the church. Moreover, insofar as the Bible contains, in its own way, the history of the world, the spiritual understanding of scripture is also the interpretation of history qua history in accordance with the gospel of Jesus Christ. As de Lubac insists in the preface to the first volume of his *Medieval Exegesis*, spiritual exegesis contains "*a whole theology of history*, which is connected with a theology of Scripture. It organizes all of revelation around a concrete center, which is fixed in time and space by the Cross of Jesus Christ."[107]

In equating a theology of history with a theology of scripture, de Lubac thus locates the meaning of history itself within the biblically inscribed history of salvation. The historical reality designated by the canonical narrative is not a particular subset of a more general "universal history." The latter is in fact coextensive with the former. Biblical history is, to borrow Lindbeck's well-worn phraseology, "world absorbing."[108] If the Christ event is the concrete center of this history, then God's creative and consummative acts delineate its circumference. The intervening history—the passage *through Christ* from protology to eschatology—is the history of God's redemptive economy, which de Lubac defines succinctly as "the recovery of lost unity."[109] This theme of unity, buttressed in particular by the biblical concept of *koinonia* (communion), is crucial for de Lubac's theology of history and serves as the primary interpretive framework for his soteriology. We might summarize this soteriology (and the theology of history that it engenders) as follows: The history of redemption designates the supernatural restoration of humanity's original unity. This work of spiritual reunion is accomplished in Jesus Christ, extended historically through the sacramental ministry of his mystical body, the church, and finally consummated at the eschaton.

History as the Restoration of Unity

The Protological Unity of the imago Dei

Insofar as the history of redemption constitutes a process of *restoration*, it presupposes the deprivation of a more original unity. In the opening chapter of *Catholicism*—a work devoted in its entirety to the social and historical dimensions of the Christian faith—de Lubac locates this unity in the creation of human beings in the *imago Dei*. "For the divine image does not differ from one individual to another," writes de Lubac. "The same mysterious participation in God which causes the soul to exist effects at one and the same time the unity of spirits among themselves."[110] Following a host of patristic authors, de Lubac describes the original unity of the human race *ontologically*, insisting that the image of God resides, not primarily in individuals, but rather in humanity as a whole. Thus, according to Gregory of Nyssa, "the whole of human nature from the first man to the last is but one image of him who is."[111] In language as evocative as it is potentially problematic, de Lubac speaks of this nature as "a single being."[112] The image of God "makes us so entirely one that we ought not to speak of man in the plural any more than we speak of three Gods."[113] Without dwelling on the potential consequences of such a claim for one's doctrine of God—the specter of tritheism is scarcely dispelled by likening the unity of the divine essence to the unity of a common human nature—de Lubac's appeal to the unity of the *imago Dei* is, at the very least, metaphysically underdetermined. Taken at face value, it would seem to indicate that human nature has a being of its own, a position that Thomas Aquinas roundly criticized, for instance, in the philosophy of Plato and his followers.[114] For de Lubac, however, the point is not to advocate for a general metaphysic, but rather to enlist the patristic authors for the purpose of maintaining the inherently social nature of human being. Without therefore committing himself to a strictly Platonic rendering of the "Form" of human nature, de Lubac suggests a number of potential resources for describing humanity's primordial accord. Thus, according to de Lubac, the original unity of the human race may be considered as a consequence of a shared derivation. The unity of God's creative act—indeed, the unity of God's very being—betokens an essential unity in and among those creatures created according to the divine image. In language more familial (and thus inherently social), de Lubac insists that monotheism postulates "the brotherhood of all men."[115] The common Fatherhood of God mitigates against any and all forms of sectarianism. Humans exist as sons and daughters of the living God, united to one another by virtue of their divine pedigree. Finally, it is this spiritual family that, according to Augustine, is intended "to form the one city of God," a communion of citizens united by love and the common worship of their Creator.[116] Whatever register one chooses to describe this paradisial reality (civic, familial, ontological, etc.), the fundamental point that de Lubac seeks to convey is that human beings were created for communion with God and fellowship with one another. The self attains its completeness only in relation to another. Thus, just as in God "there is no selfishness but the exchange of a perfect Gift," so human existence is marked by an essential reciprocity.[117] In the likeness of the Trinity itself, human persons belong within "a unity of circumincession."[118] Human nature is essentially social.

Sin and the Dissolution of Unity

"In these conditions," that is, presupposing the unifying nature of humanity's creation in the image of God, "all infidelity to the divine image that man bears in him, every breach with God, is at the same time a disruption of human unity."[119] Without wholly eliminating the natural unity of the human race—the *imago Dei* is damaged without being destroyed—the rupturing of fellowship with God results in the alienation of human beings from one another. Reciprocity gives way to individualization, and human sociality becomes marred by exclusion and exploitation. Under these conditions, humans continually oscillate between a strict individualism and a false collectivism, between the idolatry of the isolated self and the instrumentalization of the individual by society. With the introduction of sin, therefore, "'the one nature was shattered into a thousand pieces' and humanity which ought to constitute a harmonious whole . . . is turned into a multitude of individuals . . . all of whom show violently discordant inclinations."[120] Just as the *imago Dei* must be considered collectively and also individually, so the disintegrating consequences of sin must be applied equally to humanity's social and inner disruption. The discord introduced within the heart of every individual corresponds to a discord introduced *between* every individual.

Christ and the Recovery of Lost Unity

The subsequent history of redemption consists in the undoing of humanity's undoing, the recovery of both the unity of humanity with God and the unity of human beings with one another. God accomplishes both aspects of this restoration—the *vertical* reunion between God and humanity and the *horizontal* reunion between human beings—in the person and works of Jesus Christ. In *Catholicism*, de Lubac's treatment of the social and historical aspects of salvation is directed primarily against a tendency in modern theology to reduce the Christian faith to an individualist doctrine of escape. As such, it is the horizontal view that receives the bulk of de Lubac's attention. This is not, however, to diminish the significance of the vertical dimension of the work of redemption. Indeed, according to de Lubac, the latter remains the necessary cause of humanity's horizontal restoration.[121] De Lubac writes, "Christ, by completing humanity in himself, at the same time made us all complete—but in God. Thus we can say . . . that we are fully persons only within the Person of the Son, by whom and with whom we share in the circumincession of the Trinity."[122] For de Lubac, the perfection of human being—the telos of Christ's redemptive activity—consists in humanity's graced participation in the life of the Trinity. In uniting himself to our humanity, Christ permits us to share in the unity that he enjoys eternally by virtue of his divinity with the Father and the Holy Spirit.[123] Moreover, as Jesus's "high priestly prayer" makes clear, unity among human beings is a necessary correlate of humanity's union with God.[124] Thus, according to de Lubac, just as it was humanity as a whole that was created in the unity of the *imago Dei*, and just as it was this same humanity that was subjected by sin to disintegration, so it is "universal humanity" that is reconciled (both to God and to one another) in the person and work of Jesus Christ:

> Christ from the very first moment of his existence virtually bears all men within himself. . . . In making a human nature, it is *human nature* that he united to himself, that he enclosed in himself, and it is the latter, whole and entire, that in some sort he uses as a body. . . . Whole and entire he will bear it then to Calvary, whole and entire he will raise it from the dead, whole and entire he will save it.[125]

Once again, taken at face value, de Lubac's theology of the Incarnation would seem to suggest an untenable hypostatization of humanity's common nature. Again, it was Thomas who argued against such Platonic renderings of Christ's humanity, insisting that "the Word of God did not assume human nature in general but in particular, i.e. in the individual . . .

otherwise every man would be the Word of God as Christ is."[126] And yet, once again, we must not assume that what de Lubac is offering here is a general metaphysic. Influenced as the church fathers may have been by the Platonic doctrine of essential being or the Stoic conception of universal being, patristic speculation on the unity of humanity in Christ was driven first and foremost by adherence to the testimony of scripture. It was John the evangelist who insisted that Christ died "to gather together in one the children of God that were dispersed."[127] It was the Apostle Paul who declared in his letter to the Galatians, "There is no longer Jew or Greek, there is no longer slave or free, there is no longer male and female; for all . . . are one in Christ Jesus."[128] It is from the Epistle to the Ephesians that we learn that "those who once were far off have been brought near by the blood of Christ," for in his flesh Christ has ended the hostility between alienated peoples.[129] *Divisa uniuntur, discordantia pacantur,* de Lubac declares in the words of Fulgentius, "What was divided is united, discord becomes peace."[130] If sin was the cause of humanity's disintegration, Christ brings about the restoration of communion, both with God and among human persons. In his incarnation, Christ unites our humanity in himself. Through his death on the cross, "the humanity which he bore whole and entire in his own Person renounces itself and dies."[131] Christ puts to death the disintegrating powers of sin and death. Finally, in his resurrection, Christ inaugurates a new form of social existence. Christ bestows his Spirit upon the church as the principle of our terrestrial unification and the pledge of our future resurrection.[132] In Christ the promises to Abraham are fulfilled, and in him history itself attains its completion.

The Church as the Continuation of Christ

To say that history finds its completion in Christ is not, of course, to suggest that historicity ceases to be a necessary condition of creaturely existence after Jesus's resurrection. De Lubac notes that there is a certain discrepancy between the "fulfillment" of history as accomplished in Jesus Christ and the apocalyptic expectations recorded, for instance, in the book of Daniel. According to the latter, the definitive triumph of Yahweh "appears as the *end of history*, and it is allied with the physical transformation of the universe."[133] As the intervening centuries attest, however, the end of history as envisioned by Daniel did not coincide with the Christ event. The epoch inaugurated in the life, death, and resurrection of Jesus Christ is the final epoch in terms of history (contra Joachimism), but the Christian still awaits the passing of history into eternity. Only then, with the liberation of all creation, will human society attain its perfection in the eschatological enjoyment of God. In the meantime—that is, in the time between the resurrection of Christ and the general resurrection of humanity—the work of unification accomplished in the person and works of Jesus Christ is continued in and through the ministry of his body, the church. The church is, according to de Lubac, the *sacrament* of Christ's restorative presence.

More attention has been devoted to de Lubac's ecclesiology in Anglo-American literature than nearly any other aspect of his work.[134] This is hardly surprising. De Lubac authored numerous publications on the church,[135] and his writings on the subject have contributed enormously to developments in twentieth-century Roman Catholic (and also Protestant and Eastern Orthodox) ecclesiology. A full analysis of de Lubac's ecclesiology is well beyond the scope of this chapter. Our interests lie rather in the function of the church in de Lubac's theology of history, that is, in the particular relation that the church bears to the restoration of human unity. According to de Lubac, the church is both the continuation of the unifying work of Jesus Christ and the anticipation of the completion of that work in the eschaton. The church is the divinely appointed means by which and in which human beings are united, both to the mission of Christ in history and the *totus Christus* toward which history is teleologically ordered.

As early as *Catholicism*, de Lubac articulates this relation between Christ and his church in terms of the church's *sacramentality*. "If Christ is the sacrament of God," writes de Lubac, "the Church is for us the sacrament of Christ; she represents him, in the full and ancient meaning of the term; she really makes him present. She not only carries on his work, but she is his very continuation."[136] In one sense, the church is the recipient of Christ's restorative benefits. She is a creature of divine grace, brought to life by the vivifying agency of the Holy Spirit. In this sense, the church names the sociohistorical *consequence* of the unification of humanity in Jesus Christ. In another sense, however, in her mode of being in relation to the world, the church *effects* the restoration of humanity. The church is not only the "assembly which results from the reuniting of all peoples," she is also the one who unites humanity in herself.[137] "The Church which is 'Jesus Christ spread abroad and communicated' completes—so far as it can be completed here below—the work of spiritual reunion which was made necessary by sin."[138]

According to de Lubac, the church carries out this sacramental vocation in a number of ways. First, in her kerygmatic witness to the Christ event, the church relays the narrative of humanity's disintegration and the restoration of creaturely fellowship with God. The church "completes" the work of Christ precisely by bearing witness to his completed work. As the Apostle Paul declares to the congregation in Corinth, the church's *ministry* of reconciliation coincides with the church's *message* of the reconciling work of Jesus Christ.[139] Second, the church effects the unification of humanity by virtue of its own visibility as a sign of Christ's restorative agency. The church's sociality is—or at least *ought* to be—a demonstration of the possibility of restored human fellowship. In the church, the world discovers its own finality, what Rowan Williams describes as "a 'belonging together' of persons in community in virtue of nothing but a shared belonging with or to the risen Christ."[140] The church's mission is therefore to extend the gratuity of its own identity as the creature of God's unifying grace. The church offers and embodies that fellowship which it first receives from Jesus Christ. Third, the church's sacramentality is evident in the church's sacramental *cultus*. That is, in the celebration of the individual sacraments, the church actualizes its own vocation as the historical extension of Christ's restorative work.[141] "Since the sacraments are the means of salvation," de Lubac writes, "they should be understood as instruments of unity. As they make real, renew or strengthen man's union with Christ, by that very fact they make real, renew or strengthen his union with the Christian community."[142] To be baptized is thus to be incorporated into the mystical body of Christ. To partake of the consecrated elements is to become the consecrated body; the Eucharist unites the individual to Christ and, in so doing, unites the members of Christ's body one to another. In the performance of her sacramental *cultus* the church therefore exhibits both her active participation in the unification of humanity *and* her essential passivity in relation to Christ. The church is at once the one who baptizes and the congregation of the baptized. The church is both produced by the Eucharist and the one who produces the Eucharist.[143] As the sacrament of Christ, the church *in via* thus remains always and at once both the recipient and the appointed instrument of Christ's restorative benefits.

In the decades following the publication of *Catholicism*, this understanding of the church as sacrament took on something of a life of its own in Roman Catholic ecclesiology. Thinkers as diverse as Otto Semmelroth, Edward Schillebeeckx, and Karl Rahner each devoted considerable attention to the idea, and the church's sacramentality received explicit conciliar sanction in the documents of Vatican II.[144] By the late-1960s, the "Church as sacrament" had become one of the primary models in Roman Catholic and ecumenical ecclesiology for relating the mystical/invisible and institutional/hierarchical aspects of the church.[145] Despite its popularity, however, this sacramental identification of Christ and the church has also been the subject of severe theological criticism, particularly among Protestant theologians. Thus, according to Karl Barth, "to speak of a continuation or extension of the incarnation in the Church is not only out of place but even blasphemous."[146] More recently, John Webster has raised concerns that such an ecclesiology transgresses the necessary distinction between the agency of Christ and the activity of the church. According to Webster, such an ecclesiology "is characteristically insecure (even casual) about identifying Christological boundaries: it is not possible to determine the point at which Jesus stops and the church begins." In extending the efficacy of the Incarnation to the community of the church, de Lubac and others risk disturbing "the fundamental asymmetry of Christ and the church." The two become, as it were, co-constitutive.[147]

De Lubac's sacramental ecclesiology is scarcely immune from such critiques. On a number of occasions, de Lubac does indeed appear to collapse the agency of Christ into the activity of the church, thus compromising the proper freedom of Christ's lordship over the community gathered in his name. For instance, we've seen that de Lubac insists the church *completes* the work of reunion begun at the Incarnation. As

Eberhard Jüngel argues, to claim that the church completes the work of Christ is to risk conflating the necessary soteriological distinction between the *accomplished* work of Christ—the Johannine promise: "It is finished" (Τετέλεσται)[148]—and the ecclesial *appropriation* of that *opus operatum* by the power of the Holy Spirit.[149] Elsewhere, moreover, de Lubac speaks of a "communication of idioms" between Christ and his ecclesial body,[150] "so much so that the two names 'Church' and 'Christ' would seem to be interchangeable."[151] Once more, we are left searching for the point at which Jesus ends and the church begins.

Such assertions, were they to exhaust de Lubac's treatment of the subject or even stand without further qualification, would certainly risk absorbing the mystery of Christ into the mystery of the church. As it is, however, de Lubac puts a number of measures in place to mitigate precisely this threat to Christ's unilateral freedom and authority in relation to his church. First, in considering the church as the mystical body of Christ, de Lubac insists that the relation between body and head is one predominantly of *subordination.* The church is subject to Christ as one governed and directed by another.[152] The church's authority is therefore wholly derivative and subordinate; it is always an authority "under authority." Second, in stark contrast to the sinlessness of Christ, the church is and remains a sinner in each of her members until that day in which she is transformed into the likeness of Christ. Through the sacrament of the unity of humanity in Christ, the church continually betrays her divinely given vocation, resisting the very communion (with God and among her members) that she is called to represent. Drawing on the image of the sun and moon, de Lubac follows a number of church fathers in speaking of the church as *mysterium lunae.* The church depends entirely on the sun of Christ for her brilliance. She produces no light of her own, but shines only insofar as she is illumined by another. Thus, according to de Lubac, "while the sun remains always in glory, the moon (that is, the Church) continually passes through phases, now waxing, now waning. . . . Though her normal duty may be to reflect the light of her sun on men, it may happen that she interposes herself so successfully that an eclipse results, the earth finds itself plunged into darkness."[153] Any account of the church's sacramentality must therefore take into consideration the church's paradoxical (and often contradictory) condition as both *de trinitate* and *ex hominibus*. The church is first and foremost a creature of divine grace. The efficacy of the church's sacramental mission thus depends, not primarily upon her own faithfulness to Christ, but rather upon the faithfulness of Christ to the church and, through her, to all of humanity. Finally, as we noted above with respect to de Lubac's treatment of the spiritual posterity of Joachim of Fiore, de Lubac insists that the church's visible and temporal aspects—by which he means, in particular, the church's hierarchy and sacramental *cultus*—are wholly relative to our status as *viatores*.[154] Without succumbing to the millenarianism of certain forms of Joachimism, de Lubac nevertheless opposes those forms of ecclesial triumphalism by which the visible church is perceived as an end in itself. The church *in via* is not the kingdom toward which history is teleologically ordered: "The sacramental element in the church, being adapted to our temporal condition, is destined to disappear in the face of the definitive reality it effectively signifies."[155] The sacramentality of the church is thus strictly provisional. The church's mediation, de Lubac insists, "will have no *raison d'être* in the Heavenly Jerusalem; there, everyone will hear God's voice directly and everyone will respond to it spontaneously, just as everyone will see God face to face."[156] The church, insofar as it is visible, exists solely to put us in relation to Christ. It will therefore cease to exist on that day when, according to Augustine, "erit unus Christus, amans seipsum" (there will be one Christ, loving himself).[157]

The Church and the End of History

This last point, concerning the relation between the visible/temporal church and the Heavenly Jerusalem, is of tremendous importance for de Lubac's theology of history. For though de Lubac insists that the church is not yet the kingdom of heaven, he is no less adamant that the church in time participates proleptically in this eschatological reality. According to de Lubac, the church stands to our eschatological finality "in a relation of mystical analogy in which we should perceive the reflection of a profound identity. It is indeed the same city which is built on earth and yet has its foundations in heaven. . . . The Church, without being exactly coextensive with the Mystical Body, is not adequately distinct from it."[158]

For de Lubac, the church's sacramentality is thus twofold: it is both a representation of a past reality (the continuation of the unification of humanity in the person and works of Jesus Christ) and a making-present of a future reality (an anticipation of the *totus Christus*). Or rather, as Joseph Flipper argues, the church's making-present of Christ "is equally a making the end of time present to us since Christ has entered into that fullness in his own person. The eschatological Church, the whole Christ, is what the sacrament makes present."[159] De Lubac's ecclesiology is thus shot through with an eschatological tension between the *already* and the *not-yet.* The church is temporary, provisional, destined to disappear. It is also "the heavenly kingdom in embryo," the "sheltering womb and matrix of the new world," the "new universe already active at the very heart of our earthly existence."[160] The church continues to share in the apocalyptic expectations of the Jewish prophets as recorded, for instance, in the book of Daniel. The end has not yet come. The definitive triumph of Yahweh, the passage of time into eternity, the ultimate restoration of the cosmos (and with it, the perfection of human fellowship) are still, properly speaking, objects of hope. And yet, according to de Lubac, there is a fundamental difference between Christian hope and the hope of the Old Testament. For according to the former, the Kingdom of God is *already present* in the person and works of Jesus Christ. The church awaits the coming of one who has already come. And it is by virtue of this *hope* that the church *in via* already participates in the promises of eternity.[161] The time of the church is the final epoch in world history—the *age of the Spirit* during which the church participates in both the event that gave it birth and the reality to which it will ultimately give way.

Salvation *extra Ecclesiam*?

Before concluding our reflections on de Lubac's theology of history, it is worth noting a certain ambiguity with respect to his construal of the church's sacramental vocation, one that bears directly upon our interpretation of the supernatural insufficiency of nature in de Lubac's hermeneutics of human existence. Although de Lubac claims that "it is through the Church that salvation will come, that it is already coming to mankind,"[162] he nevertheless insists that "the Son, from the very beginning and in every part of the world, gives a more or less obscure revelation of the Father to every creature, and that he can be the 'Salvation of those who are born outside the Way.'"[163] Like Hans Urs von Balthasar, de Lubac thus maintains the possibility that *all* will be included in the eschatological reconstitution of humanity.[164] De Lubac does not thereby deny the axiom *extra Ecclesiam nulla salus* ("there is no salvation outside the Church"). He continues to affirm with Ambrose, "Sola Ecclesiae gratia, qua redimimur" (It is only by the grace of the Church that we are redeemed).[165] However, given his insistence on the mystical unity that human beings share by virtue of their common nature and the assumption of that nature by Jesus Christ, de Lubac is convinced that humanity's common salvation does not necessitate the inclusion of the totality of the redeemed within the visible (i.e., Roman Catholic) church. According to de Lubac, unbelievers do not themselves belong to the "normal" way of salvation, but "they will be able nevertheless to obtain this salvation by virtue of those mysterious bonds which unite them to the faithful. In short, they can be saved because they are an integral part of that humanity which is to be saved."[166] In a footnote to this passage, de Lubac notes that this is not the place to treat "the problem of the objective or subjective conditions necessary for salvation or to study how the infidel can arrive at faith."[167] Unfortunately, de Lubac nowhere returns to an investigation of these important conditions. He is content simply to assert that no human being lacks the concrete means of salvation.[168] This reticence to specify the conditions necessary for the salvation of the unbeliever leads, once more, to a certain ambiguity with respect to the relation between human being and humanity's supernatural finality. For if human beings are always already united to the saving work of Christ and the grace of the church by virtue of their common humanity, is human existence not always already under the condition of grace? De Lubac seems to suggest as much in *Catholicism*, noting "that grace is diffused everywhere and that there is no soul that cannot feel its attraction."[169] If there is any justification for the charge of intrinsicism in de Lubac's thought, it is here in his treatment of the common election of humanity in union with the mystical body of Christ.

Already in *Catholicism*, however, de Lubac insists that the unity of humanity in Christ and with the church does not negate the necessity of *metanoia* for the attainment of humanity's supernatural finality: "There is no man, no 'unbeliever,' whose supernatural conversion to God is not possible from the dawn of reason onward."[170] The rectifying work of Jesus Christ and the sacramental mediation of that work in and through the church accomplish the restoration of humanity, providing, as it were, the objective condition for the possibility of humanity's subjective appropriation. And though the normal means of such appropriation are faith and the sacrament of baptism, it is possible, according to de Lubac, for one to respond by grace to the call of the gospel *anonymously*, that is, outside the visible frontiers of the church. In *The Church: Paradox and Mystery*, de Lubac returns to this question of the relation between the restoration of humanity in Christ and the mystical body:

> By his incarnation the Word assumed all human nature. . . . It follows immediately that every man, Christian or not, in the "state of grace" or not, oriented towards God or not, whatever his knowledge or lack of it, has an organic link with Christ. . . . But this primordial relationship is altogether different from that uniting the members of the "mystical body" with their head. They alone are the beneficiaries of this union—this second relationship—who have received Christ and have made him welcome, in an implicit or explicit manner. In other words, by virtue of the assumption of all human nature by the Word incarnate, a primordial, essential and inalienable bond unites all men to Christ. [But this] must be carefully distinguished from the mystical body. The mere fact of being man does not entail automatic membership in the latter.[171]

This passage makes clear that, for de Lubac, the common restoration of humanity in Christ does not mean that human beings are always and everywhere in the "state of grace." The latter corresponds with a particular mode of being in relation to the "mystical body" of Christ. However, it is possible (indeed, de Lubac believes that it is likely) that when the church attains her own finality in the *totus Christus*, she will bring with her *all* of humanity. All of humanity will then converge upon that eschatological reality of which the church *in via* participates proleptically and sacramentally. And they will do so precisely by virtue of the mysterious relation that they bear to the church's present/earthly mediation of Christ's restorative ministry.

CONCLUSION

Reflecting on *Surnaturel* thirty years after its publication, de Lubac acknowledged a shortcoming in the work's abstraction from the history of revelation and redemption. Referring to an important article by Henri Bouillard,[172] de Lubac suggests that questions pertaining to "the supernatural order" might be more adequately addressed in terms of "the Christian mystery," that is, in terms of the relation of creation to the person and works of Jesus Christ.[173] We've seen in previous chapters that de Lubac's theology of human existence often proceeds on the basis of concepts and methodological commitments inherited from late Scholastic debates on the gratuity of humanity's supernatural finality. The conceptual parameters suggested by these debates, however necessary for de Lubac's critical engagement with extrinsicist accounts of grace, often prevented him from operating within more dramatic and biblical modes of theological exposition. For this reason, de Lubac's theology of history serves as an indispensable correlate to his theology of human existence, providing the world-historical narrative within which each individual drama finds its meaning. De Lubac's theology of history informs and conditions his hermeneutics of human existence in a number of important respects. First, de Lubac's theology of history allows him to qualify the supernatural end toward which human beings are teleologically ordered in terms of sociality. The "end of a reasonable creature . . . is to attain beatitude," de Lubac continues to affirm. However, as Thomas argues, such beatitude "can only consist in the kingdom of God, which in turn is nothing other than the well-ordered society of those who enjoy the vision of God."[174] Second, in narrating humanity's supernatural vocation in terms of the restoration of human unity, de Lubac is able to devote due theological attention to the present social and historical dimensions of human existence. Human beings exist in time and in relation to one another. Eschatology does not abrogate the Christian occupation with history. To the contrary, it is this forward-looking hope in an eschatological future that situates human beings within a meaningful history, a history constituted by the dissolution and restitution of human relations.[175] Third, de Lubac's theology of history names the concrete means by which the supernatural is socially and historically mediated. That is, the work of grace by which human beings are adopted into fellowship with God and liberated for communion with one another is accomplished in the person and works of Jesus Christ and extended historically through the ministry of the Holy Spirit in the church. Finally, in terms of the argument I have advanced throughout this book that de Lubac's theology of human existence is predicated on the supernatural insufficiency of nature, his theology of history—his confrontation with Marx in particular—demonstrates a corresponding logic with respect to history as a whole and the totality of human beings. As we have seen, for de Lubac, "it is the same for Humanity, taken as a whole, as for each individual. . . . [It] cannot reach completion without . . . a turning around of the whole being, a mysterious passage through death, a revival and a recasting that are nothing other than the evangelical *metanoia*."[176] Without denying the importance of temporal advancements in the task of social liberation, de Lubac insists that such achievements are only ever proximate to the eschatological transfiguration of human society. The resolution of social antagonism is only finally secured in the Kingdom of God. The church *in via* participates proleptically—though always imperfectly—in this eschatological reality, but the "end of history" as envisioned by Marx and the "eternal gospel" heralded by the disciples of Joachim are wholly contingent on the passage of time into eternity. Only then will the drama of history reach its conclusion.

FIVE

Being in Mystery

INTRODUCTION

To this point we have treated de Lubac's hermeneutics of human existence primarily in terms of the supernatural *insufficiency* of human nature. Human beings (and the shared history within which each individual narrative unfolds) are naturally ordered to an end that infinitely surpasses the powers of nature to attain—the beatifying gift of Godself. This line of interpretation is crucial for distancing de Lubac's project from the intrinsicism with which it is often associated, but it would be a serious misreading of the Lubacian corpus to thereby conclude that nature only ever participates in the supernatural *eschatologically* in the elevation of human being to the beatific vision. Indeed, as I have indicated throughout this book, though the dynamism of human existence does not proceed *by its own momentum* to the supernatural, God nevertheless intervenes, answering his own call on our nature and allowing the spirit *in via* to participate by grace in the supernatural beatitude that awaits it. Thus, in his confrontation with the immanentism of atheist humanism, de Lubac alludes to the possibility of a truly *converted* humanism. Moreover, though de Lubac insists that the natural desire for God "does not constitute as yet even the slightest positive 'ordering' to the supernatural," he maintains that upon receiving the indwelling of the Holy Spirit and the gift of sanctifying grace, human beings are so ordered to their supernatural perfection.[1] While de Lubac argues that the dynamism of human reason terminates at the acknowledgment of its own insufficiency, he also insists that the intellect is subsequently reborn under the aegis of the supernatural. The revelation of God encounters the *intellectus quaerens fidem*, providing the intellect with a share in God's own self-knowledge and the means thereby to interpret all things in relation to their divine *principium et finis*. Finally, though de Lubac argues against Marx and the spiritual posterity of Joachim of Fiore that the perfection of human society is only achieved at the eschaton, he maintains that the church militant participates proleptically in this eschatological reality.

Having therefore treated the dynamism of human being principally in terms of nature's insufficiency, we follow de Lubac in this chapter "beyond the threshold" of the Christian mystery, turning our attention to the drama of human existence *under the condition of grace*. In so doing, it is perhaps helpful to distinguish three stages in the spirit's journey toward God. As we have seen, de Lubac typically narrates humanity's vocation in terms of the binomial nature/supernatural. According to this binomial, "Anything that does not derive from divine adoption in man, even if it does derive from the spirit and liberty in him, can be called natural."[2] To humanity's nature, therefore, belong the innate desire for the supernatural and the transcendental affirmation of God. Nature designates humanity's status as creature; it is that which perdures in human being under the conditions of sin and grace. What the supernatural designates, meanwhile, "is not so much God or the order of divine things considered in itself, in its pure transcendence, as . . . the divine order considered in its relationship of opposition to, and in union with, the human order."[3] The supernatural names the condescension of God to humanity by grace and the corresponding elevation of human beings to fellowship with God. It is humanity's being in relation to God within the economy of redemption. This binomial may succeed in protecting the "radical heterogeneity" between "the existent nature and the supernatural to which God destines it,"[4] but a further distinction is in order to distinguish between humanity's participation in the supernatural *in via* and the perfection of humanity's supernatural finality. For this we may turn to Thomas and his threefold rendering of the *imago Dei*.[5]

Following Peter Lombard, Thomas distinguishes between the image of "creation" (*creationis*), of "re-creation" (*recreationis*), and of "likeness" (*similitudinis*). That is, according to Thomas, there is a threefold conformity of the human being to God according to *nature*, *grace*, and *glory*. As Jean-Pierre Torrell notes, this threefold *conformitas* allows Thomas to showcase "the personal dynamism of each realization of the image within the movement of *regiratio*, which brings humanity back to God."[6] The first conformity (according to nature) is found in every human being and pertains to humanity's natural aptitude for knowing and loving God. The second conformity (according to grace) belongs only to the "just" and refers to an individual's actually/habitually knowing and loving God in this life, however imperfectly. The final conformity belongs to the blessed, who enjoy a perfect knowledge and love of God in the beatific vision. It is at this stage that human beings finally attain the divine "likeness." De Lubac nowhere explicitly takes up this threefold *conformitas* from Thomas, but it is nonetheless possible to discern a similar logic in his own account of the dynamism of human existence. Like Thomas, de Lubac insists that human beings are created in the *image* of God in order that they may attain the divine *likeness*. Although the latter is, strictly speaking, an eschatological reality, de Lubac nevertheless insists on a certain participation in the likeness of God for those belonging in time to the mystical body of Christ. De Lubac treats this mediating stage of the dynamism of human existence throughout his writings on nature and the supernatural and ecclesiology, but it receives its most concise and explicit articulation in de Lubac's account of Christian mysticism. It is to de Lubac's 1965 article "Mysticism and Mystery," therefore, that we will devote the majority of our attention in what follows.

By de Lubac's own admission, his interest in mysticism played a decisive role in the development of his theology. Prior to the suspension of his teaching responsibilities in 1950, de Lubac had intended to teach a course on Christian mysticism at the Université Catholique de Lyon, considering the topic especially in its relation to what he refers to as "natural mysticism" (to which we shall return shortly). While in exile in Paris in the early 1950s, de Lubac began compiling notes for a book on the subject. But according to de Lubac, the project was too ambitious, and it remained uncompleted. De Lubac recounts in 1956:

> I truly believe that for a rather long time the idea for my book on Mysticism has been my inspiration in everything; I form my judgments on the basis of it, it provides me with the means to classify my ideas in proportion to it. But I will not write this book. It is in all ways beyond my physical, intellectual, spiritual strength. I have a clear vision of how it is linked together. I can distinguish and more or less situate the problems that should be treated in it. . . . I see the precise direction in which the solution of each of them should be sought—but I am incapable of formulating that solution. . . . The center always eludes me.[7]

De Lubac's book on mysticism remained unwritten at the time of his death in 1991, but a précis of some of the basic ideas that, according to de Lubac, would have been developed in several volumes can be clearly discerned in his 1965 article. Originally published in a condensed form as the preface to André Ravier's edited volume *La mystique et les mystiques*,[8] "Mysticism and Mystery" forms "a microcosm of [de Lubac's] entire writings on the Christian life."[9] In it, de Lubac organizes a number of key themes treated elsewhere throughout his corpus—the relationship between nature and the supernatural, the spiritual interpretation of scripture, the nature of the church, and de Lubac's critique of secular immanentism—around the question concerning the relationship between mysticism and the Christian *mysterium.* De Lubac argues that Christian mysticism (as opposed to other religious or atheistic forms of mystical occurrence) is a Trinitarian mysticism of likeness, centered on the mystical interpretation of scripture within the mystical body of Christ, the church. Rather than naming a strictly esoteric mode of religious experience, therefore, mysticism designates the conscious actualization of humanity's supernatural vocation. It is the "taking up" (and hence the "making intelligible") of the dynamism of human existence by the dynamism of faith. De Lubac's account of Christian mysticism is at once a phenomenology of graced existence and an interpretation of humanity's "mystical condition" in the light of human being's basic ordination to the supernatural. In addition to narrating the drama of human existence beyond the threshold of the Christian mystery, de Lubac's article on mysticism continues to hold in tension both the intrinsic relation between human nature and humanity's supernatural finality and the "transcendent newness" of the gift of grace. "Mysticism and Mystery" both extends de Lubac's refutation of extrinsicism and rigorously protects against the error of intrinsicism. Indeed, de Lubac considers the latter to be the principal illusion of what he refers to as a purely immanentist mysticism, "the most profound kind of atheism."[10]

MYSTICISM AND THE MYSTERY OF FAITH

As its title suggests, de Lubac's central concern in "Mysticism and Mystery" is to provide an account of the relationship between Christian mysticism and the mystery to which it adheres. To what extent is mysticism directly dependent on the self-giving of God in Jesus Christ? De Lubac notes that more than one theologian insists that Christian mysticism is, to put it rather bluntly, a contradiction in terms. Thus, according to Karl Barth, the manner in which the mystic speaks of God is nearly indistinguishable from that of the agnostic philosopher, both of them insisting that to speak of God is ultimately beyond the realm of human possibility. "But by God they do not mean the Creator of heaven and earth, the Lord and Judge and Saviour of man," declares Barth. "What they mean is the unutterableness of the ultimate depth of the mystery of the world and the human soul."[11] Barth's analysis is thus characteristic of a more general suspicion of Christian mysticism within modern (typically Protestant) theology. Construed as an agnostic apophaticism or an esoteric spiritualism, mysticism is placed in stark theological opposition to biblical faith in the Word of God.[12] For what likeness is there between that "Darkness which is beyond light"[13] and the God who is light and "in whom there is no darkness at all"?[14] To what extent does the "cloud of unknowing" correspond to the One "in knowledge of whom standeth our eternal life"?[15] What's more, a strictly phenomenological account of mystical experiences would seem to indicate an underlying unity of mysticism across religious (and even nonreligious) traditions. There are a number of "mystical phenomena"—de Lubac mentions, for instance, clairvoyance, visions, and moments of extraordinary concentration—that transcend creedal boundaries.[16] What distinguishes Christian mysticism then from the Sufism of Rumi or the "atheistic mysticism" of Friedrich Nietzsche?[17] Is Christian mysticism merely a type of a larger genre of numinous experience?

In responding to the above interpretations/critiques of Christian mysticism, de Lubac readily grants that mysticism is an analogical concept, one that is perhaps all too easily susceptible to overgeneralizations and theological distortions. Nevertheless, when properly considered according to the logic of the Christian faith and the history of Christian spirituality, mysticism names an essential mode of relating to the Christian mystery. De Lubac argues at the outset, "If 'mysticism' is to be understood as a kind of perfection attained in spiritual life, a form of actual union with the Divinity, then, for the Christian, it can only mean the union with the tripersonal God of Christian revelation, a union realized in Jesus Christ and through his grace."[18] In response to the theological opponents of Christian mysticism—those who maintain that mysticism is antithetical to faith in the revealed Word of God—de Lubac thus insists that the origins of Christian mysticism are coterminous with the origins of Christianity. Rather than being a later addition to Christian thought and praxis—the imposition of Neoplatonism on biblical/Hebraic forms of thought—mysticism belongs already to the writings of the New Testament. De Lubac mentions, for instance, the "christological mysticism" of St. Paul, the doctrine of union with Christ and the continuing activity of the Holy Spirit within the church.[19] Without denying the eschatological/apocalyptic tenor of Pauline mysticism, de Lubac quotes Louis Bouyer to the effect that for Paul "there is a real anticipation of the life of the resurrection in the life of the Spirit, which is inaugurated by baptism and sustained by faith."[20] Moreover, according to de Lubac, one might just as easily speak of the mysticism of St. John, the affirmation that Jesus dwells in the hearts of believers by the Spirit of Christ. Christian mysticism does not, therefore, as some of its critics fear, entail the absolute identification of the mystic with being itself (*ipsum esse*). It rather names that union of the believer with God accomplished in the person of Jesus Christ and mediated by the Holy Spirit.

De Lubac is sympathetic to the theological charges brought against mysticism (he is just as eager as the opponents of Christian mysticism to avoid any identification of created and uncreated being), but he is decidedly less patient with those who insist that Christian mysticism is merely one particular instantiation of a universal genre of numinous experience. There is a growing consensus, notes de Lubac, "that not only is mysticism to be found everywhere but that it is everywhere the same."[21] There is some prima facie warrant for this thesis. As we have already indicated, there are a number of mystical phenomena that appear across religious and nonreligious lines. Moreover, there is often a mutual self-recognition among mystics of various religious traditions that can even elude the adherents of a common religion. "'My banner is larger than Mohammed's,' cries the Muslim mystic Vistami. And the Sufi, Djelâl el Dûr Rumi, writes, 'I am not Christian, Jew, Mazdaist or Muslim, I belong to the supreme Spirit.'"[22] Nevertheless, de Lubac argues that this thesis concerning the unity of mysticism is based on a superficial reading of the mystical writings "lifted out of their spiritual milieu in which they are shrouded, and on insufficient attention to the qualitative differences of the religions in which the described experiences occur."[23] For de Lubac, it is historically inaccurate and sociologically naïve to claim to discover an underlying mystical kernel beneath the various husks of substantively diverse religious practices and communities. Every mysticism presupposes a common human nature (and hence a common supernatural vocation), but the polyphony of cultural and linguistic conditions determining the various "mysticisms" makes it just as problematic to speak of a universal mysticism as of the transcendent unity of all religious experience.[24] Moreover, in terms of the specificity of Christian mysticism itself, de Lubac argues that the effect of Christian mysticism on the religion within which it emerges is profoundly different from the effect that mysticism generally has elsewhere. Apart from Christianity, de Lubac argues, the mystical élan tends to surpass the religious element that gave it birth. The mystic eventually dispenses with the religious husk in his or her pursuit of sheer interiorization (what the Buddhist, for instance, refers to as nirvana).[25] The Christian mystic, meanwhile, "knows that it is the unique reality, to which he adheres by faith, that is the bearer of a universal fruit. He knows that he, in turn, nourishes himself with a unique and infinitely fruitful mystery on which his experience is always totally dependent."[26] Generally speaking, whereas the non-Christian mystic seeks to transcend the religious myth, the Christian mystic seeks to inhabit the Christian mystery. Thus, according to de Lubac, "in Christian mysticism, the mystery is first and last."[27]

Christian mysticism, de Lubac insists, "is nourished by something other than itself. The Christian mystic receives the mystery as something not only to be professed with his lips or understood with his intelligence but also to be, in a genuine sense, lived."[28] Insofar as it is nourished by something other than itself, Christian mysticism entails an essential passivity. The mystical state is one neither of enstasis nor of some alien gnosis, but of subservience and receptivity to the Christian *mysterium.* It is, as de Lubac puts it, the *interiorization* of the Christian mystery.[29] Mysticism is utterly dependent on this mystery, and yet, according to de Lubac, without an at-least-incipient mysticism, the mystery risks falling into a wholly extrinsic relation to the Christian believer. Rather than being a source of life, the mystery is thereby reduced to mere theological abstractions. There is a "reciprocal fertilization," therefore, between the mystery and Christian mysticism. The mystery nourishes the mystical life, and mysticism, in turn, assimilates the Christian mystery, giving life to the mystery for those who receive it. Even so, mysticism remains ever subservient to the mystery; for "*the mystery always surpasses the mystic.* It dominates his experience, specifies it, and is its absolute norm."[30]

We have alluded throughout this book to the significance of mystery (and the adjective "mystical") in de Lubac's theology. De Lubac writes at length of the Eucharistic mystery,[31] the mystery of the new Man,[32] the mystery of the church,[33] the mystery of the supernatural,[34] and the mystical interpretation of scripture.[35] Moreover, drawing on the philosophy of Ricoeur and Marcel, we have indicated a twofold application of the term "mystery" to de Lubac's hermeneutics of human existence. In one sense, the "mystery of human being" refers to the "irreducible opacity" of human existence in abstraction from the revelation of humanity's supernatural vocation. In another sense (one more germane to de Lubac's account of Christian mysticism), "mystery" refers to humanity's basic relation to the sacred. One of de Lubac's most expansive treatments of the term "mystery" can be found in *Corpus Mysticum,* where he investigates the transference of the title "mystical body" [*corpus mysticum*] from the Eucharistic body to the ecclesial body during the eleventh and twelfth centuries. According to de Lubac, the Greek noun μυστήριον, to which both the Latin *mysterium* and *sacramentum* correspond, refers at one level to the mutual relationship between a divinely instituted sign and that which it signifies.[36] In respect to the particular distinction between *mystery* and *sacrament*, the latter tends to be construed as "a visible sign signifying something," while the former is "something hidden that it signifies."[37] Thus, the sacrament is the exterior symbol, but the mystery is "the interior component, the reality hidden under the letter and signified by the sign, the truth that the figure indicates; in other words, the object of faith itself."[38] To borrow the language of Ferdinand de Saussure, we might say that even though "sacrament" performs the function of a *signifiant* (a form that signifies), "mystery" refers at once both to the *signifié* (the idea signified) and the *sign* itself (that union of *signifiant* and *signifié*).[39] However, insofar as it designates *the object of faith itself*, mystery is scarcely reducible to a mere semiotic phenomenon. It is rather, in the words of Paul VI, "a reality impregnated by the presence of God and of a nature, consequently, that permits a constant self-exploring."[40] For de Lubac, to speak of the Christian mystery is to speak of the very means whereby God graciously communicates himself to his creatures. To speak of the Christian mystery is ultimately to speak of the person and works of Jesus Christ.

"'The epiphanic Word of God,' manifestation of his being and of his salvific design, Christ is not only *a* mystery: he is *the* mystery—there is no other."[41] In designating the Christian mystery in strictly Christological terms, de Lubac intentionally employs the language of St. Paul, according to whom Christ is "the mystery of our religion [εὐσεβείας]," "God's mystery . . . in whom are hidden all the treasures of wisdom and knowledge."[42] It is likewise the language of St. Augustine, whose adage *Non est aliud Dei mysterium, nisi Christus* ("There is no other mystery of God, apart from Christ") factors heavily in de Lubac's own account of the Christian mystery.[43] For de Lubac, the mystery of Christ does not stand alongside other mysteries (such as the mystery of the Eucharist or the mystery of the church) as one particular instantiation of a more general dynamism between sign and signified. Christ is rather *the* mystery to which all other Christian mysteries bear a strictly derivative relation. As such, Christian mysticism ought to be considered only in its relation to the primal mystery of the Incarnation. Referring to a passage from Divo Barsotti, de Lubac insists that

> the mystery is Christ. Inasmuch as it is the revelation of God who loves, the mystery is all of theology. Inasmuch as it is the act of God who descends to meet man, it is Christian worship, the mystery of faith. Inasmuch as it is the act of man who assimilates himself to God, it is all of mysticism. All revelation is fulfilled in Christ, author and consummator of our faith, as the Letter to the Hebrews says. All worship culminates in the unique and eternal sacrifice, and *all mysticism consists of living in Christ*, the goal of the law.[44]

For de Lubac, Christian mysticism is participation in the reality of Christ. It is that union with the divinity accomplished in the person of Jesus Christ and realized in the individual through the operation of the Holy Spirit. As such, the mystical life is not directed toward a particular *experience* desired as an end in itself, but rather toward "a blossoming of Christian life"—that life inaugurated in baptism and "defined primarily by its triple and unique relationship to the mystery that is realized in faith, hope and love."[45] Further, insofar as Christian mysticism is a participation in the reality of Christ, it is likewise a participation in the very Triune life of God. Jesus communicates the divine life to us—that life which finds its original source in the Father—in communicating to us his Spirit. Christian mysticism is therefore a Trinitarian mysticism, for "in Jesus Christ, all the Trinity reveals and gives itself."[46]

If the mystery of God's self-revelation in Jesus Christ is the objective principle of Christian mysticism—the exterior *datum* to which the interiorization of mysticism corresponds—then, for de Lubac, faith is the subjective condition for the mystic's assimilation of the Christian mystery. De Lubac signals the necessary relation between faith and mysticism throughout "Mysticism and Mystery." "In the highest stages of mysticism," writes de Lubac, "there is a blossoming of the radical passivity inherent in the act of faith. It becomes a 'life of pure faith,' 'a way of pure faith.'"[47] Christian mysticism "falls within the logic of a life of faith."[48] Rather than being a deepening of *self*, therefore, Christian mysticism is a deepening of *faith*.[49] De Lubac thus goes to great lengths to remind his readers that faith is a necessary condition for Christian mysticism, but a more thoroughgoing treatment of the nature of faith itself is necessary to determine their precise relation. Such a treatment is largely absent from "Mysticism and Mystery." The closest that de Lubac comes to defining faith in this article is his claim that faith is essentially "the submission to the word that resounds on the exterior."[50] In order to supplement de Lubac's account of the necessary relation between faith and mysticism with a more detailed exposition of the former, we must therefore turn to another of de Lubac's publications from the 1960s, *La Foi chrétienne* (*The Christian Faith*).

Somewhat loosely organized as a commentary on the Apostles' Creed, *The Christian Faith* is devoted as much to the faith *by which* Christians believe as it is to the faith which Christians profess (the content of Christian belief). We saw in chapter 3 that de Lubac was generally suspicious of the mode of conceptual analysis that led some Scholastic theologians to a categorical distinction between the faculties of will and intellect. De Lubac's own consideration of faith is therefore more indebted to existential and patristic modes of thought (most notably that of Augustine) than to what he takes to be the "intellectualism" of St. Thomas and his followers.[51] De Lubac affirms that faith "necessarily includes an act of intellectual adherence to a series of beliefs," or rather "a belief in a series of revealed acts, which we come to know through the apostolic preaching."[52] To believe *in* God, one must certainly believe a number of things *about* God. And yet, unlike a simple belief, the act of faith is not reducible to a mere intellectual assent. For de Lubac, faith is "an essentially personal act which, if rightly understood, involves the depths of one's being."[53] It is a total response to the Word of God, "the disposition by which man, through the powers of grace, corresponds to the call of God revealing himself."[54] Faith is therefore the human/creaturely correlate to the divine self-disclosure. It is the graced movement of the creature toward God, a movement elicited and always sustained by the gift of God in Jesus Christ. Moreover, insofar as it is a response *to* the saving love of God, faith is itself the response *of* love. Faith and charity are inseparable and indeed nearly indistinguishable in de Lubac's thought. If, by de Lubac's account, certain trends in Scholasticism risk driving a wedge between the intellect and the will (and the corresponding virtues of faith and charity), de Lubac comes close to conflating faith and charity in humanity's supernatural movement toward God. So, for instance, de Lubac claims that faith "includes within itself hope and charity which are the very names of its own movement; they constitute as it were faith's definition."[55] For de Lubac, faith designates the entire dynamism of graced existence, a dynamism elicited by the self-revelation of God, inaugurated in baptism (the *sacramentum conversionis et fidei*), and finally ordered to the perfect enjoyment of God. Returning therefore to the question concerning the relation between mysticism and faith, we might say that the former designates the means by which the Christian *mysterium* is interiorized and assimilated under the general impulse of the latter: "Mysticism is the interiority of faith by the interiorization of the mystery."[56] It is the performative and contemplative means by which "the word that resounds on the exterior" is made to dwell ever more deeply in the believer.

THE PRINCIPAL CHARACTERISTICS OF GRACED EXISTENCE

Having argued for a particular construal of Christian mysticism with respect to its relation to the Christian mystery and the dynamism of faith, de Lubac provides a brief survey of the principal characteristics that distinguish Christian mysticism from other forms of mystical occurrence. In this short section, de Lubac draws together, with a clarity and an economy of exposition often missing from some of his other works, the various loci heretofore treated in our analysis of his hermeneutics of human existence. Indeed, it is scarcely an exaggeration to say that the main themes and theological commitments occupying de Lubac throughout his entire career converge here upon his treatment of the defining features of Christian mysticism. According to de Lubac, these fundamental traits "define all Christian reality."[57] They name, as it were, the primary means and effects of grace in the life of the Christian believer. In attending to these characteristics, one therefore catches a glimpse of the eschatological reality that consummates the dynamism of human existence. The mystical life is defined, no longer strictly in terms of humanity's supernatural insufficiency, but as the first fruits of humanity's supernatural vocation.

A Mysticism of Likeness

First of all, writes de Lubac, Christian mysticism "is a mysticism of 'likeness.' 'God, who is completely present everywhere, does not, however, dwell in everyone.' In other words, the divine image is inalienable in every human being, but the union with God is 'a union of likeness.' "[58] In designating Christian mysticism a mysticism of likeness, de Lubac takes up a number of crucial moves made elsewhere throughout his hermeneutics of human existence, demonstrating with great precision their mutual interdependence. First, de Lubac continues to employ a particular reading of the biblical creation narrative in which God created human beings in his *image* (εἰκών) in view of ultimately leading them to his *likeness* (ὁμοίωσις). De Lubac often refers to this understanding of Genesis 1:26 as that of the "Fathers of the Church" or the "Christian tradition" (as we saw above, Thomas Aquinas makes similar use of the distinction between image and likeness), but it is important to note that the progenitors of this theological distinction—notably, Irenaeus, Origen, and Clement of Alexandria—were scarcely in accord on the precise relation between image and likeness. Thus, though the most significant passages in Irenaeus seem to indicate that the likeness was somehow lost at the Fall of Adam while the image of God in humanity was retained,[59] there are other passages in which he appears to be using the two terms as synonyms.[60] For Origen, meanwhile, the lack of any reference to the likeness of God in Genesis 1:27 ("So God created man in His own image, in the image of God He created him; male and female He created them") can only mean "that man received the dignity of God's image at his first creation; but that the perfection of his likeness has been reserved for the consummation."[61] Despite the obvious discrepancies among such thinkers, each is in resolute agreement that *the likeness can only be attained within the economy of God's salvific dealings with humanity.* Thus, according to Irenaeus, in taking on flesh, the Word of God "both showed forth the image truly, since He became Himself what was His image; and He re-established the similitude after a sure manner, by assimilating man to the invisible Father through means of the visible Word."[62] Similarly, in meditating upon the Bread of Life discourse in the Gospel of John, Origen declares, "The true bread is He who nourishes the true Man, made in the image of God; and the one who has been nourished by it will come to be in the likeness of Him who created him."[63] De Lubac likewise locates the transformation of human being into the divine likeness strictly within the economy of God's grace. "The divine resemblance is something to be realized," writes de Lubac, "through the action of the Holy Spirit, by man's dependence on the redeeming Incarnation."[64] This likeness is thus only ever consummated in the beatific vision. For, as St. Augustine notes in his reading of 1 John 3:2, "the apostle John says, 'Beloved, we are now sons of God, but that which we shall be has not yet appeared. We know that when he appears we shall be like him, because we shall see him as he is.' *From this it is clear that the image of God will achieve its full likeness of him when it attains to the full vision of him.*"[65] In qualifying Christian mysticism as a mysticism of likeness, de Lubac thereby insists that although the telos of Christian mysticism (and the telos of human existence more generally) is only granted eschatologically in the beatific vision, the Christian mystic nevertheless participates proleptically in this union with God in and through the life of the Spirit. Christian mysticism is an anticipation in this life of the glorious life to come.

Second, as a mysticism of likeness, Christian mysticism is located historically in relation to a particular telos. It looks forward to the fulfillment of its own dynamism in a future event of divine self-bestowal: "It presupposes a process that can never be finished, and it contains an element of eschatological hope."[66] In insisting that Christian mysticism is directed toward an eschatological terminus, de Lubac thus reaffirms the irreducibly historical dimension of human existence. The mystic's participation in the blessedness of his or her supernatural perfection does not obviate the temporal conditions of his or her present status as *homo viator*. Christian mysticism entails neither an escape from time nor a "nostalgia for a lost paradise." Rather, "Christian mysticism is directed toward a goal, toward God who calls to us and beckons us to meet him at the end of the road."[67] As we noted in our investigation of his theology of history in chapter 4, for de Lubac, anagogy does not entail the eclipse of eschatology. The mystic's "vertical ascent" to God (the contemplation and enjoyment of the One who is both immanent and transcendent to history) is always accompanied and informed by a certain apocalyptic expectation. Only at the "end of history" will the mystic attain the reality she seeks.

Finally, in considering Christian mysticism in terms of "likeness," de Lubac positions himself once more against both extrinsicist and intrinsicist construals of the relation between human nature and humanity's supernatural finality. De Lubac is careful to distinguish between "the union that already exists between God and his creatures" and the "union of likeness" of those indwelled by the Holy Spirit. The former indicates the natural participation of all beings in the being of God. The latter refers strictly to the supernatural union "of the soul with God and its transformation by his love."[68] For de Lubac, therefore, the union of image and the union of likeness do not simply designate differing degrees of participation in the divine mystery. They do not belong, as it were, along the same ontological continuum. There is a difference in kind, not just degree, between the *conformitas* of image and that of likeness, between nature and the supernatural. The following passage is thus characteristic not only of the argument set forth in "Mysticism and Mystery" but of de Lubac's overall thesis concerning the relation of nature and the supernatural:

> God has made man in his image with the idea of bringing man to resemble him—a resemblance that must be consummated in the "beatific vision". . . . The divine resemblance is something to be realized, through the action of the Holy Spirit, by man's dependence on the redeeming Incarnation. . . . The aspiration is inherent in human nature, since man is made for this union. In other words, there must be in our nature a certain capacity for the appropriation of the mystery that is both given and revealed in Jesus Christ. It is a capacity that is naturally accompanied by desire, a desire that must be described as ontological. Illusion, with its procession of distortions and various corruptions, arises when one believes he has found or desires to find

> in this capacity—*which is only a faculty for receiving, in itself empty and powerless*—its own object or a substitute for this object.[69]

De Lubac begins this summary of the paradox of humanity's supernatural vocation with the familiar disavowal of a strictly proportionate human finality. Human beings were created for the supernatural enjoyment of God in the beatific vision. This alone is their transcendent end, their *raison d'être.* The telos of human being infinitely exceeds the faculty of human nature. De Lubac then proceeds to name the means by which human beings attain the divine likeness: the union of nature and the supernatural in the mystery of the Incarnation and the appropriation of that mystery by the Holy Spirit. Third, de Lubac insists on the intrinsic relation of being and finality. The aspiration for the supernatural is inherent in human nature. There is in our nature a certain capacity (what de Lubac elsewhere defines as a passive aptitude)[70] for the appropriation of the Christian *mysterium.* Fourth, this natural capacity corresponds to a natural longing—the desire of our nature for the gratuitous disposal of our supernatural finality. This desire is ontological. It is not, therefore, as the advocates of pure nature argue, merely elicited and conditioned. It is absolute. As such, the desire to see God could not be frustrated without an essential suffering on the part of the creature.[71] Finally, de Lubac insists that the capacity for the supernatural (and the corresponding desire of nature) is strictly *a faculty for receiving*; it does not yet participate in the object that fulfills it. This reinforces what de Lubac describes as the essential passivity in Christian mysticism. The mystic receives the mystery by faith in response to the self-revelation of God. This is precisely what distinguishes Christian mysticism from what de Lubac refers to as natural mysticism. Natural mysticism is the hypostatization of the mystical intuition, a turning toward oneself in the pursuit of that which can only be received as a supernatural gift from God. It is, according to de Lubac, "the most profound kind of atheism."[72] For de Lubac, there is therefore no confusing humanity's natural ordination to the supernatural with the supernatural object of humanity's desire. Atheistic immanentism and Christian intrinsicism are alike mistaken in considering the aspiration at the heart of human existence as anything other than a faculty for receiving, as anything other than a longing born entirely of lack.

An Understanding of Scripture

Second, "since Christian mysticism develops through the action of the mystery received in faith, and the mystery is the Incarnation of the Word of God revealed in Scripture, Christian mysticism is essentially an understanding of the holy Books. The mystery is their meaning; mysticism is getting to know that meaning."[73] By insisting that Christian mysticism is commensurate with a particular understanding of scripture, de Lubac reinforces the subservience of Christian mysticism to the mystery to which it adheres. The mystical élan does not proceed in abstraction from the revelation of the Christian *mysterium*. The mystic *receives* the mystery primarily through the instrumental ministry of sacred scripture.

In his 1966 commentary on the first chapter of *Dei verbum*, Vatican II's *Dogmatic Constitution on Divine Revelation*, de Lubac follows the council fathers in conveying the role of scripture within the economy of revelation and redemption by way of an analysis of 1 John 1:2–3: "We proclaim to you the eternal life which was with the Father and was made manifest to us—that which we have seen and heard we proclaim also to you, so that you may have fellowship with us; and our fellowship is with the Father and with his Son Jesus Christ."[74] In this passage, notes de Lubac, one discovers (1) the object of revelation, (2) its mode, (3) its transmission, and (4) its finality. The *object* of revelation is eternal life, that is to say, the one who, from all eternity, has life in himself. The object of revelation is not, therefore, a set of assertions *about* God, which, once apprehended, may be abstracted from the Triune life of God. It is the very gift of Godself, the personal being of God revealed in the divine economy. The *mode* of this divine self-disclosure is the incarnate life and ministry of Jesus Christ, "the eternal life which dwelt with the Father and was made visible to us." According to de Lubac, "Jesus is for us the 'exegete' and the 'exegesis' of the invisible Father."[75] He reveals God, not simply by virtue of the message that he proclaims, but "by his active presence, by his entire being."[76] The divine glory is made manifest in the humanity of Jesus Christ to the eyes of faith, to those indwelled by the Spirit of Christ. The *transmission* of this revelation is carried out in the first place by the testimony of the apostles, that testimony recorded and preserved for the church in sacred scripture: "What we have seen and heard we announce to you." The apostles are ambassadors to Christ, witnesses to the revelation that they received from God. The church is in important respects a creature of this apostolic testimony. She is "the 'communion' of those who, having listened to the Apostles and their successors," believe the Word of God and are charged with transmitting in turn that which they have received.[77] The mystery revealed in Jesus Christ and entrusted to his apostles is subsequently transmitted through the church's kerygmatic ministry. Finally, the *end* of revelation is coterminous with the end of human being and the telos of universal history, namely, communion with God and fellowship among human beings: "that which we have seen and heard we proclaim also to you, *so that you may have fellowship with us; and our fellowship is with the Father and with his Son Jesus Christ.*" According to de Lubac, it is impossible to dissociate the object of revelation from its end: both are expressed by the words "eternal life." In revealing to human beings the fellowship of love that belongs to God from all eternity, God grants humanity a share in this fellowship by grace and in union with Christ. Revelation is therefore indissolubly bound to redemption: "The announcement of salvation contains the salvation announced."[78] As the divinely appointed witness to God's saving acts in history, holy scripture belongs firmly within the economy of redemption. The apostolic testimony recorded in scripture "is not a pure announcement, a pure attestation that is exterior to the mystery of salvation; it coincides with the work of reconciliation that Christ works through those whom he instituted not only as witnesses, but as stewards, as *mediators of his mystery*."[79] Christian mysticism is "essentially an understanding of the holy Books" precisely insofar as the latter mediate the mystery of God revealed in Jesus Christ.

Having identified Christian mysticism with a particular interpretation of scripture, de Lubac insists that this "mystical understanding" is best encapsulated by the fourfold sense of scripture: history, allegory, tropology, and anagogy. This fourfold interpretation of sacred scripture—the most frequent medieval ordering of the multiple senses and, according to de Lubac, the one that provides the most complete rendition of the Christian mystery—is summarized succinctly in a popular distich dating from the thirteenth century: *Littera gesta docet, quid credas allegoria, / moralis quid agas, quo tendas anagogia* ("The letter teaches events, allegory what you should believe, morality teaches what you should do, anagogy what mark you should be aiming for").[80] In chapter 4, we noted the significance of the first two senses for de Lubac's theology of history. The *letter* refers to the saving acts of God in human history, the calling of a people to himself, the manifestation of God's theophanic glory, the acts of deliverance whereby God liberates his people from the tyranny of captivity and idolatry. The letter is therefore of the utmost importance for the mystical understanding of scripture insofar as our salvation is accomplished historically: "God has intervened in human history: the first thing to do is to learn the history of his interventions from the Book where they have been recorded by the Holy Spirit."[81] The spirit of scripture does not therefore negate the letter but fulfills it. As such, it is not the letter that is to be avoided, but rather the *mere letter*, that reading of scripture which attempts to abstract the historical facts from the mystery to which they ultimately signify. The *allegorical* sense of scripture (what de Lubac describes elsewhere as the *spiritual* interpretation) is, we have noted, the interpretation of the entirety of scripture (and the events to which the scriptures bear witness) in the light of the mystery of Christ. "In short," writes de Lubac, "the spirit of the letter is Christ. The Gift prophesied by the Law is Christ. 'The New Testament is Christ.' 'The Gospel is Christ.'"[82] According to de Lubac, the final two senses—*tropology* and *anagogy*—ought not to be considered in abstraction from the previous two meanings, but rather as integral components to the allegorical interpretation of scripture. In other words, one does not move *beyond* the spiritual sense in reading the text tropologically and/or anagogically. Tropology and anagogy name instead two modes of inhabiting the mystery conveyed by the spiritual understanding of scripture. As the distich indicates, the third sense "teaches what you should do." Tropology thus concerns the moral doctrine that ensues from the mystery revealed in scripture. Tropology indicates not merely the ethical command and corresponding response to the Word of God, but *the very indwelling of that Word* in the soul of the believer: "It is by the tropological sense thus understood that Scripture is fully *for us* the Word of God, this Word which is addressed to each person, *hic et nunc* [here and now] as well as to the whole church, and telling each 'that which is of interest to his life.'"[83] Lastly, anagogy teaches "what mark you should be aiming for"—the telos toward which the mystical understanding of scripture is properly ordered. Anagogy refers as much to an eschatological reality (the end of each person and humanity as a whole in the *totus Christus*) as to the mystical life of the Christian believer (the contemplation of "things above").[84] Thus, whereas the allegorical sense refers to the coming of Christ in the Incarnation, and the tropological sense refers to the coming of Christ in each individual, the anagogical sense refers to the coming of Christ at the end of history. It is also the sense by which the Christian *in via* enjoys "a unique intuition" of the One who alone satiates the desire of our nature. As such, the anagogical sense "has the richness of the three preceding dimensions concentrated within itself."[85]

As his commentary on *Dei verbum* and his article "Mysticism and Mystery" make clear, for de Lubac, Christian mysticism is commensurate with a "mystical" understanding of scripture because the mystery to which the mystic adheres and the mystery mediated in and through scripture are one and the same. In addition to being the "exegete" and the "exegesis" of the invisible Father, Jesus Christ is both the exegesis of sacred scripture (its primary object and its ultimate end) and the scriptural exegete par excellence, explaining in himself the mysteries revealed throughout.[86] It is likewise by the illumination of the Spirit of Christ that believers are brought to a spiritual understanding of the biblical text. For "Christ cannot be recognized except through the Spirit, and . . . this Spirit is always the Spirit of Christ. . . . All of Scripture is evangelical when it is contemplated, as it should be, 'in the Spirit of the Lord.'" Undergirding de Lubac's treatment of the spiritual understanding of scripture is therefore an account of divine agency whereby the Spirit of God (the *interior principle* of mystical exegesis) unlocks to us the mystery of the scriptures, the self-revelation of God in Jesus Christ (the essential *object* of mystical exegesis).[87] As with the eschatological perfection of human being into the divine likeness, the spiritual sense is not achieved by means of some progressive impulse of wholly natural tendencies, but is rather received as a divine gift. Mystical exegesis is not, therefore, the product of hermeneutical ingenuity, but rather "arises from the all-powerful Act posited by the Word of God and revealed by his Spirit."[88] This process of spiritual understanding—a process identical, according to de Lubac, with the process of conversion to Christ[89]—*is* the very interiorizing of the Christian mystery spoken of above.[90] For in discovering the spiritual meaning of scripture, the mystic is brought to participate in the divine mystery and is thereby transformed by the Word of God evermore deeply into the divine likeness.

A Nuptial Mysticism

Insofar as "all mystical thought must be expressed in symbols," Christian mysticism "is very much attached to the symbolism of 'spiritual marriage.'"[91] De Lubac is scarcely alone among modern Roman Catholic theologians in privileging the analogy of marriage in his construal of Christian mysticism. As Fergus Kerr has demonstrated, the nuptial motif (and the development of various "nuptial mysticisms") factored heavily in twentieth-century Roman Catholic thought. Moreover, according to Kerr, it was the recovery of Origen (and Origen's *Homilies on the Song of Songs* in particular) by de Lubac and others that led to the predominance of this theme "in papally endorsed and papally inspired Catholic theology at the end of the twentieth century."[92] De Lubac undoubtedly belongs within this "nuptial trajectory" in twentieth-century Catholicism, but his employment of the symbolism of marriage is less encompassing (and in many ways less innovative) than that of such contemporaries as Hans Urs von Balthasar or John Paul II.[93]

De Lubac's primary reason for adopting the nuptial motif in his account of Christian mysticism is its predominance in scripture. In the book of Hosea, the Lord instructs his prophet to take to himself "a wife of whoredom" as a testimony to Israel's adultery and the Lord's fidelity: "Go, love a woman who has a lover and is an adulteress, just as the Lord loves the people of Israel, though they turn to other gods."[94] Likewise, the Song of Songs, with its evocative depictions of marital intimacy, has a long and consecrated history of interpretation (both Jewish and Christian) relating the love between the bride and the bridegroom to the relationship between God and his people.[95] For "as the bridegroom rejoices over the bride," declares the prophet Isaiah, "so shall your God rejoice over you."[96] This nuptial motif continues well into the writings of the New Testament. In both Ephesians and 2 Corinthians, Paul likens the relationship between Christ and his church to the union of husband and wife, and in the book of Revelation, the Seer of Patmos refers to the eschatological Jerusalem as the bride of the Lamb.[97] Following a host of patristic and medieval expositors of scripture (not only Origen, but also Jerome, Bernard of Clairvaux, and St. John of the Cross), de Lubac therefore readily adopts this biblical motif as an apposite expression of the mystic's relation to God.

Beyond its obvious biblical precedent, de Lubac finds in the symbolism of marriage an effective means of safeguarding the "personalist" element of Christian mysticism. The mystic's relation to God is not the abandonment of the self to a transcendent principle without concern for the soul that seeks it. Nor is it reducible to that "dwelling in the nearness of being" lauded by Heidegger as the meaning of human "ek-sistence."[98] Christian mysticism is a personal response to the Trinitarian bestowal of divine charity: "It involves mutual love even though all the initiative comes from God."[99] There is therefore a "bond of reciprocity" in Christian mysticism that sets it apart from all forms of natural mysticism. As de Lubac argues elsewhere with respect to the relation between faith and the faithfulness of God, Christian mysticism entails "the encounter of two persons offering themselves to each other in a fullness of presence, a total engagement."[100]

Finally, according to de Lubac, the symbol of marriage illustrates "an unsurpassable feature of Christian mysticism," because "between the human soul and its God, as in the marriage of the Church and the Lamb, there is always a union, not absorption. . . . It is, if you wish, a unification but not an identification."[101] For de Lubac, the symbol of marriage thus mitigates the temptation to pantheism (or panentheism) in Christian accounts of deification. The mystic's union with God does not trespass the infinite qualitative distinction between created and uncreated being. The expression "spiritual marriage" allows personal duality to survive without thereby denying the profound unity that results from the mystical process.

As a number of de Lubac's interpreters have recently noted, this personal duality is often obfuscated in more "radical" construals of de Lubac's thought.[102] In *The Suspended Middle*, for instance, John Milbank describes "the subtle heart of de Lubac's theology" as follows:

> The gift of deification is guaranteed by *no* contrast, not even with Creation, never mind nature. . . . In the ultimate experience of the supernatural which orients it, namely the beatific vision, our entire being is transfigured by the divine light. Here we *become* the reception of this light and there is no longer any additional "natural" recipient of this reception.[103]

As Chad Pecknold and Jacob Wood note, Milbank's claim that the gratuity of humanity's deification is guaranteed without contrast to nature can, without violence to de Lubac's thought, be taken as a mere indication of the priority of divine agency.[104] As we demonstrated in our own investigation of the *desiderium naturae* in chapter 2, de Lubac is adamant that the gratuity of the supernatural does not require, as a methodological or ontological prerequisite, the supposition of a self-contained nature. The gratuity of the supernatural resides in God's free decision to elevate human beings to the supernatural vision of God. It is precisely because God wills for us this supernatural finality that God wills for us to be.[105] But what does Milbank mean by insisting that we *become* the reception of this divine gift, that there is no longer *any additional natural recipient* of the supernatural? As Adam Cooper argues, Milbank would appear to envision deification "along the lines of an unmodified Plotinian Neoplatonism, where 'to be' and 'to be God' mean essentially the same thing. . . . The final union of God and the human creature is of such a kind that no real distinction between them remains: giver and receiver share one and the same divine existence."[106] Whether or not this "Neoplatonist radicalism" adequately captures Milbank's intent (as the above passage indicates, Milbank's own position is hardly transparent),[107] it is clearly at variance with the mysticism of de Lubac. For de Lubac, grace elevates and perfects human nature without thereby erasing the radical heterogeneity between nature and the supernatural. As I have sought to demonstrate throughout this book, de Lubac never demurs from the Blondelian insistence that humanity's supernatural vocation in no way eliminates the "state of nature." Indeed, according to Blondel, "the latter remains immanent to the divine adoption itself."[108] In his employment of the symbolism of spiritual marriage, therefore, de Lubac adamantly rejects any identification of finite and infinite being in favor of a mysticism of *mutual love*. That is, just as the husband and wife become "one flesh" without in any way nullifying their individual identities, so the mystic becomes "one spirit" (*unus spiritus*) with God by "the union of love that is a unity of desires."[109] According to de Lubac, this union of the soul with God "takes place when two wills, that of the soul and that of God, are in agreement, and one has nothing that repels the other. Thus, when the soul completely rejects in itself all that is repugnant or does not conform to the will of God, *it is transformed into God through love*."[110] Such is the transformation of human being into the divine likeness. Such is what Thomas refers to as the image of re-creation, the *conformitas* according to grace: the participation of creaturely knowledge and love in God's own eternal knowledge and love of himself.

An Ecclesial Mysticism

Fourth, Christian mysticism is necessarily an ecclesial mysticism. As early as *Catholicism*, de Lubac defends Christian mysticism from widespread charges of individualism and religious subjectivism. Drawing on Joseph Maréchal's *Études sur la psychologie des Mystiques*, de Lubac insists "that the Catholic mystic is not merely a separated being in comparison with the rest of the faithful, an escapist in search of some hazy transcendence."[111] Rather, the mystic supports the Christian community (through prayer, acts of charity, and, indeed, through the very manifestation of a life informed by grace) and is in turn supported by the community. Mysticism entails the fulfillment, not the suspension, of a truly catholic mode of social existence. This ecclesial rendering of Christian mysticism is given further theological justification in the 1965 article on mysticism. Here, de Lubac states unequivocally,

> If mystical life at its summit consists of an actual union with the Divinity, such a union could be possible only through a supernatural grace whose normal setting is the Church and whose normal conditions are the life of faith and the sacraments. In this sense, one can agree with Dom Anselm Stolz that it is only in the Church that a "true mysticism" can be found; "outside of the Church, no mysticism."[112]

If, as we have argued, Christian mysticism names the principal means and effects of grace in the life of a believer—the shape of human existence under the vivifying conditions of the supernatural—then it is scarcely surprising that de Lubac locates the mystical life within the mystical body of Christ. For it is in the church, remarks de Lubac, that the Incarnation achieves "the marriage of the Word and humanity."[113]

As we saw in chapter 4, for de Lubac, the church continues and conveys the unifying work of Jesus Christ through the ministry of word and sacrament. In terms of the mystical interpretation of scripture (the second aspect of Christian mysticism), the mystic encounters (or is rather encountered by) the Word of God *within* the one, holy, catholic, and apostolic church. Critical of what he perceives as an unnecessary bifurcation of scripture and the church's tradition in certain post-Tridentine renditions of the "two source" theory of revelation,[114] de Lubac insists on a real unity of reciprocity between the church and scripture. In the first place, again, the church is a creature of the Word of God; Christ speaks in and to his church through the mediation of scripture, and it is precisely in the hearing of this Word that the church is built up for all eternity.[115] In another sense, however, in terms of both its origin and its historical reception, the church is the bearer of scripture, the one from whom and through whom the scriptures are delivered: "The books which make the Gospel of Jesus known to us . . . have been prepared, formed, edited and circulated within the Church; they have been preserved and canonized within the Church. . . . Today, just as from the very beginning, it is still through the Church that the Gospel is transmitted to us."[116] It is within the church, therefore, that the mystic hears the voice of Christ speaking through scripture: "It is only in the Church, through the effect of the Church's preaching, that this Scripture ceases to be a simple mass of letters in order to become a living language."[117]

This relation of mutual causation between the church and scripture clearly parallels de Lubac's account elsewhere of the relationship between church and Eucharist, between the ecclesial and sacramental bodies of Christ. As de Lubac argues in a number of places—most famously in *Corpus Mysticum*—the church both produces *and is produced by* the Eucharist.[118] De Lubac first of all insists that it is the church that produces the Eucharist, "and it was principally to that end that her priesthood was instituted."[119] In the celebration of the Lord's Supper, Christ acts through the instrumental ministry of the "hierarchic" church, through the *ordo sacerdotalis* of the bishop and his attendant clergy, to unite the members of his body to himself and, in so doing, to communicate the gift of eternal life. Moreover, in uniting the individual members of his body to himself, Christ unites them to one another, and it is precisely in this sense that de Lubac insists that the Eucharist "makes" the church: "The cup of blessing that we bless, is it not a sharing in the blood of Christ? The bread that we break, is it not a sharing in the body of Christ? *Because there is one bread, we who are many are one body, for we all partake of the one bread.*"[120] Debates in the eleventh and twelfth centuries (anticipating later debates at the time of the Reformation) concerning the "real presence" of Christ in the elements served to obscure the importance of this ecclesial body, effectively elevating individual Eucharistic piety over the formation of ecclesial unity, but de Lubac is adamant that "the communion of saints is not an effect that is exterior to the sacrament; it cannot be detached from it. It is the definition of its fruitfulness." The communion of saints (*sanctorum communio*) is the culmination, "the final and substantial reality" of sacramental communion.[121] Those who partake of "holy things" (*sancta*) become thereby a "holy people" (*sancti*).[122] Thus, just as it is within the church that the mystic receives the mystery of Christ conveyed in scripture, so it is by means of the church's sacramental ministry that the mystic "passes into the body of Christ."[123] And just as "the announcement of salvation contains the salvation announced," so the recipient of Christ's body becomes the gift that is received.

For de Lubac the church is not only a provisional means of uniting humanity to Christ; it is also "the heavenly kingdom in embryo," the end toward which the incarnate life and ministry of Jesus Christ is oriented. To speak of Christian mysticism as an ecclesial mysticism is therefore to locate the Christian mystic within this eschatological community, among the recipients of Christ's restorative benefits. The Christian mystic belongs in time to the society of those gathered together in Christ for all eternity. And as Christ, the eternal Logos made flesh, acts always and inseparably with the Father and the Holy Spirit, so it is in Christ that the mystic participates now in the blessed unity of the Trinity.

A Trinitarian Mysticism

This brings us to the final characteristic of Christian mysticism: "Christian mysticism is a trinitarian mysticism since, in Jesus Christ, all the Trinity reveals and gives itself."[124] This statement serves in many respects as the culmination of de Lubac's insistence that in Christian mysticism the mystery is first and last, for as de Lubac argues elsewhere, Christian faith consists primarily in the mystery of the divine Trinity.[125] To speak of Christian mysticism as a Trinitarian mysticism is therefore to name, with all the specificity, all the theological and metaphysical precision that such a confession requires, the unique subject of the mystery to which the mystic adheres. The God to whom the mystic relates is not some abstract, undifferentiated deity. "He is not," de Lubac insists, "the 'All-Possibility' or 'the place of indefinite possibilities.' Neither is he the *Ungrund*, the original chasm, the obscure core of being—or nonbeing—from which persons emerged."[126] The God of Christian mysticism is the God revealed in Jesus Christ; it is from this unique reality that the other characteristics of Christian mysticism derive their theological significance. Thus, Christian mysticism is "an understanding of the holy Books," because the latter convey the works *ad extra* of the one by whom, through whom, and for whom all things exist. In dwelling upon these works, in meditating upon the saving acts of God recorded in scripture, the mystic is brought to participate in the blessed knowledge of God's inner life. The divine economy attested in scripture opens the way for the mystic to theology proper, to the "praise and silent adoration" of this unfathomable Trinitarian mystery.[127] Likewise, Christian mysticism is an ecclesial mysticism because the church is "a mysterious extension of the Trinity in time, which not only prepares us for this life of union and gives us a sure guarantee of it, but also makes us participate in it already."[128] The church's unity is not primarily voluntary or juridical; indeed, it is often obscured by the visibility of the church's discordant members. Rather, the church's unity is essential to it. It is ontological. It is a unity grounded in the intra-Trinitarian unity of God and accomplished in the mystical body of Christ through the ministry of the Holy Spirit. What is true of the church corporately is likewise true of the soul individually. The mystic's union with

God—that union of love described above in terms of spiritual marriage—everywhere bears the mark of this Trinitarian structure. It is always through the Son and by the Holy Spirit that the mystic is brought to deeper fellowship with God the Father.[129]

Finally, in designating Christian mysticism a Trinitarian mysticism, de Lubac seeks to illumine the irreducibly relational nature of humanity's supernatural vocation.[130] More specifically, de Lubac points to the self-relatedness of the divine persons as both the analogical exemplar and the efficient cause of humanity's graced participation in the divine "likeness." It is difficult to overstate the importance of this Trinitarian principle for de Lubac's "mysticism of likeness" and his hermeneutics of human existence more generally, but one must be careful not to overextend the analogy between the intra-Trinitarian relations and the communitarian shape of humanity's graced existence. De Lubac narrates humanity's supernatural vocation in terms of the restoration of social unity, and in doing so he often avails himself of the paradox of unity and distinction at the heart of Christian reflection on the tripersonal being of God. Between the individual members of the *Civitas Dei*, notes de Lubac, "there obtains no scale of the degrees of being, but in the likeness of the Trinity itself—and, by the mediation of Christ in whom all are enfolded, within the Trinity itself—a unity of circumincession."[131] In his foreword to the 1988 edition of *Catholicism*, Joseph Cardinal Ratzinger (Benedict XVI) intimates that this is the key insight of de Lubac's book: "He [de Lubac] shows how the idea of community and universality, rooted in the trinitarian concept of God, permeates and shapes all the individual elements of Faith's content."[132] The Trinitarian concept of God is indeed fecund in de Lubac's rendering of the social aspects of Christian dogma. It is *the* mystery that governs and contains all others. Attention to this foundational doctrine provides the basic heuristic principles for navigating a host of other dogmatic "paradoxes" elsewhere.[133] However, de Lubac's employment of the doctrine of the Trinity as an *analogue* for human relations is far less determined and/or strained than what is typically offered as "relational" models of God's Trinitarian life in a great deal of modern theology.[134] The Trinity is not, for de Lubac, a "social program." It is not primarily by imaging *among ourselves* the reciprocity of God's intra-Trinitarian life that we come to resemble God. It is rather by *our relatedness to God*—by that particular mode of relatedness given and received in Christ—that we finally attain the divine likeness. To return to an earlier quotation by de Lubac, "Christ, by completing humanity in himself, at the same time made us all complete—but in God. Thus we can say . . . that we are fully persons only within the Person of the Son, by whom and with whom we share in the circumincession of the Trinity."[135] In his 1942 lecture on the "internal causes" of the disappearance of the sacred, de Lubac relates this Christologically inscribed participation in the divine circumincession explicitly to the eschatological attainment of the divine likeness. Man was created to resemble God, "which is to say, that he was destined to live eternally in God, to enter into the inner movement of the trinitarian Life."[136]

"In the all-sufficient Being there is no selfishness but the exchange of a perfect Gift."[137] Christian mysticism is the "conscious actualization" of the reception of this gift.[138] The mystic knows herself as known and loved by God, and through the grace of the Holy Spirit, she is made capable of responding to God in love. Likewise, the mystic knows herself as belonging to that humanity united in Christ, and by the Spirit of Christ that dwells within her, she too is made to share in the love of God for her fellow members. The eschatological reality in which the mystic participates is therefore as much a transformed *relationship* as a transfigured *nature.* Or rather, it is the latter precisely because it is the former. Reason and will are perfected and perfectly integrated in "the knowledge of love," that creaturely participation in the eternal knowledge and love of God. According to de Lubac, it is only in this light, by means of the supernatural enjoyment of God, that the mystic comes to understand the meaning of his or her own existence. We may therefore apply to de Lubac an insight attributed elsewhere to St. Augustine: "We find our nature as loved creatures through the experience of being redeemed creatures. That we can be saved only by sheer gift is the revelation that gives us access to the unknown but always presupposed ground of all our distinctly human activity, the ground in gift, in the turning of God to what is not God in uncaused love."[139] In a more Lubacian key: it is in receiving the gift of the supernatural, in receiving the very gift of Godself, that the mystic is brought to an awareness of the original gratuity of her created nature, a gratuity ordered precisely (and paradoxically) to the *donum perfectum* of the supernatural. As we have argued throughout, this "perfect gift," though presupposing the prior gift of nature, always retains its transcendent newness. The "union of likeness," de Lubac reminds us, is not to be confused with "the union that already exists between God and all his creatures." Michel Sales succinctly captures the position of de Lubac on this point: Christ "does not only bring to man a key for understanding *what he is*, but the Gift of *a new Being which he is not.* If Christ reveals man to himself, it is for the purpose of opening him up to a Gift which will convert and transfigure his being into a being with a radical ontological newness."[140] In order for human being to attain its finality, the dynamism of human existence must be taken up into the dynamism of faith. The mystical life, the climax of the drama of human existence, must therefore begin in mortification.

CONCLUSION

Henri de Lubac's mystical theology is in many respects the capstone of his theological hermeneutics of human existence. It names the "converted humanism" to which de Lubac alludes throughout his confrontation with contemporary atheism, the essential community of persons gathered together in the person of Christ. It thus designates the only means capable of procuring *l'homme nouveau* sought after by the immanentist eschatologies of the twentieth century. In the community of the church, and by virtue of the grace conferred therein, the mystic participates already in the end toward which all of history is oriented: the reconciliation of all things in Jesus Christ. It is in the eschatological promise of this "well-ordered society" (the *totus Christus*) that the personal good of each perfectly coincides with the good of the greater human totality. De Lubac's mystical theology likewise narrates what Pierre Rousselot refers to as the *renaissance of reason*,[141] the transfiguration of the *intellectus quaerens fidem* into the *fides quaerens intellectum.* The dynamism of reason anticipates its final repose in "the interiority of faith by the interiorization of the Christian mystery."[142] The mystical aspiration animating (and always transcending) the dialectic of the idea of God discovers, and thereby *recognizes*, its own supernatural object in the biblically mediated revelation of God in Jesus Christ. Finally, in terms of humanity's *desiderium naturae*, de Lubac's mystical theology contains one of his clearest expositions of the paradoxical relation between the supernatural insufficiency of human nature and humanity's supernatural vocation. According to de Lubac, humanity's "capacity for the appropriation of the Christian mystery"—that capacity to which the desire of our nature corresponds—is strictly "a faculty for receiving, in itself empty and powerless."[143] What de Lubac refers to as Christian mysticism is not therefore the mere thematization of humanity's latent mystical condition. It is not the "making explicit" of some preconscious union with the divinity. It is the conscious actualization of a wholly new and wholly gratuitous relation to God (a union of "likeness"); it is a graced mode of being corresponding to the revelation of God within a particular community created and sustained by the reconciling work of Christ. Christian mysticism thus contributes to a hermeneutics of human existence, not by interpreting a heretofore uninterpreted *datum*, but by gesturing toward, through the performance of certain practices (prayer, the reading of scripture, participation in the Eucharist, an active commitment to more just social relations, etc.) and through the realization of a new form of social and spiritual existence, that "for which" human persons were created. Under the conditions of grace, Christian mysticism attests to humanity's supernatural vocation. And as de Lubac asserts throughout his writings, "It is in his divine vocation that man learns to know himself."[144]

Conclusion

Paradox and Postconciliar Theology

PARADOX AND THEOLOGICAL POLEMICS

Toward the end of his reflections in *Catholicism*, in a chapter devoted to the "present situation" of Christian theology, de Lubac alerts his readers to the dangers inherent in theological polemics. "It is a great misfortune," de Lubac famously remarks, "to have learned the catechism *against* someone."[1] A theology forged in the fires of controversy often results in a narrowness of outlook and a lack of proportion that amount to serious doctrinal error. The systematic coherence of the church's faith—a coherence properly attested, de Lubac insists, by constant vigilance to a series of *seemingly* antinomous convictions[2]—is obfuscated by one-sided attempts to fortify "the faith that was once for all entrusted to the saints"[3] against a particular theological aberrance. In combatting doctrinal error, the theologian often unwittingly adopts the vantage of his opponent. He accepts the line of questioning presented by his interlocutor, "so that without sharing the error he may make implicit concessions to his opponent, which are the more serious the more explicit are his refutations."[4] A number of de Lubac's own writings were devoted precisely to unmasking and thus tempering the results of such one-sided theological polemics. The ecclesiology set forth in works such as *Catholicism* and *The Splendor of the Church*, for instance, and the sustained attention devoted therein to the church's *mystical* relation to the reconciling work of Christ, was intended to supplement the disproportionately juridical and hierarchical ecclesiologies arising in the wake of Gallican and Protestant challenges to the Roman Catholic Church's secular and sacerdotal authority. Similarly, as a result of controversies surrounding the work of Berengar of Tours (d. 1088), who claimed that the Eucharistic elements symbolically *represent* the body and blood of Christ without thereby undergoing an essential change, late medieval theologians tended to emphasize the real presence of Christ in the Eucharist to the neglect of the sacrament's role in the formation of the *ecclesial* body of Christ. The historical investigations in de Lubac's *Corpus Mysticum* constitute a sustained argument to the effect that Eucharistic realism and ecclesial realism are co-determinative.[5] Finally, in an attempt to combat the "bastard Augustinianisms" of Baius and Jansenius, both of whom appeared to compromise the gratuity of the supernatural by insisting that the reward of eternal life was somehow *owed* to human beings prior to the Fall, certain Thomists in the sixteenth century and thereafter attempted to protect the gratuity of the supernatural by recourse to a purely immanent teleology. In each of these cases—in the church's confrontation with Gallicanism, Lutheranism, Berengarian symbolism, and Bainism—the fullness and coherence of the Catholic faith is obscured by the exigencies of polemic. The delicate balance of Christian dogma and the serene confidence of the church's theological reflection are mitigated, however unwittingly, in the fog of theological controversy.

But is de Lubac himself immune from such a line of critique? It is possible that de Lubac's own confrontation with theological extrinsicism left him ill-protected against the correlative and equally deleterious threat of theological intrinsicism. De Lubac's commitment to the intrinsic relation between human being and humanity's supernatural finality, his constant appeal to a natural "capacity" for the supernatural (and a corresponding *desiderium naturae*), and perhaps most controversially his insistence that "*L'esprit* est *donc désir de Dieu*"[6] would appear to prevent him from affirming what Thomas Joseph White happily refers to as a *good extrinsicism*, "the radical gratuity and transcendence of the order of grace to that of nature."[7] In a 1985 interview with Angelo Scola, then professor at the Pontifical Lateran University (now cardinal and archbishop of

Milan), de Lubac acknowledges that much of his work on nature and the supernatural was indeed deeply informed by the line of inquiry adopted by his neo-Scholastic interlocutors, even though, according to de Lubac, this manner of "attacking the problem" owed more to his role as a historian than as a polemicist.[8] This explains the relative dearth of theological attention to Christology and/or humanity's sinful postlapsarian condition in many of de Lubac's writings on the supernatural. Moreover, as a number of his critics have recently pointed out, de Lubac largely neglects to pursue the implications of his theology of nature and the supernatural into other theological arenas, most notably into the realm of moral theology. As Steven A. Long argues, one of the primary (if unintended) implications of de Lubac's denial of the intelligibility of human nature in abstraction from the supernatural "consists in a certain antinomian rejection of the Church's intelligibly authoritative direction in moral teaching."[9] It is not sufficient, Long contends, "to instruct people that something is wrong 'because the Church and Scripture say so,' with no further consideration."[10] The ethical quagmire confronting the church and society today—Long has in mind attacks upon the "natural" institution of heterosexual marriage and debates surrounding the use of contraception and abortion—requires deliberate attention to "the ontological density and proportionate end of human nature."[11] In both cases—that is, with respect to de Lubac's consideration of the supernatural in abstraction from sin and Christology and the moral implications of his refusal to consider human nature in abstraction from the supernatural—the problems facing de Lubac's theology are hardly insurmountable. As we sought to demonstrate at length in chapter 4, de Lubac's theology of history provides the necessary Christological framework within which to locate his theology of nature and the supernatural. Moreover, in response to Long's criticisms, it is not at all self-evident that de Lubac's refusal of a purely immanent human teleology bars the way to an "ontologically dense" ethic of created nature. As Oliver O'Donovan argues to great effect, one must not conclude from the *epistemological* difficulties confronting an "ethic of nature" that there is "no objective order to which the moral life can respond. We may only conclude that any certainty we may have about the order which God has made depends upon God's own disclosure of himself and of his works."[12] The persuasiveness of the church's moral vision resides first and foremost in the persuasiveness of the gospel to which the church must continually bear witness—the vindication of God's created order, the restoration of human being and human fellowship, in the person and works of Jesus Christ. Theology may have recourse to the findings of moral philosophy in order to demonstrate that its ethical teachings are not *against* reason (again, grace does not destroy God's created order but vindicates it by bringing it to its supernatural perfection), but it is only within the domain of revelation that we perceive "the natural order as it really is and overcome the epistemological barriers to an ethic that conforms to nature."[13]

None of this, of course, settles the more basic question pertaining to de Lubac and intrinsicism, and it is perhaps here that de Lubac's remarks on the dangers of theological polemics fall closest to home. For all of his protestations to the contrary, the sheer prevalence of intrinsicist interpretations of his theology (among critics and disciples alike) would seem to indicate that de Lubac's opposition to extrinsicism often prevented him from expressing with due clarity and theological precision the necessary distinction between nature and the supernatural. What de Lubac describes as the paradox of a nature always already ordered to the wholly gratuitous disposal of an end that infinitely surpasses the capacities of that nature to attain easily (perhaps all too easily) gives way to the supposition of a nature always already graced. The paradoxical tension necessary for describing the mystery of human being is thereby relaxed in favor of an easy resolution. But reading de Lubac charitably at this point (which is not, I hasten to add, the same as reading him *radically*) requires that we take him at his word when he argues that "between the existent nature and the supernatural to which God destines it, the distance is as great, the abyss is as profound, the heterogeneity is as radical as between nonbeing and being";[14] when he maintains that "the longing that surges from [the] 'depth' of the soul is a longing 'born of a lack,' and not arising from 'the beginnings of possession'";[15] and when he insists that "it is the same for Humanity, taken as a whole, as for each individual. . . . [It] cannot reach completion without a totally different process—or rather a 'passion': a turning around of the whole being, a mysterious passage through death, a revival and a recasting that are nothing other than the evangelical *metanoia*."[16] Throughout his voluminous corpus—not simply in his "later" writings, but already in those works antedating *Humani generis*—de Lubac was devoted to maintaining that "good extrinsicism" of the order of grace to that of nature, albeit without recourse to a theory of pure nature. As we have sought to demonstrate throughout, in his confrontation with atheist humanism, in his account of humanity's natural desire for the supernatural, his theological epistemology, his theology of history, and his mystical theology, de Lubac remained committed to the "supernatural insufficiency of human nature." Any attempt to remain faithful to the fundamental theological insight of Henri de Lubac—not simply in his confrontation with neo-Scholasticism but in the development of a genuinely theological hermeneutics of human existence—must seek to move beyond the polemics in order to maintain the paradox.

INTRINSICISM AND THE NEW INTEGRISM

While the "good extrinsicism" of grace to nature was potentially obscured by de Lubac's decades-long polemic against pure nature (however unwittingly and despite de Lubac's explicit arguments to the contrary), shifts in the theological landscape following Vatican II brought into relief his persistent commitment to the radical heterogeneity of nature and the supernatural. Even before the council's close, de Lubac expressed serious misgivings about an ascendant "progressivism" masquerading as the authentic interpretation of Vatican II.[17] De Lubac decried the emergence of a "new integrism" galvanizing public opinion and exercising considerable influence over both Catholic laity and the teaching office of the church.[18] According to de Lubac, this "para-Council" sought "radical 'transformation,' which is to say, the secularization of the Church, which is to say, by its true name, apostasy. It is apostasy that is covered up by the successive tinsel of the 'spirit of the Council,' 'secularization,' 'pluralism,' and so on."[19] Having vigorously confronted the neo-Scholastic integrism of the 1940s and 50s, de Lubac set himself with equal resolve against "an opposite but analogous integrism" in the final decades of his life.[20]

Postconciliar debates on the proper reception of Vatican II and the nature of Catholic theology—debates typified, for instance, by thinkers associated with the "opposing" journals *Concilium* and *Communio*—are notoriously complex and resist superficial categorization along "liberal" and "conservative" lines. As Tracey Rowland notes, the leading Catholic theologians of the 1960s and 70s were largely in agreement in their opposition to the "monolithic system" of neo-Scholasticism. Tensions arose over competing visions of an alternative way forward.[21] De Lubac's own misgivings about certain trends in postconciliar theology revolved around a confluence of methodological, theological, and ecclesial concerns. De Lubac worried, for instance, that the "openness to the world" suggested by and evinced in the conciliar documents (notably *Gaudium et spes*) was being pressed into the service of a theological conformism to foreign (and often hostile) intellectual fads. Uncritical employment of Hegel, Marx, or Nietzsche, no less than strict neo-Scholastic adherence to Aristotle, risked compromising the Christian faith and/or blunting its critical edge. According to de Lubac, this slavishness to contemporary intellectual trends led to an impatience with, if not an open disregard for, the common judgments and habits of thought sustained throughout the church's theological tradition. Thus unmoored from the church's living tradition, the faith was all too easily distorted in the very attempts to render that faith intelligible and persuasive to the modern unbeliever. The impulse for theological and ecclesial renewal ultimately gave way to *mutation*: "a difference not of degree but of nature."[22]

De Lubac's rhetoric is no doubt severe and often lacking in concrete engagement with the thinkers and ideas alluded to in his critique of the "para-Council." The dangers attending theological polemics are therefore just as prevalent in de Lubac's confrontation with the new integrism as they were in his confrontation with the old. Nevertheless, where de Lubac *does* offer substantive commentary on postconciliar theology, it is clear that his misgivings are every bit as indebted to a particular construal of the relationship between nature and the supernatural as his refusal of pure nature. That is to say, de Lubac was convinced that both neo-Scholasticism and certain trends in postconciliar Catholicism mitigate the necessity of the supernatural. The former, in its avowal of a purely natural teleology, relegated the supernatural to an arbitrary "superstructure." The latter had a tendency to "naturalize" the supernatural, eliding the necessary distinction between nature and the economy of grace. This particular line of criticism may sound surprising coming from de Lubac. After all, a number of the thinkers and intellectual trajectories critiqued by de Lubac appeal directly to his theses on the supernatural. So, for instance, in their defense of an "anonymous" and "implicit" Christianity, both Karl Rahner and Edward Schillebeeckx adopt a typically Lubacian line of critique against two-tiered portrayals of the relationship between nature and the supernatural.[23] Gustavo Gutierrez (who received private tuition from de Lubac while a student at the Institut Catholique in Lyon) likewise articulates his proposal for a theology of liberation in the wake of de Lubac's dismantling of the theory of pure nature: "In the concrete situation there is but one vocation: communion with God through grace. In reality there is no pure nature and there never has been; there is no one who is not invited to communion with the Lord, no one who is not affected by grace."[24] Gutierrez's equivocation between the *invitation* to communion with God and the universal *reception* of grace already indicates an intrinsicist inflection on de Lubac's original thesis. It is precisely here, according to de Lubac, that so much postconciliar theology misses the mark. Intrinsicist construals of nature and grace, no less than extrinsicist appeals to pure nature, relax the necessary tension, thereby dissolving the paradox, of a created nature oriented to a supernatural finality. De Lubac's response to postconciliar intrinsicism—typified in his engagement with Rahner, liberationist theologies, and Schillebeeckx—thus provides a useful vantage for demonstrating his enduring commitment to the good extrinsicism of grace to nature.

As we indicated in chapter 2, Rahner articulates his own theology of nature and grace as a *via media* between neo-Scholastic accounts of pure nature and de Lubac's account of the *desiderium naturae*. For Rahner, as for de Lubac, human beings are always already ordered to a supernatural end. According to Rahner, however, this ordering, which entails "room and scope, understanding and desire" for the supernatural gift of God is already the work of divine grace.[25] Humanity's abiding ordination to the supernatural (what Rahner terms the supernatural existential) is not merely a potency antecedent to the divine self-communication; it is the very self-communication of God already present in every human being "at least in the mode of an offer."[26] This self-communication of God as offer is the condition for the possibility of the acceptance of

God's beatifying self-bestowal. It is the grace given in and with human existence prior to (and for the sake of) the grace of justification. In this sense, as Karen Kilby notes, the supernatural existential is identical to what Rahner refers to elsewhere as transcendental revelation.[27] According to Rahner, what human beings encounter in the "categorical" history of revelation and salvation (as witnessed in the Old and New Testaments), and especially in the self-revelation of God in Jesus Christ, is "the necessary and historical self-interpretation of that original, transcendental experience which is constituted by God's self-communication."[28] The self-disclosure of God in Christ is therefore the climactic thematization of God's prior self-revelation in the depths of human existence. Categorical revelation makes explicit, thus bringing to reflexive consciousness, that which is always already implicit in every act of knowing and willing.

De Lubac's response to Rahner's account of the supernatural existential is initially somewhat ambivalent. He suggests at one point that Rahner misunderstood his position, that their respective arguments were actually closer than Rahner seemed to think, and that Rahner's employment of Heideggarian vocabulary only muddied the waters.[29] Elsewhere de Lubac argues that such an existential, "conceived as a kind of 'medium' or 'linking reality,'" was "a useless supposition, whereby the problem of the relationship between nature and the supernatural is not resolved, but only set aside."[30] At the very least, Rahner's articulation of a supernatural existential is theologically redundant, doing the work that might just as easily be accomplished by a sufficient doctrine of creation. As we argued in chapter 2, humanity's abiding orientation to the supernatural is gratuitous, not because it is graced, but precisely because it is *created.* The unexacted character of humanity's desire for God is secured by the very contingency of all created being upon God.

Although de Lubac's treatment of the supernatural existential is somewhat muted, his rejoinder to the "anonymous Christianity" entailed in Rahner's account of transcendental revelation is more urgent and direct.[31] On the one hand, notes de Lubac, conceiving of revelation transcendentally as the interpretation of a basic preconceptual experience dangerously abstracts revelation from its particular rootedness in/as history. Revelation is essentially *dramatic,* the self-interpretation of God in history culminating in the person and works of Jesus Christ. For de

Lubac there is therefore no circumventing the scandal of particularity. Because revelation is identical with God's saving acts in history, it demands attention to "a definite place and at a definite time" through the mediation of scripture within the interpretive community of the church.[32] Moreover, according to de Lubac, such appeals to an implicit or anonymous Christianity undermine the necessity of *metanoia* and faith as the subjective correlates to divine revelation: "In Jesus, there has appeared to us not only someone who reveals to man what man already was but also 'through the perfect illumination of the Light' from God someone who, revealing the depths of God, changes man radically."[33] Appropriation of the Christian mystery is not simply the explication and/or realization of what "man himself truly is, and what he himself experiences in the depths of his existence."[34] As Joseph Ratzinger argues, "Just to accept one's humanity as it is (or, even as it should be, 'in its ultimate unconditionality')—that is not redemption; it is damnation."[35] Salvation is the undoing of humanity's own undoing, the restoration of human being by virtue of the restoration of human fellowship with God. Participation in the mystery of Christ therefore entails "a rupture, a radical change of position," nothing less than "the recreation of existence."[36] The supernatural gift of revelation is indissolubly united in Christ to the supernatural gift of salvation, a newness not only of knowing but of one's entire being.

Whereas de Lubac's appraisal of Rahner demands greater theological attention to the contingencies of history as the appointed locus of God's revelatory and salvific activity, his critique of liberation theology centers upon the latter's restriction of Christian hope to the immanent processes of history. De Lubac's criticism of liberation theology has been the cause of some confusion and consternation among even his most sympathetic interpreters. As Gemma Simmonds argues, liberation theology is in many respects an attempt to take seriously de Lubac's own retrieval of the social and historical aspects of salvation.[37] Joseph Flipper likewise registers a tension between de Lubac's sacramental ecclesiology and his criticisms of liberationist accounts of social progress. That is, though de Lubac insists that the church historically mediates the supernatural reunification of humanity, he nevertheless maintains that the temporal advancement of human liberation is not to be confused with the supernatural inbreaking of God's kingdom. Thus, according to Flipper, de Lubac ultimately fails to elaborate upon "how social and political practices, the struggle for justice, or the social aspects of ecclesial communion could be anticipatory of the consummation of God's plan."[38]

As Balthasar notes in a brief survey of contemporary trends in Catholic theology, there is indeed a certain family resemblance between de Lubac's work on "the essentially communitarian character of the Catholic Church" and the theologies of liberation arising in the second half of the twentieth century.[39] Like de Lubac, for instance, Gutierrez insists on a single finality for human beings,[40] provides an account of sin as the rupturing of relationship among humans with God,[41] and defines salvation in terms of "the communion of men with God and among human beings" and as something that "embraces all human reality, and leads it to its fullness in Christ."[42] However, despite the similarities (or perhaps precisely because of the proximity of liberation theology to his own project), de Lubac expresses serious reservations with liberationist accounts of salvation.[43] For starters, de Lubac was suspicious of the uncritical appropriation of Marx in certain liberationist theologies of history. As we indicated in chapter 4, de Lubac was convinced that Marxist social theory was predicated on a Marxist metaphysic, on, that is, the absolute negation of transcendence. History marches along according to its own immanent dialectic, propelled through social antagonism in pursuit of the final emancipation of humanity from all forms of alienation. Thus relegated to the immanent domain of history, liberation can only be understood as a "strictly human undertaking," an attempt to bring about "by human means certain changes in the organization of temporal society."[44] It is man who "transforms himself by conquering his liberty throughout his existence and his history."[45] The oppressed are thus invited "to break with their present situation and *take control of their own destiny*."[46] De Lubac readily grants the Christian imperative "to contribute to a better organization of human society," even insisting that such endeavors provide "a certain sketch of the age to come."[47] He refuses, however, to equate such earthly progress with the growth of the kingdom of God—refuses, that is, to equate liberation with salvation. Once again, de Lubac appeals to the necessity of *metanoia.* Liberation from social, economic, political, and ideological oppression is insufficient for securing human freedom so long as the self remains in captivity to sin. Human nature is not only infinitely disproportionate to its own supernatural finality; sinful humanity actively resists the divine invitation to share collectively in the life of God. To be saved, therefore, "man must first be freed from his own sins, *liberated from himself*."[48] Moreover, as we argued at length in chapter 4, history itself must similarly undergo a radical transfiguration in order to attain its fulfillment in the eschaton. However much temporal advances may foreshadow the world to come, they remain always imperfect, ambivalent, and liable to retrogression. History itself is immanently incapable of arriving at its own destiny, for the end of history, like the end of every individual human being, is supernatural.

In many respects, the above lines of criticism converge in de Lubac's response to Schillebeeckx's work during and immediately following Vatican II concerning the relationship between the church and the world. Like Rahner, Schillebeeckx argues for an "implicit Christianity" operating outside the church and constituting a universal condition of human existence. Anticipating and indeed informing the arguments of liberationist theologians, Schillebeeckx likewise articulates the nature of salvation in terms of the reconfiguration of social relations within history.[49] Both convictions are taken up and mutually explored in Schillebeeckx's account of the church as the "sacrament of the world." According to Schillebeeckx, "The Church manifests, as in a sacrament, what grace . . . is already accomplishing everywhere in human-existence-in-the-world."[50] In the Incarnation, Christ confers upon human existence and the whole of human history "a new religious meaning," such that history itself is sanctified.[51] In "the acceptance of human existence,"[52] in the human capacity to "make history" through the "humanization of the world,"[53] and most definitively in acts of love ordered to the service of others,[54] humanity exemplifies the grace conferred upon the world by Christ. It is in the church, however, that this new religious meaning "takes on the form that establishes an historical, visible, concrete community."[55] The church makes explicit, bringing to full consciousness, the assumption of humanity and human history in Christ. The world is therefore an *implicit Christianity*, "a distinctive, non-sacral, but sanctified expression of man's living community with the living God," while the church, in her visible structures, her worship, sacraments, and confession of faith, "is the 'set-aside,' sacral expression of this implicit Christianity."[56]

De Lubac's response to Schillebeeckx constitutes one of his most sustained and damning appraisals of trends in postconciliar theology. In his personal notebooks written throughout Vatican II, de Lubac records a conversation with a fellow priest in which he was asked what he thought of the theory that was beginning to spread among Parisian clergy that "the world has always been Christian; it is only Christian revelation that makes us say so." De Lubac recounts, "I replied to him that I am one hundred percent opposed to it; that, objectively, it is a betrayal of the Gospel."[57] Indeed, it was largely in response to Schillebeeckx's project that de Lubac resigned from the editorial committee of *Concilium*. Having initially (albeit unenthusiastically) accepted the invitation from Rahner and Schillebeeckx to serve on the committee,[58] de Lubac soon registered serious misgivings on reading Schillebeeckx's recently published article "The Church and the World."[59] In a letter to Rahner, de Lubac notes, "I have become greatly troubled. Not only is it impossible for me to associate myself with such a theological orientation—but, if I had the power, I would believe it my duty to combat it.—If such an orientation must be that of *Concilium*, it would be better for me to withdraw immediately from the editorial committee."[60] Despite Rahner's assurance that Schillebeeckx's argument was in no way indicative of the overall direction of *Concilium*, de Lubac's concerns were only exacerbated by his reading of the journal's first five issues. On May 24, 1965, de Lubac submitted to Rahner a letter of formal resignation, stating, "It is, in my opinion, a betrayal to present a propaganda tool in the service of an extremist school as if it were a theological effort in line with the council."[61]

We have already gone some way toward anticipating de Lubac's response to Schillebeeckx's position in our treatment of Rahner and liberation theology. De Lubac continues to insist on the particularity of the gospel and the historical means by which God is revealed and God's creatures are redeemed. De Lubac likewise accuses Schillebeeckx of falsely equating salvation with the "technical construction of a new politico-social world."[62] Schillebeeckx's conflation of social progress and the kingdom of God immanentizes the eschaton, thus robbing history of the means by which it ultimately attains its appointed end. Beyond such shared criticisms, de Lubac argues that Schillebeeckx's portrayal of the church as the "sacrament of the world" denigrates the church as the divinely appointed instrument by which and within which human beings participate in the saving benefits of Christ. For de Lubac, as we noted in chapter 4, the church is not the "sacrament of the world" but "the sacrament of *Christ*."[63] The difference between these two construals is more than semantic. Whereas for Schillebeeckx the church manifests a sanctification that appears to take place without her, for de Lubac the church is an "efficacious sign" that actually accomplishes in history what it signifies.[64] The church is "a sign and instrument of the world's *salvation*."[65] However provisional, however imperfect, and however resistant she may often be to her own vocation, the church extends that which she first receives from Christ, the grace of spiritual reunion and a foretaste of humanity's supernatural vocation. Thus, according to de Lubac, "the Church of Christ's primary, essential, irreplaceable mission is to remind us constantly, *opportune*, *importune*, of our divine supernatural vocation and to communicate to us through her sacred ministry the seed, still fragile and hidden, yet real and living, of our divine life."[66]

The above foray into de Lubac's postconciliar provocations is hardly exhaustive, and more could easily be said about the lines of divergence between de Lubac and those theologies of nature and grace emerging especially after Vatican II. De Lubac scholarship has long been occupied with de Lubac's confrontation with preconciliar extrinsicism; it is to be hoped that future scholarship will devote similar energy to his critical engagement with postconciliar intrinsicism.[67] At the very least, however, we have begun to indicate the ways in which de Lubac's later work reinforces, sharpens, and clarifies the paradox always at the heart of his theological hermeneutics of human existence. As we have argued throughout, such a hermeneutics insists equally on the intrinsic relation between nature and the supernatural *and* the infinite disproportion between human being and humanity's supernatural vocation. It is only by the gift of grace that human beings are elevated to the place of reason's repose and the perfect enjoyment of humanity's deepest desire. It is only in the light of this gift, therefore, that the drama of human existence finds its ultimate meaning.

NOTES

Acknowledgments

1. Xavier Tilliette, "Henri de Lubac achtzigjährig," cited in Rudolf Voderholzer, *Meet Henri de Lubac: His Life and Work* (San Francisco: Ignatius, 2008), 48–49.

Introduction

1. Innocent VI, "Sermo de *S. Thoma*"; cited in Leo XIII, "*Aeterni Patris*: Encyclical Letter on the Restoration of Christian Philosophy," *Acta Sanctae Sedis* 12 (1879): 21.
2. Leo XIII, *Aeterni Patris*, 31.
3. Ibid. (emphasis added).
4. Erich Przywara, "Le Mouvement théologique et religieux en Allemagne," *Nouvelle revue théologique* 56 (1929): 567; cited in "Apologetics and Theology," *TF*, 98.
5. At the time, de Lubac was lodged at the Jesuit residence on rue d'Auvergne, "an old shack that was demolished shortly afterward." De Lubac arrived in Lyon without a single book and, much to his dismay, discovered that the library of the Catholic Faculties was wholly insufficient. Fortunately, de Lubac discovered a "treasure" in the attic of a local day school: "a library, particularly of literature, which had long been neglected but which contained several tiers of theology well furnished with old books" (*ASC*, 16).
6. *ASC*, 25. De Lubac did eventually publish this essay in Henri de Lubac, *Théologies d'occasion* (Paris: Desclée de Brouwer, 1984).
7. According to de Lubac, one of the students in attendance at his inaugural lecture came to tell him a few days later "that it was too academic and that it was not easy to draw any precise ideas from it" (*ASC*, 16).
8. By the time de Lubac delivered his inaugural lecture, debates over the nature and methods of apologetics in the face of scientism and neo-Kantian rationalism had occupied French Catholics for the better part of four decades. At

one extreme was the position criticized by de Lubac (following Blondel, Lucien Laberthonnière, and others), which sought to demonstrate the existence of God by traditional metaphysical arguments (from motion, causality, contingency, etc.) and the authority of biblical revelation on the basis of the miracles and fulfilled prophecies contained therein. At the other extreme, Catholic Modernists such as Alfred Loisy sought to commend the Christian faith wholly on the basis of "the conformity of religion with the needs and aspirations of man"; see Loisy, "Les Preuves et l'économie de la revelation," *Revue du clergé français* 22 (March 1900): 128; cited in Avery Dulles, *A History of Apologetics* (San Francisco: Ignatius, 1999), 277. Between these two extremes, a number of thinkers, such as Ambroise Gardeil and Ambroise de Poulpiquet, sought to hold together the objective/intellectual and subjective/affective approaches to apologetics, arguing for the validity of Christian beliefs on the basis of both external evidence and the faith's ability to satisfy the moral and spiritual impulses of human beings. See Dulles, *A History of Apologetics*, 271–84; Avery Dulles, "Faith and Reason: From Vatican I to John Paul II," in *The Two Wings of Catholic Thought: Essays on "Fides et Ratio,"* ed. David Ruel Foster and Joseph W. Koterski (Washington, DC: Catholic University of America Press, 2003), 195–96; Reginald Garrigou-Lagrange, *God, His Existence and His Nature*, vol. 1, *A Thomistic Solution of Certain Agnostic Antinomies* (St. Louis: B. Herder Book Co., 1939), 8–60.

9. "Apologetics and Theology," *TF*, 92.

10. Thus, in his contribution to the *Dictionnaire apologétique de la foi catholique*, Xavier-Marie le Bachelet insists, "As in every science, one must take the apologetical object itself as the starting point, that being the rational credibility of the Christian and Catholic religion, or the demonstration of the fact of divine revelation . . . : on the positive side, proofs which form the constitutive part of the demonstration, with their supports and annexes; on the negative side, the defence of these proofs against attacks which undermine their foundations or directly invalidate them"; see le Bachelet, "Apologétique," in *Dictionnaire apologétique de la foi catholique*, ed. Adhémar d'Alès (Paris: Beauchesne, 1911), 244–45; cited in Noel O'Sullivan, *Christ and Creation: Christology as the Key to Interpreting the Theology of Creation in the Works of Henri de Lubac* (Oxford: Peter Lang, 2009), 95–96; see also Jean-Pierre Wagner, *La théologie fondamentale selon Henri de Lubac* (Paris: Cerf, 1997), 24.

11. *Dogmatic Constitution on the Catholic Faith*, chap. 3, "Vatican I," in *Decrees of the Ecumenical Councils*, vol. 2, *Trent to Vatican II*, ed. Norman P. Tanner (London: Sheed and Sheed, 1990), 804.

12. Pius X, "The Oath against the Errors of Modernism," in *The Sources of Catholic Dogma*, ed. Heinrich Denzinger (St. Louis: Herder Book Co., 1957), 550. As Fergus Kerr notes, the oath against Modernism was "treated effectively as the formulary of orthodoxy for clerics throughout the first half of the century"; see

Kerr, *Twentieth-Century Catholic Theologians: From Neoscholasticism to Nuptial Mysticism* (Malden, MA: Blackwell, 2007), 223.

13. See "Apologetics and Theology," *TF*, 95.

14. Ibid., 93. De Lubac's critique of two-tiered apologetics follows closely and builds on the work of the controversial Blondelian theologian and philosopher Lucien Laberthonnière. See Laberthonnière, "L'Apologétique et la méthode de Pascal" (1901), in *Le réalisme chrétien et l'idealisme grec* (Paris: Seuil, 1966). De Lubac sent an early copy of "Apologetics and Theology" to Laberthonnière, who responded positively but reproached de Lubac for his overreliance on Aquinas (*ASC*, 16). Though they were allied in their critiques of extrinsicism, Laberthonnière's construal of apologetics pushed in a more explicitly intrinsicist direction. Thus, according to Laberthonnière, "in all human life . . . is there not always the desire to possess God, the desire to be God? But this desire is not natural . . . [I]f man desires to possess God and to be God, it is that God has already given himself to him. This is how nature even finds itself and finds in itself the demand for the supernatural. These demands do not belong to nature qua nature, but they belong to nature as already penetrated and invaded by grace"; Laberthonnière, "L'Apologétique et la méthode de Pascal," 151; cited in John Kirwan, *An Avant-garde Theological Generation: The "Nouvelle Théologie" and the French Crisis of Modernity* (Oxford: Oxford University Press, 2018), 65.

15. Ibid., 94–95.

16. Ibid., 91.

17. Already in "Apologetics and Theology," de Lubac insists that what is commonly considered the "classical" position with respect to the relations between nature/grace, reason/faith, etc. (that is, the position of neo-Scholasticism) is actually "something completely modern, in form and spirit" ("Apologetics and Theology," *TF*, 95–96, n15; see *MS*, 5).

18. De Lubac, "Apologetics and Theology," *TF*, 96 (emphasis original).

19. Ibid., 96–97.

20. Ibid., 98 (emphasis original).

21. This is not to say that de Lubac denies the necessity of grace for the assent of faith. Like Pierre Rousselot (1878–1915), de Lubac insists on both the intellect's natural dynamism toward God *and* the necessity of the supernatural illumination of faith (*lumen fidei*) in order for the mind "to savor the supernatural beauty of doctrine" (ibid., 100–101); see also Rousselot, *The Eyes of Faith* (New York: Fordham University Press, 1990), 27–28. We will return to a more exhaustive treatment of de Lubac's theological epistemology in chapter 3.

22. "Apologetics and Theology," *TF*, 97.

23. In "Apologetics and Theology," de Lubac describes the discipline of fundamental theology rather vaguely as "an in-depth study of essential religious problems that, while being at the base of theology, are of the first order of

importance for apologetics" (ibid., 104). For a detailed treatment of de Lubac's contribution to fundamental theology, see Wagner, *La théologie fondamentale selon Henri de Lubac.*

24. In the summer of 1950, de Lubac was removed from his teaching duties at the Faculty of Theology on account of "pernicious errors on essential points of dogma." De Lubac was finally permitted to resume teaching in November 1959 until March 1, 1960, at which time he resigned in good standing (*ASC*, 68, 91). See chapter 3 herein for a more detailed account of what would come to be known as the "Fourvière affair."

25. Later published as Henri de Lubac, "Nature and Grace," in *The Word in History*, ed. T. Patrick Burke (New York: Sheed & Ward, 1966), 24–40.

26. A portion of the second chapter of *Athéisme et sens de l'homme* has been translated into English as "The Total Meaning of Man and the World," *Communio* 35 (Winter 2008): 613–41.

27. De Lubac, "Nature and Grace," 32; de Lubac, "The Total Meaning of Man and the World," 619.

28. De Lubac's notes taken during Vatican II have recently been translated into English as *Vatican Council Notebooks*, 2 vols. (San Francisco: Ignatius, 2015, 2016). For an insightful evaluation of de Lubac's involvement in and response to Vatican II, see Aaron Riches, "Henri de Lubac and the Second Vatican Council," in *T&T Clark Companion to Henri de Lubac*, ed. Jordan Hillebert (London: T&T Clark, 2017), 121–56.

29. De Lubac, "The Total Meaning of Man and the World," 620; see de Lubac, "The 'Supernatural' at Vatican II," *BC*, 177–90.

30. De Lubac, "Nature and Grace," 26.

31. Ibid., 24.

32. See *DAH*, 24–25.

33. De Lubac, "Nature and Grace," 26.

34. *C*, 353.

35. See Ludwig Feuerbach, *The Essence of Christianity* (New York: Prometheus Books, 1989). We will return to a more detailed consideration of Feuerbach's project in chapter 1.

36. De Lubac, "Nature and Grace," 29–30.

37. De Lubac, "The Total Meaning of Man and the World," 626–27.

38. Ibid., 625. De Lubac is here drawing on the work of his *confrère* Henri Bouillard. See Bouillard, "Croire et comprendre," in *Mythe et foi*, ed. Enrico Castelli (Paris: Aubier, 1966), 294–300.

39. Paul Ricoeur, "Sciences humaines et conditionnements de la foi," *Recherches et Débats* 14 (1965): 140; cited in de Lubac, "The Total Meaning of Man and the World," 628 (emphasis added).

40. Henri de Lubac, "On Christian Philosophy," *Communio* 19, no. 3 (1992): 482–83. On Blondel's "method of immanence," see Blondel, "The Letter on

Apologetics," in *The Letter on Apologetics and History and Dogma* (Grand Rapids, MI: William B. Eerdmans, 1964), 156; Oliva Blanchette, *Maurice Blondel: A Philosophical Life* (Grand Rapids, MI: William B. Eerdmans, 2010), 136–39.

41. De Lubac, "Nature and Grace," 25.

42. Hans Urs von Balthasar, *The Theology of Henri de Lubac: An Overview* (San Francisco: Ignatius, 1991), 23. Though never officially one of de Lubac's students, Balthasar was a student at the scholasticate in Fourvière, where de Lubac lived while lecturing in the Faculty of Theology at the Université Catholique. As Balthasar recalls, "fortunately Henri de Lubac was in residence, and he referred us beyond scholasticism to the church fathers, generously making his notes and excerpts available to us"; see Balthasar and Angelo Scola, *Test Everything, Hold Fast to What Is Good* (San Francisco: Ignatius, 1989), 11–12.

43. *ASC*, 143.

44. For an insightful treatment of this natural debt (*debitum naturae*), see Andrew Dean Swafford, *Nature and Grace: A New Approach to Thomistic Ressourcement* (Eugene, OR: Pickwick Publications, 2014), 10–12, 100–106. According to Swafford, the construal of the *debitum naturae* by the extrinsicist tradition maintains that "God's justice to the creature entails that He provides whatever is necessary for a given creature to reach its *natural* end—which is the end given to it on account of its nature, and which is accessible by way of its own natural principles. In this sense, God is *not* free in His offer of man's natural end; that is, He could not have withheld this end from man without injustice on His part" (10).

45. On the place of paradox in Christian anthropology, see *S*, 483–85.

46. De Lubac, "The Total Meaning of Man and the World," 627.

47. *S*, 487–88.

48. Ibid., 488.

49. "The Mystery of the Supernatural," *TH*, 288.

50. See ibid., 302; "The Search for a New Man," *DAH*, 465–66; *AMT*, 91; *MS*, 31, 83–84; *BC*, 32; *ASC*, 59n23.

51. De Lubac, "The Mystery of the Supernatural," 302.

52. See John Milbank and Catherine Pickstock, *Truth in Aquinas* (London: Routledge, 2001), 38; Fergus Kerr, "A Catholic Response to the Programme of Radical Orthodoxy," *Radical Orthodoxy?—A Catholic Enquiry*, ed. Laurence Paul Hemming (Aldershot: Ashgate, 2000), 55–56; Milbank, *The Suspended Middle: Henri de Lubac and the Renewed Split in Modern Catholic Theology*, 2nd ed. (Grand Rapids, MI: William B. Eerdmans, 2014), 44–45; Paul J. DeHart, *The Trial of the Witnesses: The Rise and Decline of Postliberal Theology* (Malden, MA: Blackwell, 2006), 271; David Grumett, *De Lubac: A Guide for the Perplexed* (London: T&T Clark, 2007), 16–17; John Wright, *Postliberal Theology and the Church Catholic* (Grand Rapids, MI: Baker Academic, 2012), 18–21; David Brown, "Sacramentality," in *The Oxford Handbook of Theology and Modern European Thought*, ed.

Nicholas Adams, George Pattison, and Graham Ward (Oxford: Oxford University Press, 2013), 627; Joshua B. Davis, *Waiting and Being: Creation, Freedom, and Grace in Western Theology* (Minneapolis: Fortress Press, 2013), 48–52; Adam G. Cooper, *Naturally Human, Supernaturally God: Deification in Pre-Conciliar Catholicism* (Minneapolis: Fortress Press, 2014), 160.

53. "Internal Causes of the Weakening and Disappearance of the Sense of the Sacred," *TH*, 231. Yet even here, in the sentences immediately preceding this assertion, de Lubac argues: "There is an absolute distinction, a radical heterogeneity between nature and the supernatural, and it is good to stress this first in order to avoid certain deadly and sacrilegious confusions."

54. This is the interpretation provided by Fergus Kerr, "French Theology: Yves Congar and Henri de Lubac," in *The Modern Theologians*, 2nd ed., ed. David Ford (Malden, MA: Blackwell, 1997), 113.

55. De Lubac, "The Mystery of the Supernatural," 291–92.

56. Ibid., 292.

57. Edward T. Oakes, "The Paradox of Nature and Grace: On John Milbank's *The Suspended Middle: Henri de Lubac and the Debate Concerning the Supernatural*," *Nova et Vetera* 4, no. 3 (2006): 693 (emphasis original).

58. The affinities between Radical Orthodoxy and the *nouvelle théologie* (and de Lubac in particular) were made explicit already in the movement's original "manifesto": John Milbank, Catherine Pickstock, and Graham Ward, eds., *Radical Orthodoxy: A New Theology* (London: Routledge, 1999), see 2. Shortly after publication, at a conference held at Heythrop College on the subject of Radical Orthodoxy, Milbank claimed that "Radical Orthodoxy considers that Henri de Lubac was a greater theological revolutionary than Karl Barth, because in questioning a hierarchical duality of grace and nature as discrete stages, he transcended, unlike Barth, the shared background assumption of all modern theology. In this way one could say, anachronistically, that he inaugurated a postmodern theology" (Milbank, "The Programme of Radical Orthodoxy," in Hemming, ed., *Radical Orthodoxy?—A Catholic Enquiry*, 35).

59. Milbank, *The Suspended Middle*, 44. Unless otherwise indicated, all citations of this text are from the 2nd edition.

60. *MS*, 84–85.

61. Milbank, *The Suspended Middle*, 9.

62. Oakes, "The Paradox of Nature and Grace," 693–94.

63. Irenaeus, *Adversus Haereses* IV, 34, i.

64. See *C*, 239; "The Light of Christ," *TH*, 218; *ME*, 1:236; "Mysticism and Mystery," *TF*, 83; *CPM*, 5, 78; *PS*, 1:156.

65. Milbank, "The Programme of Radical Orthodoxy," 35. According to Milbank, this is the radical implication of de Lubac's work.

66. *CF*, 93–94.

67. See ibid., 298–99.

68. "The Light of Christ," *TH*, 213.

69. *BC*, 41.

70. See Aquinas, *ST* Ia IIae, q. 110, a. 2.

71. See 2 Peter 1:4. By divinization, de Lubac wishes to affirm "that the influx of God's Spirit does not remain external to man; that without any commingling of natures it really leaves its mark *on* our nature and becomes in us a principle of life" (*BC*, 42; emphasis original). For an excellent treatment of de Lubac's understanding of deification, see Cooper, *Naturally Human, Supernaturally God*, 151–215.

72. See Swafford, *Nature and Grace*, 7.

73. *S*, 483.

74. Maurice Blondel, "La notion et le rôle du miracle," *Annales de philosophie chrétienne* (July 1907): 346–47; cited in *BC*, 32.

75. See *ST* Ia, q. 44, a. 1.

76. See *BC*, 48–52.

77. "Mysticism and Mystery," *TF*, 62.

78. *S*, 483.

79. "The Search for a New Man," *DAH*, 465. We will return to a fuller evaluation of the significance of this lecture in chapter 4.

80. *BC*, 119.

81. *MS*, 28.

82. See Dennis J. M. Bradley, *Aquinas on the Twofold Human Good* (Washington, DC: Catholic University of America Press, 1997); John Milbank, *The Suspended Middle: Henri de Lubac and the Debate Concerning the Supernatural*, 1st ed. (Grand Rapids, MI: William B. Eerdmans, 2005); Ralph McInerny, *Praeambula fidei: Thomism and the God of the Philosophers* (Washington, DC: Catholic University of America Press, 2006); Oakes, "The Paradox of Nature and Grace"; David Braine, "The Debate between Henri de Lubac and His Critics," *Nova et Vetera* (2008): 543–90; Nicholas J. Healy, "Henri de Lubac on Nature and Grace: A Note on Some Recent Contributions to the Debate," *Communio* 35 (Winter 2008): 535–64; Guy Mansini, "The Abiding Theological Significance of Henri de Lubac's *Surnaturel*," *The Thomist* 73 (2009): 593–619; Lawrence Feingold, *The Natural Desire to See God according to St. Thomas Aquinas and His Interpreters*, 2nd ed. (Ave Maria, FL: Sapientia Press, 2010); Steven A. Long, *Natura Pura: On the Recovery of Nature in the Doctrine of Grace* (New York: Fordham University Press, 2010); Christopher J. Malloy, "De Lubac on Natural Desire: Difficulties and Antitheses," *Nova et Vetera* (2011): 567–624; Edward T. Oakes, "The *Surnaturel* Controversy: A Survey and a Response," *Nova et Vetera* 9, no. 3 (2011): 625–56; Bernard Mulcahy, *Aquinas's Notion of Pure Nature and the Christian Integralism of Henri de Lubac* (New York: Peter Lang, 2011); Reinhard Hütter, *Dust Bound for Heaven: Explorations in the Theology of Thomas Aquinas* (Grand Rapids, MI: William B. Eerdmans, 2012); Swafford, *Nature and Grace*; Milbank, *The Suspended Middle*;

Thomas Joseph White, "Imperfect Happiness and the Final End of Man: Thomas Aquinas and the Paradigm of Nature-Grace Orthodoxy," *The Thomist* 78 (2014): 247–89; Nicholas J. Healy, "The Christian Mystery of Nature and Grace," in Hillebert, ed., *T&T Clark Companion to Henri de Lubac*, 181–204.

83. For a helpful summary of the ongoing debate, see Santiago Sanz Sánchez and John Watson, "The Revival of the Notion of Pure Nature in Recent Debates in English Speaking Theology," *Annales Theologici* 31 (2017): 171–250. For recent defenses of de Lubac's thesis, see Oakes, "The *Surnaturel* Controversy"; Healy, "Henri de Lubac on Nature and Grace" and "The Christian Mystery of Nature and Grace."

84. There is, of course, a certain irony in seeking to distance de Lubac's project from the polemics it has engendered. De Lubac himself was often guilty of impatient readings of the neo-Scholastic tradition in the service of his own critique of pure nature. One of the great services of Feingold's work is the clear and detailed exhibition of such thinkers as Cajetan, Báñez, and Suárez on the natural desire to see God.

85. Mulcahy, *Aquinas's Notion of Pure Nature*, 59. Feingold is more nuanced than Mulcahy on this point, noting a fundamental ambiguity in de Lubac's thought as to whether the *desiderium naturae* is natural or already supernatural (see Feingold, *The Natural Desire to See God*, 329–38). Feingold nevertheless concurs that an abiding supernatural disposition in human beings prior to the gift of sanctifying grace would imply that humans are *constituted* in grace, thus undermining the doctrine of original sin as traditionally construed (ibid., 391).

86. According to Mulcahy, "In de Lubac's judgment, to suggest a distinction between knowing God naturally (as first cause, through metaphysics) and knowing God supernaturally (through deification, personal communion, and vision of the divine essence) is a distinction with no real foundation. In *The Mystery of the Supernatural*, he attributes this distinction to the Dominican commentator Sylvester Ferrara (1474–1528) and to his own least-favourite teacher Pedro Descoqs, SJ (1877–1946), but dismisses it out of hand" (Mulcahy, *Aquinas's Notion of Pure Nature*, 59, referring to *MS*, 46. Mulcahy makes similar accusations on 154, 214–15). This is a serious mischaracterization of de Lubac's argument in *MS*. De Lubac's argument is not against the possibility of a natural knowledge of God per se, but rather against a construal of humanity's final end, beatitude, and perfection as consisting in a purely natural contemplation of God. De Lubac summarizes the concern alluded to (and misrepresented) by Mulcahy as follows: "Take, then, the great traditional texts, from Augustine, say, and Thomas, dealing with *man's final end and beatitude*: they will be systematically brought down [by proponents of pure nature] to a natural plane and their whole meaning thus perverted. They will no longer be taken to be anything but affirmations of a purely natural philosophy. The 'perfection' of human nature spoken of in these texts, *a perfection which was recognized as meaning its supernatural consummation*, will thus be-

come a *completely natural perfection* which can be adequately defined by pure philosophy" (*MS*, 37; emphasis added).

87. *DG*, 35, 39; citing Thomas Aquinas, "Omnia cognoscentia cognoscunt implicite Deum in quolibet cognito" (*De veritate* q. 22, a. 2, ad 1). For de Lubac's distinction between "objective" and "subjective" revelation, see *DG*, 89–90.

88. Mulcahy, *Aquinas's Notion of Pure Nature*, 155.

89. See Mansini, "The Abiding Theological Significance of Henri de Lubac's *Surnaturel*," 4. For a thorough critique of overly Platonist interpretations of de Lubac's work, see Joseph Flipper, *Between Apocalypse and Eschaton: History and Eternity in Henri de Lubac* (Minneapolis: Fortress Press, 2015), 108–15.

90. "Mystery of the Supernatural," *TH*, 292.

91. Long, *Natura Pura*, 11 (emphasis added). In defense of this claim, Long appeals often to Thomas's distinction between human and angelic natures on the basis of their "proximate and natural ends" (see *ST* Ia, q. 75, a. 7, ad 1; Long, *Natura Pura*, 13, 73). According to Long, if human nature is defined in terms of its supernatural finality, then it would be impossible to distinguish between human and angelic natures, for humans and angels have the same supernatural *finis ultimus* (namely, eternal happiness). However, as Nicholas Healy has argued, Long's own definition of human nature in terms of humanity's proximate end runs into precisely the same difficulty, for even in this account human and angelic natures are ordered alike to a strictly natural knowledge and love of God. Thus, according to Healy, what ultimately distinguishes humans and angels "at the level of species is that this ordination is directed to different *degrees* of that knowing and loving" (Healy, "Henri de Lubac on Nature and Grace," 559; emphasis original). The same argument obviously applies to those who insist that if human beings were naturally ordered to the supernatural, then human nature itself would be divine (see Mulcahy, *Aquinas's Notion of Pure Nature*, 153; Feingold, *The Natural Desire to See God*, 321).

92. Feingold, *The Natural Desire to See God*, 314 (emphasis original).

93. Long, *Natura Pura*, 32.

94. Ibid., 13; see also Feingold, *The Natural Desire to See God*, xxxiii, 397.

95. *DG*, 209. Some of de Lubac's critics insist to the contrary upon a radical *discontinuity* between Thomas and his theological predecessors on the subject of nature and grace. According to Guy Mansini, for instance, "One will look long and hard in the Fathers, and mostly in vain, for any even implicit expression of the gratuity of grace as distinct from the gratuity of creation" (Mansini, "The Abiding Theological Significance of Henri de Lubac's *Surnaturel*," 12).

96. See *ST* Ia, q. 22, a. 2.

97. *ST* Ia IIae, q. 1, a. 2.

98. See *ST* Ia IIae, q. 5, a. 5.

99. See Aquinas, *De veritate* q. 14, a. 10; *ST* Ia IIae, q. 3, a. 8; *ST* Ia, q. 12, a. 4.

100. *ST* Ia IIa, q. 5, a. 5, ad 2; see also *De veritate* q. 14, a. 10, ad 5.

101. At the time Aquinas was writing, an apophatic tendency developed especially from encounters with the writings of Pseudo-Dionysius and John Damascene led some theologians to deny the possibility of knowing God's essence. This position was condemned by William of Auvergne, the bishop of Paris, in 1241, just about ten years before Aquinas began teaching at the University of Paris. See Jean-Pierre Torrell, *Saint Thomas Aquinas*, vol. 2, *Spiritual Master* (Washington, DC: Catholic University of America Press, 2003), 27–29.

102. *ST* Ia, q. 12, a. 1.

103. See *ST* Ia IIae, q. 1, a. 5.

104. Thomas Aquinas, *Compendium of Theology* (Oxford: Oxford University Press, 2009), §104.

105. Feingold, *The Natural Desire to See God*, xxiv (emphasis original).

106. See ibid., 397–401.

107. See ibid., xxxiii, 397.

108. See *ST* Ia, q. 12, a. 1.

109. See Feingold, *The Natural Desire to See God*, 221–23.

110. See ibid., 317–24, 442–43.

111. *AMT*, 125; see also *S*, 433–34.

112. As Aquinas argues in a subsequent question, insofar as "the general notion of happiness consists in the perfect good," and "the perfect good of a man is that which entirely satisfies his will," to desire happiness is "nothing else than to desire that one's will be satisfied. And this everyone desires" (*ST* Ia IIae, q. 5, a. 8).

113. *ST* Ia IIae, q. 3, a. 8 (emphasis added).

114. *ST* Ia IIae, q. 5, a. 8.

115. See *ST* Ia IIae, q. 1, a. 7.

116. *ST* Ia IIae, q. 3, a. 6.

117. *ST* Ia IIae, q. 5, a. 3.

118. *ST* Ia IIae, q. 5, a. 4.

119. *ST* Ia IIae, q. 3, a. 8; q. 5, a. 5.

120. Henri de Lubac, "Duplex Hominis Beatitudo," *Communio* 25 (Winter 2008): 599.

121. Oakes, "The *Surnaturel* Controversy," 635.

122. "The Mystery of the Supernatural," *TH*, 292.

123. See *CM*; "The Mystery of the Supernatural," *TH*, 281–316; *MS*; *CPM*; "Mysticism and Mystery," *TF*, 35–69.

124. David Stewart, "Existential Humanism," in *Studies in the Philosophy of Paul Ricoeur*, ed. Charles E. Reagan (Athens: Ohio University Press, 1979), 28, referring to Paul Ricoeur, "L'Homme et son mystère," in *Le Mystère* (Paris: Horay, 1960), 119.

125. *DG*, 6.

ONE. A Hermeneutics of Atheist Humanism

1. "Spiritual Warfare," *TH*, 488.

2. Ibid., 489 (emphasis original).

3. Jean Daniélou, "H. de Lubac: Le Drame de l'humanisme athée," *Etudes* (May 1945): 275, cited in Michael Kelly, "Humanism and National Unity: The Ideological Reconstruction of France," in *The Culture of Reconstruction: European Literature, Thought and Film, 1945–50*, ed. Nicholas Hewitt (Basingstoke: Macmillan, 1989), 111.

4. For what follows, see Georges Chantraine, *Henri de Lubac, Tome 1, De la naissance à la démobilisation (1896–1919)* (Paris: Cerf, 2007), 57–58; see also de Lubac, *Mémoire sur l'occasion de mes écrits* (Paris: Cerf, 2006), 425n16; Rudolf Voderholzer, *Meet Henri de Lubac: His Life and Work* (San Francisco: Ignatius, 2008), 25–26.

5. The church's reasons for opposing Dreyfus are complicated, and accusations that the church in France was the *primary* agitator against Dreyfus are certainly overstated. Nevertheless, as Adrien Dansette argues, "It matters little that Catholics did not play a leading part [in the affair]. Taken individually, they were anti-Dreyfus. The church as a whole was no less so, and it is on this general outlook that the church loses a case in which all the evidence was not on the side of the prosecution. Almost all the church's friends were opposed to Dreyfus, and almost all her enemies, the Jews, the Protestants, and the free-thinkers, were on the other side"; Dansette, *Religious History of Modern France*, vol. 2, *Under the Third Republic* (Edinburgh: Nelson, 1961), 181.

6. Roger Soltau, *French Political Thought in the Nineteenth Century* (London: Ernest Benn, 1931), 357.

7. See Nicholas Atkin, "The Politics of Legality: The Religious Orders in France, 1901–45," in *Religion, Society and Politics in France Since 1789*, ed. Frank Tallett and Nicholas Atkin (London: The Hambledon Press, 1991), 149–65; Voderholzer, *Meet Henri de Lubac*, 27–30, 37–41; and Aidan Nichols, "Henri de Lubac: Panorama and Proposal," *New Blackfriars* 93, no. 1043 (2012): 3–5.

8. See *ASC*, 35, 42.

9. Joseph Komonchak, "Theology and Culture at Mid-Century: The Example of Henri de Lubac," *Theological Studies* 51 (1990): 597.

10. See Robert O. Paxton, *Vichy France: Old Guard and New Order, 1940–1944* (London: Barrie & Jenkins, 1972), 148–52; Julian Jackson, *France: The Dark Years, 1940–1944* (Oxford: Oxford University Press, 2001), 268–71.

11. "Letter to My Superiors," *TH*, 434–35.

12. Ibid., 437–38.

13. See Henri de Lubac, *Christian Resistance to Anti-Semitism: Memories from 1940–1944* (San Francisco: Ignatius, 1990).

14. *ASC*, 53.

15. Ibid., 52.

16. "Letter to My Superiors," *TH*, 429.

17. See ibid., 430; "Spiritual Warfare," *TH*, 489, 493.

18. De Lubac acknowledges in the preface to later editions that "this work had to make its appearance during the occupation. In writing it, I had to take into account the necessities imposed by censorship; and it was printed before the liberation of Paris. This explains, on the one hand, some of the emphases and, on the other hand and in particular, some of the omissions, some of the silences" (*DAH*, 15).

19. Ibid., 11.

20. See Michael Kelly, "Humanism and National Unity: The Ideological Reconstruction of France," in Hewitt, ed., *The Culture of Reconstruction*, 103–19; Kelly, *The Cultural and Intellectual Rebuilding of France after the Second World War* (Hampshire: Palgrave Macmillan, 2004), 127–54.

21. Kelly, *The Cultural and Intellectual Rebuilding of France*, 127. According to Jacques Derrida, "this profound concordance was authorized, in its philosophical expression, by the *anthropologistic* readings of Hegel (interest in the *Phenomenology of Spirit* as it was read by Kojéve), of Marx (the privilege accorded the *Manuscripts of 1844*), of Husserl (whose descriptive and regional work is emphasized, but whose transcendental questions are ignored), and of Heidegger, whose projects for a philosophical anthropology or an existential analytic only were known or retained (*Sein und Zeit*)"; Derrida, "The Ends of Man," in *Margins of Philosophy* (Brighton: Harvester Press, 1982), 117 (emphasis original).

22. Edward Baring, "Humanist Pretensions: Catholics, Communists, and Sartre's Struggle for Existentialism in Postwar France," *Modern Intellectual History* 7, no. 3 (2010): 582–85.

23. Kelly, "Humanism and National Unity," 104–5.

24. Kelly, *The Cultural and Intellectual Rebuilding of France*, 136. See Emmanuel Mounier, "Refaire la Renaissance," reprinted in Emmanuel Mounier, *Oeuvres, Tome 1, 1931–1939* (Paris: Editions du Seuil, 1961); and Jacques Maritain, *Integral Humanism* (Notre Dame, IN: University of Notre Dame Press, 1973).

25. Maritain, *Integral Humanism*, 6–7.

26. Kelly, "Humanism and National Unity," 111.

27. Stefanos Geroulanos, *An Atheism That Is Not Humanist Emerges in French Thought* (Stanford, CA: Stanford University Press, 2010), 100–101 (emphasis original).

28. Ibid., 106.

29. Maritain, *Integral Humanism*, 27; Nicholas Berdyaev, *The Fate of Man in the Modern World* (London: Student Christian Movement Press, 1935), 25.

30. Emmanuel Levinas, "On Maurice Blanchot," in *Proper Names*, trans. Michael B. Smith (London: The Athlone Press, 1996), 127–28.

31. Thus, according to Levinas: "The unburied dead of wars and death camps accredit the idea of a death with no future, making tragic-comic the care for one's self and illusory the pretensions of the rational animal to a privileged place in the cosmos, capable of dominating and integrating the totality of being in a consciousness of self"; see Levinas, *Humanism of the Other* (Urbana: University of Illinois Press, 2006), 45.

32. Geroulanos, *An Atheism That Is Not Humanist*, 12 (emphasis original).

33. Karl Marx, "Contribution to the Critique of Hegel's *Philosophy of Right*," in *The Marx-Engels Reader*, ed. Robert C. Tucker (New York: W. W. Norton, 1978), 65.

34. Michel Foucault, *The Order of Things: An Archeology of the Human Sciences* (New York: Pantheon Books, 1970), 386–87 (emphasis added).

35. *DAH*, 65.

36. Ibid., 23.

37. Ibid., 24–25.

38. Ibid., 25. According to Maritain, *negative atheism* entails "a merely negative or destructive process of casting aside the idea of God, which is replaced only by a void." *Positive atheism*, meanwhile, entails "an active struggle against everything that reminds us of God—that is to say, antitheism rather than atheism—and at the same time a desperate, I would say heroic, effort to recast and reconstruct the whole human universe of thought and the whole human scale of values in accordance with the state of war against God"; see Maritain, *The Range of Reason* (London: Geoffrey Bles, 1953), 104.

39. *DAH*, 12.

40. Karl Marx, "Foreword to Thesis: The Difference between the Natural Philosophy of Democritus and the Natural Philosophy of Epicurus," in Karl Marx and Friedrich Engels, *On Religion* (New York: Schocken, 1964), 15.

41. Ludwig Feuerbach, *The Essence of Christianity* (New York: Prometheus, 1989), 14.

42. See ibid., 33.

43. Ibid., 26.

44. *DAH*, 32.

45. Marx is thus able to write in the introduction to his "Contribution to the Critique of Hegel's *Philosophy of Right*": "For Germany, the *criticism of religion* has been largely completed; and the criticism of religion is the premise of all criticism. . . . The basis of irreligious criticism is this: *man makes religion*; religion does not make man. Religion is indeed man's self-consciousness and self-awareness so long as he has not found himself or has lost himself again"; see Marx, "Contribution to the Critique of Hegel's *Philosophy of Right*," in *The Marx-Engels Reader*, 2nd ed., ed. Robert C. Tucker (New York: W. W. Norton and Company, 1978), 53 (emphasis original). On de Lubac's interpretation of the relation between Feuerbach and Marx, see *DAH*, 36–42, 433.

46. Paul Vignaux, "Retour à Marx"; quoted in *DAH*, 38. We will return in chapter 4 to a more detailed account of de Lubac's interaction with Marx.

47. *DAH*, 42–44.

48. Ibid., 44.

49. See Nietzsche, *The Will to Power* (New York: Vintage, 1968), 86–87.

50. Nietzsche, *Thus Spoke Zarathustra* (New York: Cambridge University Press, 2006), 65 (emphasis original).

51. Nietzsche, *The Will to Power*, 145.

52. Nietzsche, *The Gay Science*, quoted in *DAH*, 59.

53. See the section devoted to the work of Auguste Comte (*DAH*, 215–61).

54. Henri de Lubac, *Athéisme et sens de l'homme: Une double requite de "Gaudium et Spes"* (Paris: Éditions du Cerf, 1968), 24.

55. *DAH*, 422; see also de Lubac, *Athéisme et sens de l'homme*, 29. On the relation between the Old and New Testaments in the theology of Origen, see *HS*, 109–203.

56. De Lubac, *Athéisme et sens de l'homme*, 29.

57. Ibid., 24.

58. Hegel, *Lectures on the Philosophy of Religion*, ed. Peter C. Hodgson (Berkeley: University of California Press, 1984, 1985, 1987), 1:84 (emphasis original).

59. Ibid., 1:186–87.

60. Ibid., 1:318.

61. Ibid., 3:233. Thus, in the Hotho transcript of the 1824 lectures, Hegel asserts: "Religion is therefore the relation of [finite] spirit to absolute spirit. But, as knowing, spirit is thus what is known or absolute spirit itself, and religion is the *self-consciousness of absolute spirit*—its relation to itself as the object of its knowing, which is *self*-knowing. . . . Religion is also consciousness, and has therefore finite consciousness within it, though sublated as finite because absolute spirit is itself the other that it knows, and it is only by knowing itself that it becomes absolute spirit. Consequently, however, it is only mediated through consciousness or finite spirit, so that it has to *finitize* itself in order by this finitization to come to know itself" (ibid., 1:318; emphasis original).

62. Feuerbach, *The Essence of Christianity*, 2–3 (emphasis added).

63. Stanislas Breton, *La Passion du Christ et les philosophes*; cited in de Lubac, *Athéisme et sens de l'homme*, 28.

64. Feuerbach, *The Essence of Christianity*, 14.

65. Ibid., 46–47.

66. Ibid., 53.

67. Ibid.

68. *DAH*, 162. The material on Comte included in *DAH* was taken from a course that de Lubac taught in the Faculty of Theology at the Université Catholique de Lyon (*ASC*, 40).

69. *DAH*, 158–59.
70. Ibid., 163 (emphasis original).
71. Ibid., 171.
72. See Auguste Comte, *The Catechism of Positive Religion* (London: John Chapman, 1858), 128.
73. *DAH*, 188, 220.
74. Ibid., 222.
75. Ibid., 233.
76. Ibid., 235–36.
77. Ibid., 227; quoting Edward Caird, *La Philosophie sociale et religion d'Auguste Comte* (Glasgow: J. Maclehose & Sons, 1885), 130, 132–33.
78. Ibid., 29.
79. De Lubac, *Athéisme et sens de l'homme*, 30.
80. *DAH*, 14.
81. Nietzsche, *Ecce Homo* (Oxford: Oxford University Press, 2007), 88–89; de Lubac references this passage in *DAH*, 64 (emphasis original).
82. *DAH*, 67–68.
83. *C*, 359.
84. *DAH*, 67.
85. John Webster, "The Human Person," in *The Cambridge Companion to Postmodern Theology*, ed. Kevin J. Vanhoozer (Cambridge: Cambridge University Press, 2003), 219.
86. Acts 17:28.
87. D. Stephen Long, *Speaking of God: Theology, Language, and Truth* (Grand Rapids, MI: William B. Eerdmans, 2009), 43.
88. See Eberhard Jüngel, *God as the Mystery of the World* (Edinburgh: T&T Clark, 1983), 19–20.
89. Henri de Lubac, "The Search for a New Man," *DAH*, 399.
90. *DG*, 193.
91. See *C*, 358–59.
92. *DAH*, 404.
93. Ibid., 259–61.
94. Nietzsche, *Ecce Homo*, 35.
95. Ibid., 65 (emphasis added).
96. Levinas, *Proper Names*, 127–28.
97. Jean-Paul Sartre, *Existentialism and Humanism* (London: Methuen & Co., 1968), 55.
98. See Geroulanos, *An Atheism That Is Not Humanist*, 223.
99. Sartre, *Existentialism and Humanism*, 28 (emphasis added).
100. De Lubac makes a similar observation, noting that among the heirs of humanism, "there is competition as to who will proclaim himself, in one sense or another, the most resolutely 'anti-humanist' " (*BC*, 95).

101. See Heidegger, "Letter on Humanism," in *Pathmarks*, ed. William McNeill (Cambridge: Cambridge University Press, 1999), 250.

102. See Derrida, "Ends of Man," in *Margins of Philosophy* (Brighton: Harvester Press, 1982), 124.

103. Maurice Blanchot, "On Nietzsche's Side," in *The Work of Fire* (Stanford, CA: Stanford University Press, 1995), 292.

104. Ibid., 296.

105. Geroulanos, *An Atheism That Is Not Humanist*, 256.

106. Blanchot, "On Nietzsche's Side," 296 (emphasis added).

107. Ibid., 293.

108. Sartre, *Existentialism and Humanism*, 33–34. According to Sartre, "The existentialist . . . finds it extremely embarrassing that God does not exist, for there disappears with Him all possibility of finding values in an intelligible heaven. There can no longer be any good *à priori*, since there is no infinite and perfect consciousness to think it. It is nowhere written that 'the good' exists, that one must be honest or must not lie, since we are now upon the plane where there are only men. Dostoevsky once wrote 'If God did not exist, everything would be permitted'; and that, for existentialism, is the starting point" (ibid., 33).

109. See *ASC*, 41, 240–42. We will return in chapter 4 to a more detailed account of de Lubac's criticism of this "new catechism" among Roman Catholic thinkers.

110. *C*, 368.

TWO. The Desire of Nature

1. "Christian Explanation of Our Times," *TH*, 441–42. As Michael Kelly notes, the École des cadres d'Uriage "was a leadership training institute, aiming to form the next generation of the country's elite, and sponsored in the early stages by Vichy before being closed down. Many of the staff and students joined the Resistance and became prominent in postwar public life" (Kelly, "Humanism and National Unity," 117n15).

2. De Lubac, "Christian Explanation of Our Times," 442.

3. The Chantiers de Jeunesse were compulsory youth camps set up under the Vichy government dedicated to "work of national importance," such as road-building and forestry. See Debbie Lackerstein, *National Regeneration in Vichy France: Ideas and Policies, 1930–1944* (Farnham: Ashgate, 2011), 194–96.

4. "Internal Causes of the Weakening and Disappearance of the Sense of the Sacred," *TH*, 225.

5. Ibid., 227.

6. Ibid., 233.

7. Gerald O'Collins helpfully (if somewhat reductively) summarizes this form of theology as: "(1) 'regressive' in method, (2) conceptualist rather than historical or biblical, (3) legalistic and worried about errors, (4) non-liturgical, and (5) non-experiential"; O'Collins, *The Second Vatican Council: Message and Meaning* (Collegeville, MN: Liturgical Press, 2014), 5.

8. "Internal Causes," *TH*, 232.

9. "The Mystery of the Supernatural," *TH*, 292; see also *MS*, 54.

10. Henri de Lubac, "Deux augustiniens fourvoyés," *Recherches de science religieuse* 21 (1931): 422–43, 513–40; de Lubac, "Remarques sur l'histoire du mot 'surnaturel,'" *Nouvelle Revue théologique* 61 (1934): 225–49, 350–70; de Lubac, "Esprit et liberté dans la tradition théologique," *Bulletin de literature ecclésiastique* 40 (1939): 121–50, 189–207; de Lubac, "La recontre de 'superadditum' et de 'supernaturale' dans la théologie medieval," *Revue du Moyen Âge Latin* 1 (1945): 27–34; de Lubac, "À propos de la conception medieval de l'ordre surnaturel (Échange de vues avec J. De Blic)," *Melanges de science religieuse* 4 (1947): 365–73; de Lubac, *Surnaturel: Ètudes historiques*; de Lubac, "*Duplex hominis beatitudo*," *Recherches de science religieuse* 35 (1948): 290–99; de Lubac, "Le Mystère du Surnaturel," *Recherches de science religieuse* 36 (1949): 80–120; de Lubac, "Saint Thomas: *Compendium theologiae*, c. 104," *Recherches de science religieuse* 36 (1949): 300–305; de Lubac, *Augustinisme et théologie moderne* (Paris: Aubier, 1965); de Lubac, *Le Mystère du Surnaturel* (Paris: Aubier, 1965); de Lubac, "Petite catéchèse sur la 'nature' et la 'grâce,'" *Revue international Communio II*, no. 4 (1977): 11–23; de Lubac, *Petite catéchèse sur nature et grâce* (Paris: Fayard, 1980); de Lubac, *Lettres de M. Étienne Gilson adressées au P. Henri de Lubac et commentées par celui-ci* (Paris: Cerf, 1986).

11. For examples of the first series of texts, see Aquinas, *Summa contra Gentiles* 3.25, 50–51, 57; *ST* Ia, q. 12, a. 1; *ST* Ia IIae, q. 3, a. 8; *Compendium* I, chap. 104. For the latter, see *De veritate*, q. 14, aa. 2, 10, ad 2; *ST* Ia, q. 75, a. 7, ad 1; *ST* Ia IIae, q. 62, aa. 1, 3. For a complete list of the relevant texts, see Jorge Laporta, *La Destinée de la nature humaine selon Thomas d'Aquin* (Paris: J. Vrin, 1965), 147–61; Feingold, *The Natural Desire to See God*, 27–43.

12. Milbank, *The Suspended Middle*, 44.

13. According to de Lubac, "Saint Thomas himself most certainly saw it [the natural desire], not as some superficial 'velleity,' which would have in common with many a chimerical dream the fact that it arises spontaneously or 'naturally' in the spirit, but rather as the desire of nature itself—or at least its resonance in objective consciousness and its authentic expression. The effect and the sign of a profound finality. Not only *desiderium naturale* [a natural desire], but *desiderium naturae* [the desire of nature]" (*S*, 433); see also "The Mystery of the Supernatural," *TH*, 293. De Lubac attaches great significance to this distinction between *desiderium naturale* and *desiderium naturae*, but his critics have been swift

to point out that Thomas often equivocates between these two phrases. See Feingold, *The Natural Desire to See God*, 328.

14. "The Mystery of the Supernatural," *TH*, 288; see also *MS*, 33–34.

15. Philip J. Donnelly, "Discussions on the Supernatural Order," *Theological Studies* 9, no. 2 (1948): 237.

16. Pierre Rousselot, *The Intellectualism of Saint Thomas* (New York: Sheed and Ward, 1935), 178–79.

17. Auguste Valensin, the brother of Albert Valensin (who appointed de Lubac to his chair at the Université Catholique de Lyon), studied philosophy under Blondel at Aix-en-Provence before entering the Society of Jesus in 1899. Prior to World War I, Valensin attracted considerable controversy within the Society for his defense of Blondel's method of immanence in an article for the *Dictionnaire Apologétique de la Foi catholique.* This controversy resulted in the removal of Valensin from his teaching responsibilities in Jersey. After the war, Valensin was located at Ore Place, where, as Jon Kirwan notes, he mediated Blondelian thought to two generations of Jesuit students. See Kirwan, *An Avant-garde Theological Generation: The "Nouvelle Théologie" and the French Crisis of Modernity* (Oxford: Oxford University Press, 2018), 77–81.

18. De Lubac, "Jersey: Dissertations et Gribouillis, Notes de Philosophie," in *Les Archives Jésuites de Vanves*; cited in Kirwan, *An Avant-garde Theological Generation*, 112. Kirwan provides a detailed account of de Lubac's intellectual development as a student in ibid., 108–30.

19. *ASC*, 35. As Georges Chantraine notes, this likely occurred during the academic year of 1925–26; see Chantraine, "La théologie du Surnaturel selon Henri de Lubac," *Nouvelle revue théologique* 119, no. 2 (1997): 219.

20. *ASC*, 35.

21. De Lubac, "The Total Meaning of Man and the World," *Communio* 35 (Winter 2008): 618; see also de Lubac, "Nature and Grace," in *The Word in History*, ed. T. Patrick Burke (New York: Sheed and Ward, 1966), 32. The term *obediential potency* (*potentia obedientiae*) refers to "the aptitude for there to be realized in a thing whatever God has decreed to work in it" (Cajetan, Commentary on *ST* I, q. 1, a. 1; cited in Feingold, *The Natural Desire to See God*, 101). According to de Lubac, *obediential potency* thus denotes the possibility of a divine miracle—the capacity in created nature to be transformed by the will of God above its own innate powers. As we will see, de Lubac denies that this term is sufficient for defining the relationship of human nature to the supernatural, for "it does not lay sufficient stress on 'the absolutely special case of spirit'" (*MS*, 143).

22. De Lubac, "Nature and Grace," 32.

23. According to Taylor, "the coming of modern secularity . . . has been coterminous with the rise of a society in which for the first time in history a purely self-sufficient humanism came to be a widely available option. . . . [A] secular age is one in which the eclipse of all goals beyond human flourishing becomes con-

ceivable; or better, it falls within the range of an imaginable life for masses of people"; Charles Taylor, *A Secular Age* (Cambridge, MA: Harvard University Press, 2007), 18–20.

24. Ibid., 15–16.

25. Jean-Yves Lacoste, "Henri de Lubac and a Desire beyond Claim," in Hillebert, ed., *T&T Clark Companion to Henri de Lubac*, 357–58.

26. See *C*, 322.

27. *ASC*, 143.

28. *C*, 20.

29. *HS*; *ME*.

30. See "Internal Causes," *TH*, 230–31; citing Augustine, *Confessions*, 1.1.1.

31. Published together in 1965, *AMT* is a slightly revised edition of the "Première partie" of *Surnaturel*, while *MS* offers an expanded form of the argument set forth in *Surnaturel*'s concluding chapter ("Exigence divine et désir naturel") and in "The Mystery of the Supernatural."

32. The system of pure nature proved an especially useful ally in combatting the "twin errors" of Baianism and Jansenism in the sixteenth and seventeenth centuries. Michael Baius (1513–89), chancellor and professor of scriptural interpretation at the Catholic University of Leuven, argued that eternal life was humanity's *natural* end and would have been owed to Adam (had he not sinned) solely as a reward for his natural merit. Without denying the necessity of the inhabitation of the Holy Spirit for Adam's original state of innocence, Baius nevertheless understood this indwelling, not as a gift of divine *grace*, but rather as a necessity of human *nature*, for without such divine assistance, human nature would essentially remain incomplete (see *S*, 33; *AMT*, 26). Cornelius Jansenius (1585–1638) likewise instrumentalizes divine assistance prior to the Fall, arguing that Adam was "created in grace" only to the extent that he had at his disposal sufficient grace for the performance of good works and for perseverance in justice. For Jansenius, the natural rectitude of the will originally enjoyed by Adam (who was thus capable of making efficacious use of the grace available to him) was so obliterated by the Fall that postlapsarian man becomes utterly devoid of freedom. The grace of Christ comes, therefore, not to heal or to liberate, but rather to master the remnants of a decimated nature.

According to late sixteenth- and early seventeenth-century Scholastics, the chief error underlying both heresies was precisely their shared denial of pure nature. De Lubac thus goes to great lengths in the first part of *Surnaturel* and in his *Augustinianism and Modern Theology* to demonstrate that the principal offense of these two thinkers is to be found, not in their denial of a state of pure nature, but rather in their shared misunderstanding and denigration of the supernatural. Thus, according to Jansenius, God lends his assistance to Adam, not because of the "sublimity" of his (supernatural) end, but rather in deference to "the weakness of the creature which, brought out of nothingness, always retains an inclination for nothingness" (*S*, 43; *AMT*, 37). For Baius, meanwhile, the Holy Spirit is placed at Adam's disposal, not for the purpose of elevating his nature above itself, but as a necessary means for the attainment of strictly natural ends (*AMT*, 5). Baius (and Jansenius after him) thus failed to recognize that the gift of the supernatural, culminating as it does in the beatific vision, constitutes more than simply the perfection of human nature. According to de Lubac, for both thinkers, "the whole order of grace was no more than a means placed at the service of human nature and its activity; it was 'a necessary logical complement of the creation of spirit, not a privileged condition raising spirit above its natural state'" (*MS*, 93). On Baius, See P. J. Donnelly, "Baius and Baianism," *New Catholic Encyclopedia*, vol. 2 (New York: McGraw-Hill, 1967); on Jansenius, see Nigel Abercrombie, *The Origins of Jansenism* (Oxford: Oxford University Press, 1936); for a more detailed account of de Lubac's treatment of these two figures, see David Grumett, "De Lubac, Grace, and the Pure Nature Debate," *Modern Theology* 31, no. 1 (January 2015): 123–46.

33. *S*, 105; *AMT*, 109.

34. This second factor in the development of the theory of pure nature, set forth by de Lubac in *AMT* (110–12), was entirely absent from the original argument in *Surnaturel.* It is likely that de Lubac mentions the case of limbo at this point in deference to some of his earlier critics; see, for instance, Philip J. Donnelly, "The Gratuity of the Beatific Vision and the Possibility of a Natural Destiny," *Theological Studies* 11 (1950): 401.

35. Serge-Thomas Bonino, "The Theory of Limbo and the Mystery of the Supernatural in St. Thomas Aquinas," in *"Surnaturel": A Controversy at the Heart of Twentieth-Century Thomistic Thought*, ed. Serge-Thomas Bonino (Ave Maria, FL: Sapientia Press, 2009), 118. Although the doctrine of limbo finds few contemporary theological defenders and is entirely absent from *The Catechism of the Catholic Church* promulgated by John Paul II, it continues to play an important role in arguments for the theory of pure nature. See Feingold, *The Natural Desire to See God*, 350–53; Bernard Mulcahy, *Aquinas's Notion of Pure Nature and the Christian Integralism of Henri de Lubac* (New York: Peter Lang, 2011), 66–70.

36. *AMT*, 110.

37. According to Thomas Aquinas, the state of original justice prior to the introduction of original sin consisted in humanity's "reason being subject to God, the lower powers to reason, and the body to the soul. . . . Now it is clear that such a subjection of the body to the soul and of the lower powers to reason, was not from nature; otherwise it would have remained after sin. . . . Hence it is clear that also the primitive subjection by virtue of which reason was subject to God, was not a merely natural gift, but a supernatural endowment of grace" (*ST* Ia, q. 95, a. 1; see also *ST* Ia, q. 100, a. 1, ad 2; *De malo*, q. 4, a. 2, ad 1; and *Compendium* I, chap. 186).

38. See *ST* Ia IIae, q. 109, a. 2. This acknowledgment that a state of pure nature has never *actually* existed leads proponents of pure nature to an interpretation of humanity's actual/historical *condition* that is remarkably similar to de

Lubac's own position. Thus, according to Steven A. Long, one of de Lubac's severest contemporary critics, "Once ordered in and by grace at creation, thereinafter human nature will be in vain and frustrated apart from the supernatural end. That is, human nature, created in sanctifying grace, is as such remotely ordered to the supernatural by this fact" (Long, *Natura Pura*, 24). Like de Lubac, Long thus grants that from the moment of their creation human beings were called to a supernatural end (whereas for de Lubac this call is constitutive, for Long it is an effect of the original bestowal of sanctifying grace). Given the causal efficacy of grace, this call perdures even after the loss of original justice. Once created and called, therefore, no end short of the beatific vision can satisfy the longing of human nature.

39. *AMT*, 112.

40. See *ST* Ia, q. 62, a. 1.

41. See Denys, *De puritate et felicitate animae*, a. 55 (*Opera omnia*, 40, 431).

42. Ibid., aa. 56–61 (*Opera omnia* 40, 431–34); cited in *MS*, 144.

43. See *S*, 105; *AMT*, 113; *MS*, 144–45.

44. "For as the ultimate beatitude of man consists in the use of his highest function, which is the operation of his intellect; if we suppose that the created intellect could never see God, it would either never attain to beatitude, or its beatitude would consist in something else beside God; which is opposed to faith. For the ultimate perfection of the rational creature is to be found in that which is the principle of its being; since a thing is perfect so far as it attains to its principle" (*ST* Ia, q. 12, a. 1). Denis J. M. Bradley notes that this theological argument is based on the metaphysical principle that "every being achieves its perfection when it is joined to or attains its source of efficient cause" (Bradley, *Aquinas on the Twofold Human Good*, 432).

45. See *ST* Ia, q. 2, a. 3.

46. Cajetan, Commentary on *ST* 1, q. 12, a. 1, n. 10 (Leonine ed., 4:116); cited in Feingold, *The Natural Desire to See God*, 170.

47. *MS*, 163.

48. "The Mystery of the Supernatural," *TH*, 300.

49. *MS*, 76.

50. "The Mystery of the Supernatural," *TH*, 301.

51. Ibid., 302.

52. See *S*, 485.

53. Thomas Aquinas, *On Creation [Quaestiones Disputatae de Potentia Dei, Q. 3]*, trans. S. C. Selner-Wright (Washington, DC: The Catholic University of America Press, 2011), a. 1, resp.

54. John Webster, "'Love Is Also a Lover of Life': *Creatio ex Nihilo* and Creaturely Goodness," *Modern Theology* 29, no. 2 (2013): 169.

55. "The Mystery of the Supernatural," *TH*, 304; see also *S*, 114; *AMT*, 158; *MS*, 148.

56. Aristotle, *De caelo*, II, 8, 290; cited in *AMT*, 169. For examples of neo-Scholastic employment of this principle, see Suárez, *De ultimo fine hominis*, d. 16, s. 2, n. 8; and Cajetan, Commentary on *ST*, q. 12, a. 1, n. 9.

57. *AMT*, 159. De Lubac traces this maxim to the works of Dominic Soto, Robert Bellarmine, and Francis Toletus: Soto, *De natura et gratia*, bk. 1, c. 4; Soto, *In Sent.*, bk. 4, d. 49, q. 2, art. 1; Bellarmine, *De gratia primi hominis*, bk. 1, c. 7; Toletus, *In Primam Partem*, q. 1, art. 1.

58. Suárez, *De ultimo fine hominis*, d. 15, s. 2, n. 6; cited in *MS*, 149.

59. "The Mystery of the Supernatural," *TH*, 304.

60. Thomas Aquinas, *De malo*, q. 1, c. 5; cited in *AMT*, 171.

61. *ST* Ia IIae, q. 5, a. 5, ad 2.

62. "The Mystery of the Supernatural," *TH*, 304.

63. Thomas Aquinas, *Compendium of Theology* (Oxford: Oxford University Press, 2009), §68.

64. "The Mystery of the Supernatural," *TH*, 303.

65. "Internal Causes," *TH*, 230.

66. See Origen, "On Prayer," in *Origen*, trans. Rowan A. Greer (New York: Paulist Press, 1979), 27.2; Irenaeus, *Against Heresies*, 5.16.2; Augustine, *De trinitate* 14.18.24.

67. 1 John 3:2 (emphasis added).

68. "The Mystery of the Supernatural," *TH*, 296.

69. Paul Ricoeur, "L'Homme et son mystère," in *Le Mystère* (Paris: Horay, 1960), 119.

70. Cited in *AMT*, 242.

71. On the influence of Blondel on de Lubac's theology, see Antonio Russo, *Henri de Lubac: Teologia e dogma nella Storia. L'influsso di Blondel* (Rome: Edizioni Studium, 1989); Francesca Murphy, "The Influence of Maurice Blondel," in Hillebert, ed., *T&T Clark Companion to Henri de Lubac*, 57–91.

72. *BC*, 37–38.

73. Maurice Blondel, *Action (1893): Essay on a Critique of Life and a Science of Practice* (Notre Dame, IN: University of Notre Dame Press, 2007), 300–301.

74. Ibid., 305.

75. See Blondel, "The Letter on Apologetics," in *The Letter on Apologetics and History and Dogma* (Grand Rapids, MI: William B. Eerdmans, 1994), 134.

76. See Blondel, *Action*, 357.

77. These three letters are included in the appendix (1:7) of *ASC*, 183–88.

78. Maurice Blondel, *Le Problème de la philosophie catholique* (Paris: Bloud et Gay, 1932).

79. In order to assuage neo-Scholastic misgivings about his work, Blondel makes a number of allusions in *Le Problème de la philosophie catholique* to the hypothesis of a state of pure nature (see *ASC*, 184). Similarly, in *L'Etre et les êtres*

(1935), Blondel insists, "One primary datum must be maintained: A state of pure nature is conceivable and effectively realizable"; Blondel, *L'Etre et les êtres: Essai d'ontologie concrete et intégrale* (Paris: Alcan, 1935), 491; cited in Henri Bouillard, *Blondel and Christianity* (Washington, DC: Corpus Books, 1970), 95.

80. De Lubac is adamant, for instance, that the condemnation of "Baianism" in Pius V's *Ex omnibus afflictionibus* (1567) nowhere demands a theory of pure nature (see *S*, 103).

81. *ASC*, 184; de Lubac, *Mémoire sur l'occasion de mes écrits*, 188: "comment un esprit conscient peut-il être autre chose qu'un désir absolu de Dieu?"

82. *ASC*, 186.

83. Ibid., 187.

84. Blondel, "The Letter on Apologetics," 141. This is not to deny a certain ambiguity in Blondel's own account of the relationship between human nature and humanity's supernatural finality. Blondel insists, for instance, that the supernatural is both "indispensable and at the same time inaccessible for man" (161) and that "what we find in ourselves is precisely not what we have to receive [i.e., the gift of the supernatural]" (153), but he nevertheless suggests that "the need for the gift, the request for the gift is, like the gift itself, already a grace" (143). Blondel later elaborates on these distinct gifts as the gift of prevenient grace (by which human beings are originally ordered to the supernatural) and the gift of sanctifying grace (by which human beings attain their supernatural finality). On this development in Blondel's thought, see Ryan A. Longton, "A Reconsideration of Maurice Blondel and the 'Natural' Desire," *Heythrop Journal* (2015): 919–30. As we will seek to demonstrate throughout this and subsequent chapters, de Lubac's own construal of the supernatural insufficiency of human nature, however indebted to Blondel's original insights, consistently resists identifying the desire of nature with the economy of grace. This is because, for de Lubac, the gift of grace designates, not only the elevation of humanity's *created* nature, but the transfiguration of humanity's *sinful* nature. For de Lubac, therefore, the distinction between nature and grace is "much more radical than in the case of the general differentiation between nature and the supernatural" (*BC*, 119).

85. *S*, 483.

86. Ibid., 484.

87. Ibid., 483.

88. Ibid., 486–87.

89. Donnelly, "The Gratuity of the Beatific Vision and the Possibility of a Natural Destiny," 393.

90. Ibid., 392.

91. See *S*, 490.

92. In an interview toward the end of his life, de Lubac was asked: "How can you say both that the desire to see God is something natural to man, and that the vision of God is an absolutely free gift?" De Lubac responds: "I spoke at the end of

my book [*Surnaturel*] of a divine 'requirement' [*exigence*], that is, a requirement that God makes. I was referring to St. Augustine's very expressive phrase: 'He requires all of thee' (Sermon 15). People took what I had said to mean: A requirement that man makes, a right of man over God. You couldn't have a more obvious misreading"; see Henri de Lubac and Angelo Scola, *De Lubac: A Theologian Speaks* (Los Angeles: Twin Circles, 1985), 11–12.

93. *S*, 487.

94. Ibid. David Coffey's translation of the concluding chapter of *Surnaturel* unfortunately muddies the water further by translating this sentence as "one must add that it is already, in a sense, *something divine* [*quelque chose de Dieu*]"; see Coffey, "Some Resources for Students of *La nouvelle théologie*," *Philosophy and Theology* 11, no. 2 (1999): 372 (emphasis added).

95. *S*, 487.

96. Ibid., 488.

97. Feingold, *The Natural Desire to See God*, 330.

98. Milbank, *The Suspended Middle*, 44.

99. Ibid., 70.

100. Ibid., 5.

101. John Milbank and Catherine Pickstock, *Truth in Aquinas* (London: Routledge, 2001), 38.

102. Ibid. Milbank has especially in mind Jean-Hervé Nicolas, "Les Rapports entre la Nature et le surnaturel dans le Débats Contemporaines," *Revue Thomiste* 95, no. 3 (1995): 399–418.

103. Milbank, *The Suspended Middle*, 44.

104. *S*, 487.

105. *MS*, 84.

106. Ibid., 31 (emphasis added).

107. Ibid., 84.

108. Ibid., 83.

109. In the second edition, Milbank writes: "In *A Brief Catechesis*, de Lubac does little more than repeat in telescoped form his earlier post–*Humani Generis* position. Yet the significant thing is that, by citing the pre-encyclical book which sparked off the entire controversy, *Surnaturel* itself, he implies his real non-repentance of his original position" (*The Suspended Middle*, 2nd ed., 53). This is a rather bizarre argument, given that nearly all of de Lubac's postencyclical treatments of the supernatural reference his earlier writings, not to mention the fact that *Augustinianism and Modern Theology* reproduces with little alteration the entire first part of *Surnaturel*.

110. *BC*, 41.

111. Ibid., 119.

112. See *ASC*, 71.

113. Pius XII, "*Humani Generis*: Encyclical Letter Concerning Some False Opinions Threatening to Undermine the Foundations of Catholic Dogma," *Acta Apostolicae Sedis* 42 (August 12, 1950): 561–78.

114. Ibid., §26.

115. Milbank, *The Suspended Middle*, 1st ed., 7. Milbank softens this claim ever so slightly in the second edition: "After *Humani Generis*, outside his historical work, de Lubac *to a degree* comes across as a stuttering, *perhaps* traumatized theologian, *resolved to* articulate himself in somewhat oblique fragments" (*The Suspended Middle*, 2nd ed., 8; emphasis added). In this edition, Milbank likewise assigns some of the blame for de Lubac's "traumatized" condition to liberal postconciliar critiques of his theology.

116. *ASC*, 295.

117. Ibid., 266.

118. "The Mystery of the Supernatural," *TH*, 288.

119. Ibid., 302.

120. *Humani generis*, §26.

121. *ASC*, 260, 263.

122. "The Mystery of the Supernatural," *TH*, 302; see also *MS*, 79–80.

123. See *ASC*, 71.

124. *S*, 109 (emphasis added).

125. *AMT*, 128–29; de Lubac, *Augustinisme et théologie moderne*, 162.

126. See Milbank, *The Suspended Middle*, 9–10.

127. "The Mystery of the Supernatural," *TH*, 292.

128. It was not until December 1958, however, that de Lubac received a verbal approval from Rome for the resumption of his old courses. He resumed teaching from November 1959 until March 1, 1960, before handing in his resignation (*ASC*, 91).

129. See ibid., 89–91.

130. De Lubac includes Father Tilliette's review in the appendix of *ASC*, 352–53.

131. S. Dockx, "Du désir naturel de voir l'essence divine d'après saint Thomas," *Archives de philosophie* 27 (1964): 49–96; Étienne Gilson, "In Company with Father de Lubac: Faith Seeking Understanding" (*La Croix*, July 18–19, 1965), in *Letters of Étienne Gilson to Henri de Lubac*, ed. Henri de Lubac (San Francisco: Ignatius, 1988), 177–82; Jean-Pierre Torrell, "Chronique de theologie fondamentale," *Revue Thomiste* 66 (1966): 93–107.

132. Gilson, "In Company with Father de Lubac," 178.

133. Milbank, *Theology and Social Theory: Beyond Secular Reason* (Oxford: Blackwell, 2006), 207.

134. See Karl Rahner, "Concerning the Relationship between Nature and Grace," in *Theological Investigations 1* (London: Darton, Longman and Todd,

1961), 297–317; Rahner, "Nature and Grace" and "Questions of Controversial Theology on Justification," *Theological Investigations 4* (Baltimore: Helicon Press, 1966), 165–218; Rahner, *Foundations of Christian Faith: An Introduction to the Idea of Christianity* (London: Darton, Longman and Todd, 1978), 126–33.

135. This is not to deny a certain ambiguity in Rahner's own articulation of the supernatural existential. In his 1950 essay "Concerning the Relationship between Nature and Grace," Rahner grants that it would be necessary "to examine more closely how the supernatural existential is related to grace itself, and in what sense it is distinct from it," thus giving the impression that the supernatural existential is somehow a *tertium quid* alongside nature and grace. However, when he returns to the question in subsequent writings, Rahner shows less interest in delimiting between grace and the supernatural existential, insisting instead that the latter is but a lower "degree" of the former (see Rahner, "Concerning the Relationship between Nature and Grace," 316; Rahner, "Questions of Controversial Theology on Justification," 215–16).

136. For Rahner, pure nature serves as a remainder concept (*Restbegriff*), that which perdures in the hypothetical absence of grace and the abiding supernatural existential. This nature never actually exists in abstraction from the supernatural existential (there is no pure nature *as such*), but it is necessary to delineate between the two in order to protect the gratuity of God's self-giving love. In this sense, pure nature denotes the meaningful possibility of human existence *without* a supernatural ordination to grace (see Rahner, "Concerning the Relationship between Nature and Grace," 313–15).

137. See *ASC*, 62, 123; de Lubac, ed., *Letters of Ètienne Gilson to Henri de Lubac*, 98–100.

138. See Milbank, *The Suspended Middle*, 42.

139. "The Mystery of the Supernatural," *TH*, 303.

140. See *MS*, 55, 76.

141. Ibid., 83.

142. On "the call of God" as humanity's vocation, see "The Mystery of the Supernatural," *TH*, 303; de Lubac, "Nature and Grace," 30.

143. *S*, 487.

144. Ibid.

145. De Lubac is thus wholly in agreement with Long in opposing accounts of human agency as "absolutely independent of God" and the natural realm as "an utterly separate jurisdiction sealed off from providence" (Long, *Natura Pura*, 41).

146. See *ST* Ia, q. 105, a. 4.

147. Galatians 2:19–20.

148. 2 Corinthians 5:17.

149. *CPM*, 89.

150. 1 John 3:2.

151. Blondel, "The Letter on Apologetics," 141.

152. "Nature and Grace," 34.
153. *MS*, 222.
154. Ibid., 214–15.

THREE. The Knowledge of God

1. "The Conditions of Ontological Affirmation as Set Forth in *L'Action* by Maurice Blondel (1899)," *TF*, 386.
2. See ibid., 386n13.
3. *DG*, 70 (emphasis altered). "[L]'*intelligence* est *faculté* de l'être parce que l'*esprit* est *capacité* de Dieu"; de Lubac, *De la connaissance de Dieu* (Paris: Editions du Témoignage Chrétien, 1948), 76; de Lubac, *Sur les chemins de Dieu* (Paris: Aubier, 1956), 89.
4. De Lubac, "On Christian Philosophy," *Communio* 19, no. 3 (1992): 482–83.
5. *DG*, 35, 39; citing Aquinas, "Omnia cognoscentia cognoscunt implicite Deum in quolibet cognito," in *De veritate*, q. 22, a. 2, ad 1.
6. For a detailed introduction and bibliography of the Christian philosophy debates, see Gregory B. Sadler, ed., *Reason Fulfilled by Revelation: The 1930s Christian Philosophy Debates in France* (Washington, DC: Catholic University of America Press, 2010).
7. De Lubac, "On Christian Philosophy," 479.
8. Bréhier, "Is There a Christian Philosophy?," in Sadler, ed., *Reason Fulfilled by Revelation*, 127.
9. La Société française de Philosophie, "La notion de philosophie chrétienne," *Bulletin de la Société française de Philosophie* 31 (1931).
10. See Sadler, *Reason Fulfilled by Revelation*, 29.
11. *ASC*, 24.
12. Etienne Gilson, "The Notion of Christian Philosophy," in Sadler, ed., *Reason Fulfilled by Revelation*, 139.
13. Etienne Gilson, *The Spirit of Mediaeval Philosophy* (London: Sheed and Ward, 1936), 35.
14. Ibid., 37.
15. Francesca Murphy, *Art and Intellect in the Philosophy of Étienne Gilson* (Columbia: University of Missouri Press, 2004), 57.
16. Etienne Gilson, *Thomism*, 6th ed. (Toronto: Pontifical Institute of Mediaeval Studies, 2002), 10.
17. Jacques Maritain, *An Essay on Christian Philosophy* (New York: Philosophical Library, 1955), 14 (emphasis added).
18. Ibid., 15.
19. Ibid., 26.

20. Ibid., 28.

21. Maurice Blondel, "Does Christian Philosophy Exist as Philosophy?," in Sadler, ed., *Reason Fulfilled by Revelation*, 143–44.

22. Blondel, *Action*, 361–62.

23. De Lubac, "On Christian Philosophy," 482.

24. Gilson, *Thomism*, 18.

25. *ASC*, 24.

26. De Lubac, "On Christian Philosophy," 482–83.

27. Ibid., 483.

28. Ibid., 485.

29. Ibid., 486, 489.

30. De Lubac argues elsewhere: "Human knowledge is never without an a priori. Man is made in such a way that he cannot give meaning to something without choosing his perspective" ("Mysticism and Mystery," *TF*, 39).

31. De Lubac, "On Christian Philosophy," 487.

32. Ibid., 487n20.

33. See Bréhier, "Is There a Christian Philosophy?," 125–27.

34. Blondel, "Is There a Christian Philosophy?," in Sadler, ed., *Reason Fulfilled by Revelation*, 155.

35. De Lubac, "On Christian Philosophy," 497.

36. *CPM*, 14.

37. Gabriel Marcel, "A propos de *L'esprit de la philosophie medieval* par M. E. Gilson," *Nouvelle Revue de Jeunes*, March 15, 1932, 312; cited in de Lubac, "On Christian Philosophy," 501 (emphasis original).

38. De Lubac, "On Christian Philosophy," 502.

39. Maritain's work is in many respects a defense of Gilson's position on more theoretical grounds. Maritain acknowledges as much in the introduction to his essay: "Let me indicate straightway my basic agreement with [Gilson]. However, whereas he has intentionally adopted the historical standpoint, I should like to attempt to bring together some elements of a solution on the doctrinal level" (Maritain, *An Essay on Christian Philosophy*, 4).

40. Ibid., 28.

41. See de Lubac, "On Christian Philosophy," 482.

42. Ibid., 485.

43. Ibid., 489.

44. Ibid., 487.

45. See Aquinas, *ST* Ia, q. 1, a. 7.

46. Balthasar, *The Theology of Henri de Lubac*, 15.

47. See, for instance, Abbé Charles Journet, review of "Sur la philosophie chrétienne," *Nova et vetera* (1936); cited by de Lubac, *ASC*, 177–78.

48. "In the current meaning of the term," notes de Lubac, "'theology' has for a long time, and especially since the sixteenth century, evoked a more spe-

cialized knowledge, having its own life, object, and proper methodology often on the fringes of philosophical currents. It is no longer exactly the understanding of faith . . . and it is still less an understanding by faith, an intellectual synthesis operating under faith's light. . . . Today, in fact, 'theology' is the science of revealed truths; it is not . . . the science of all things in their final reasons under the light of faith. If we do not have a special word to designate this final science [the third mode of Christian philosophy], is it not because it no longer corresponds to much of our thought?" ("On Christian Philosophy," 499).

49. Ibid., 487.

50. As Blondel notes in his "Letter on Apologetics," the method of immanence "can consist in nothing else than in trying to equate, in our own consciousness, what we appear to think and to will and to do with what we do and will and think in actual fact—so that behind factitious negations and ends which are not genuinely willed may be discovered our innermost affirmations and the implacable needs which they imply" (Blondel, "The Letter on Apologetics," 156). The "method of immanence" in no way precludes the idea of transcendence (for such an idea is itself an immanent affirmation), but the "doctrine of immanence" excludes in principle the affirmation of any transcendent reality. See Oliva Blanchette, *Maurice Blondel: A Philosophical Life* (Grand Rapids, MI: William B. Eerdmans, 2010), 136–42, 288–90.

51. "Apologetics and Theology," *TF*, 98.

52. Ibid., 93.

53. De Lubac, "On Christian Philosophy," 504; citing Gabriel Marcel, *Nouvelle revue des jeunes*, December 1932, 1305.

54. As with "Apologetics and Theology," de Lubac was reluctant to include "On Christian Philosophy" in later collections of his work, because it seemed to him to have something too academic about it, "something too abstract, too distanced from human reality, from its conflicts, its tragedy" (*ASC*, 25).

55. For de Lubac's response to these critiques see "Postscript," *DG*, 205–20; and *ASC*, 310–11.

56. *ASC*, 80.

57. Ibid., 42.

58. *DG*, 206.

59. On *DG* as an exercise in natural theology, see *ASC*, 81; on the distinction between objective and subjective revelation, see *DG*, 90.

60. See the concluding chapter of *DG*, "God in Our Times," 177–97.

61. Blondel, "The Letter on Apologetics," 158.

62. Blondel, *Action*, 310.

63. Joseph Maréchal, "Cahier Five: Thomism Confronting Critical Philosophy," in *A Maréchal Reader*, ed. Joseph Donceel (New York: Herder and Herder, 1970), 96.

64. *ASC*, 31–32.

65. "The Origin of Religion," *TF*, 309–32.

66. Ibid., 330.

67. Ibid., 331, emphasis added; see also *DG*, 21.

68. *DG*, 3.

69. Ibid., 15.

70. See ibid., 36.

71. Ibid., 105.

72. Ibid., 36.

73. Ibid., 20.

74. Joseph Maréchal, *Le point de départ de la recherché métaphysique*, bk. 5; cited in *DG*, 86.

75. De Lubac includes with this acknowledgment two passages from Maréchal, *Le point de départ de la recherché métaphysique*, bk. 5, which, according to de Lubac, "sum up and provide a foundation for what precedes [chapters 2 and 3], and will help explain part of what remains to be said in the following chapter, 'The Knowledge of God'" (*DG*, 84–86; de Lubac, *Sur les chemins de Dieu*, 293–95). This note was not included in *De la connaissance de Dieu*.

76. Maréchal, *Le point de depart de la recherché metaphysique*, bk., 5; cited in *DG*, 85.

77. Maréchal, *Le point de depart de la recherché metaphysique*, bk. 5, xxxiii, in Donceel, ed., *A Maréchal Reader*, 165.

78. Anthony M. Matteo, *Quest for the Absolute: The Philosophical Vision of Joseph Maréchal* (DeKalb: Northern Illinois University Press, 1992), 108–9.

79. *DG*, 12.

80. Ibid., 7.

81. Ibid., 134.

82. See Kerr, *Twentieth-Century Catholic Theologians*, 77–79.

83. Stephan Körner, "The Impossibility of Transcendental Deductions," *The Monist* 51, no. 3 (1967): 321; Karen Kilby, *Karl Rahner: Theology and Philosophy* (London: Routledge, 2004), 41.

84. Kilby, *Karl Rahner*, 41.

85. Kerr, *Twentieth-Century Catholic Theologians*, 79.

86. See George Lindbeck, *The Nature of Doctrine: Religion and Theology in a Postliberal Age* (London: SPCK, 1984), 34–38.

87. De Lubac, "On Christian Philosophy," 484–85.

88. Paul Gilbert, "Ontologism," in *Encyclopedia of Christian Theology*, ed. Jean-Yves Lacoste (New York: Routledge, 2005), 2:1155; see also Gerald A. McCool, *Catholic Theology in the Nineteenth Century: The Quest for a Unitary Method* (New York: Seabury Press, 1977), 113–28.

89. D. Cleary, "Ontologism," in *New Catholic Encyclopedia*, 2nd ed. (Washington, DC: The Catholic University of America, 2003), 10:604.

90. *DG*, 39n7, 213.

91. Maréchal, *Le point de départ de la recherché métaphysique*, bk. 5; cited in *DG*, 86.

92. Kerr, *Twentieth-Century Catholic Theologians*, 93. By "experiential-expressivism," I mean the understanding of religious belief and behavior as derivative upon a basic, universal experience of the Absolute. See Lindbeck, *The Nature of Doctrine*, 31–32.

93. *DG*, 111.

94. Ibid., 106–7.

95. Ibid., 59–60.

96. Ibid., 48.

97. Ibid., 41.

98. Ibid., 22.

99. Ibid., 20.

100. Ibid., 106–7.

101. Ibid., 106.

102. On de Lubac's account of the *triplex via*, see ibid., 122.

103. See ibid., 53, 123.

104. See *ASC*, 80–81.

105. *DG*, 120.

106. Ibid., 126.

107. Ibid., 188.

108. Ibid., 36; see also 37, 51, 188; "The Conditions of Ontological Affirmation as Set Forth in *L'Action* by Maurice Blondel (1899)," *TF*, 384.

109. *DG*, 89.

110. Louis Bouyer, *Le sens de la vie monastique* (Turnhout: Éditions Brepols 1950), 132, cited by de Lubac, *DG*, 109–10.

111. *DG*, 109.

112. De Lubac, *De la connaissance de Dieu*, 81–82.

113. *ST* Ia, q. 2, a. 1, ad 2.

114. *DG*, 7.

115. Ibid., 76.

116. Ibid., 145–54.

117. Ibid., 148.

118. *ST* Ia IIae, q. 62, a. 1; cited in de Lubac, "Duplex Hominis Beatitudo," *Communio* 25 (Winter 2008): 599.

119. See *ST* Ia IIae, q. 3, a. 2 ad 4; a. 5; q. 5, aa. 3, 5. De Lubac treats these passages, among others, throughout "Duplex Hominis Beatitudo."

120. De Lubac, "Seigneur, je cherche ton visage: Sur le chapitre XIV du *Proslogion* de saint Anselme." This lecture was later published, along with de Lubac, "Sur la philosophie chrétienne," in *Recherche dans la foi: Trois etudes sur*

Origène, saint Anselme et la philosophie chrétienne (Paris: Beauchesne, 1979), 81–124.

121. Anselm, *Proslogion*, chap. 14, in *Anselm of Canterbury: The Major Works*, ed. Brian Davies and G. R. Evans (Oxford: Oxford University Press, 2008), 95.

122. De Lubac, "Seigneur, je cherche ton visage," 89 (emphasis added).

123. Ibid., 93 (emphasis added).

124. Ibid., 92.

125. *ASC*, 140.

126. De Lubac, "Seigneur, je cherche ton visage," 92.

127. *CF*, 298–99.

128. See John Milbank, "The Programme of Radical Orthodoxy," in Hemming, ed., *Radical Orthodoxy?—A Catholic Enquiry*, 35.

129. *CF*, 298.

130. Ibid., 292.

131. Ibid., 305.

132. On the inclusion of hope and love in the movement of faith, see ibid., 297–305; on faith as a response to an encounter with God's revelation in Christ, see ibid., 147, 301.

FOUR. Being in History

1. *C*, 331.

2. Ibid., 332.

3. "Christian Explanation of Our Times," *TH*, 450.

4. *C*, 141.

5. Rudolf Bultmann, *The Presence of Eternity: History and Eschatology* (New York: Harper, 1957), 120.

6. "The Search for a New Man," *DAH*, 429.

7. Ben Quash, *Theology and the Drama of History* (Cambridge: Cambridge University Press, 2005), 3.

8. *C*, 165.

9. Ibid., 142–43.

10. Karl Löwith, *Meaning in History* (Chicago: Chicago University Press, 1949), 5.

11. *C*, 120.

12. See Jean Daniélou, *The Lord of History: Reflections on the Inner Meaning of History* (London: Longmans, 1958); Hans Urs von Balthasar, *A Theology of History* (London: Sheed & Ward, 1964); Balthasar, *Theo-Drama: Theological Dramatic Theory*, 5 vols. (San Francisco: Ignatius Press, 1988–1998).

13. See *C*, 351–66; de Lubac, *Affrontements mystiques* (Paris: Éditions du Témoignage chrétien, 1950), 2–92; de Lubac, *Athéisme et sens de l'homme: Une*

double requite de Gaudium et Spes (Paris: Éditions du Cerf, 1968); de Lubac, *Pic de La Mirandole: Études et discussions* (Aubier Montaigne, 1974), 156–57; *PS*, 2:337–72.

14. Following the election on October 21, 1945, the three main political parties in France—the socialist SFIO (Section Française de l'Internationale Ouvriére), the Catholic MRP (Mouvement Républicain Populaire), and the communist PCF (Parti Communiste Français)—shared political power until May 1947. This short-lived political arrangement became known as *Tripartisme*. See Edward Baring, *The Young Derrida and French Philosophy, 1945–1968* (Cambridge: Cambridge University Press, 2011), 22–28.

15. *ASC*, 240.

16. This particular reading of Marx is perhaps overly indebted to Marx's earlier writings (1843–44), which are more directly concerned with the problem of religion, but de Lubac maintains that the entirety of Marx's corpus presupposes the positive suppression of religion. According to de Lubac, the final end of Marxism is "the return of man to possession of himself through the elimination of any transcendence" ("The Search for a New Man," *DAH*, 432; see also *ASC*, 241).

17. See *ASC*, 58–59.

18. Originally published as "L'idée chrétien de l'homme et la recherche d'un homme nouveau," *Etudes* (October 1947): 1–25; (November 1947): 145–69, de Lubac's lecture was later expanded in "La recherché d'un homme nouveau," in *Affrontements mystique*, 2–92. An English translation of the latter is available as "The Search for a New Man," *DAH*, 399–468.

19. *ASC*, 58–59.

20. Thus, in response to Jakob Hommes's insistence that de Lubac had undertaken to "baptize the communist philosophy"—Hommes, *Der technische Eros* (Freiburg: Herder, 1955), 40—de Lubac insists, "if he [Hommes] had discovered a propagandist for Pelagius in Saint Augustine or a partisan of Averroès in Saint Thomas, it would not have been a more revolutionary find" (*ASC*, 239).

21. See Gerroulanos, *An Atheism That Is Not Humanist*, 100–129.

22. Henri Lefebvre, *Le matérialisme dialectique* (Paris: Presses universitaires de France, 1947). Originally published in 1939, Lefebvre's text quickly became a best seller in the aftermath of World War II and an influential introduction to Marxist theory in France. See Kelly, *The Cultural and Intellectual Rebuilding of France*, 151.

23. Karl Marx and Frederick Engels, *The Communist Manifesto* (London: Verso, 1988), 62.

24. "The Search for a New Man," *DAH*, 434.

25. Ibid., 435–36.

26. Karl Marx, *A Contribution to the Critique of Political Economy* (Chicago: Charles H. Kerr & Company, 1904), 11–12.

27. For a similar critique, see Löwith, *Meaning in History*, 42. De Lubac leaves the question of genealogical inspiration unexplored in this essay, but he eventually locates Marxist apocalypticism within a Joachite trajectory. We will return to de Lubac's treatment of the legacy of Joachimism in the section that follows.

28. "The Search for a New Man," *DAH*, 442. For a similar objection to Marx's historical materialism, see Jacques Maritain, *Integral Humanism* (Notre Dame, IN: University of Notre Dame Press, 1972), 54.

29. "The Search for a New Man," *DAH*, 444.

30. *C*, 354.

31. "The Search for a New Man," *DAH*, 455.

32. *MS*, 28.

33. Gilson, *Thomism*, 10.

34. Löwith, *Meaning in History*, 18.

35. As Marx famously concludes his theses on Feuerbach, "The philosophers have only interpreted the world, in various ways; the point is to change it"; Marx, "Theses on Feuerbach," in *Writings of the Young Marx*, ed. Loyd D. Easton and Kurt H. Guddat (New York: Doubleday, 1967), 402.

36. "The Search for a New Man," *DAH*, 455.

37. Ibid., 466 (emphasis added).

38. In his own memoirs, de Lubac points to this passage as proof that he never denied the distinction between nature and the supernatural (*ASC*, 59n23).

39. *PS*, 1:14. I am grateful to Patrick Gardner and Troy Stefano for permitting me to check my own translation against their working translation of the first chapter of *La Postérité spirituelle de Joachim de Flore.*

40. Bernard McGinn notes, "What is distinctive about Joachim's theology . . . is what might be called its archaism. Strongly scriptural and symbolic in outlook, displaying an adequate, though not profound, knowledge of the Fathers, it was in conscious reaction against the Scholastic application of logical categories and distinctions to theology"; McGinn, "The Abbot and the Doctors: Scholastic Reactions to the Radical Eschatology of Joachim of Fiore," in *Apocalypticism in the Western Tradition* (Aldershot: Variorum, 1994), ix.32.

41. Cyril O'Regan, *Theology and the Spaces of Apocalyptic* (Milwaukee, WI: Marquette University Press, 2009), 17–18. For a refutation of the apocalyptic turn in modern European thought, see, especially, Hans Urs von Balthasar, *Apokalypse der deutschen Seele: Studien zu einer Lehre letzten Haltungen*, vols. 1–3 (Salzburg: Anton Pustet, 1937–39).

42. On the Sibylline legacy in medieval thought, see Bernard McGinn, "*Teste David cum Sibylla*: The Significance of the Sibylline Tradition in the Middle Ages," in *Apocalypticism in the Western Tradition*, iv. 7–35.

43. See Morton W. Bloomfield, "Joachim of Flora: A Critical Survey of His Canon, Teachings, Sources, Biography and Influence," *Traditio* 13 (1957): 263–69.

44. While abbot at the Benedictine monastery of Corazzo, Joachim worked to have the monastery incorporated into the Cistercian Order. By 1190, however, Joachim had left the Cistercians to found a house of his own in Calabria.

45. Bloomfield, "Joachim of Flora," 269.

46. Joachim, *Expositio in Apocalypsim*, f. 39r–v; cited in Bernard McGinn, *Visions of the End* (New York: Columbia University Press, 1979), 130.

47. See *C*, 148–56.

48. See *ME*, 3:359–76; *PS*, 1:19–42.

49. Joachim, *Expositio in Apocalypsim*, f. 5r–v; cited in McGinn, *Visions of the End*, 133–34 (emphasis added).

50. Ibid., 134.

51. De Lubac notes, "Each of these three terrestrial ages has, as it were, a double date of origin: that of its anticipated date of inauguration, or, as Joachim says, its 'initiation' or its 'germination,' and that of its complete foundation, its confirmation, 'clarification' or 'fructification,' while awaiting the date of its 'term' or its 'passing away'" (*ME*, 3:334).

52. See ibid., 340–41.

53. Cyril O'Regan, *The Heterodox Hegel* (Albany: State University of New York Press, 1994), 266.

54. *Liber figurarum*, table XIX; cited in *Medieval Exegesis*, 3:356. There is disagreement over the authorship of the *Liber figurarum*, but the text is generally held to be "a genuine attempt to illustrate the Abbot's views, prepared before or shortly after his death by disciples fully cognizant of his ideas" (Bloomfield, "Joachim of Flora," 259).

55. See *HS*, 247–59.

56. Ibid., 251–52; see also *ME*, 3:362–69.

57. See *SC*, 204–8. According to de Lubac, this brief section contains the outline for the doctrinal conclusion that he originally envisioned (though never included) for *PS* (*ASC*, 156n1).

58. See *ME*, 3:327–419; de Lubac, *Exégèse medieval* (Aubier: Éditions Montaigne, 1964), 4:325–44.

59. *ASC*, 156.

60. Ibid.

61. *PS*, 1:13–14.

62. De Lubac's genealogy covers a staggering array of thinkers, from the early Franciscan Joachimites (i.e., Gerard of Borgo San Donnino) to the German Romanticists (i.e., Schleiermacher, Fichte, Hölderlin), Hegel, Marx, and a number of "contemporary Joachimites" (i.e., Jürgen Moltmann and de Lubac's former

pupil Michel de Certeau). Contemporary scholars of Joachim, though generally sympathetic of de Lubac's reading of the Calabrian abbot (see Bernard McGinn, "The Abbot and the Doctors," ix.34), have raised some doubts about the criteria for Joachimite inclusion in de Lubac's genealogy; see also Marjorie Reeves, review of *La Postérité spirituelle de Joachim de Flore, T 1: De Joachim à Schelling, Journal of Theological Studies* 32, no. 1 (1981): 191–94. Given the proliferation of Joachite themes and motifs in medieval and postmedieval thought, and the ambiguity with respect to de Lubac's own criteria for genealogical inclusion, it is perhaps helpful to follow Bernard McGinn in distinguishing between "Joachimite" (thinkers/texts in genuine harmony with the writings of Joachim) and "Joachite" (thinkers/texts broadly influenced by "the body of ideas claiming Joachim as its source"); McGinn, "The Abbot and the Doctors," ix.35; see Cyril O'Regan, *Gnostic Return in Modernity* (Albany: State University of New York Press, 2001), 253n45. In what follows, we employ the Lubacian ascription "joachimisme," though with the caveat that de Lubac's genealogy is broadly inclusive of Joachite elements.

63. *PS*, 2:437.

64. De Lubac is scarcely alone in locating Joachim's theology of history at the origins of secular modernity. Both Karl Löwith and Eric Voegelin devote considerable attention to the Joachimite vision animating the history of secularization. See Löwith, *Meaning in History*, 159, 208–13; Eric Voegelin, *The New Science of Politics: An Introduction* (Chicago: University of Chicago Press, 1987), 111–24.

65. Ernst Bloch, *The Principle of Hope* (Cambridge, MA: MIT Press, 1995), 2:509–11. On the Joachimism of Bloch, see *PS*, 2:366–74.

66. Löwith, *Meaning in History*, 159.

67. *ME*, 3:343.

68. See ibid., 3:348.

69. As de Lubac notes, for instance, Joachim still acknowledges the continuance of the papacy during the age of the Spirit (*ME*, 3:356–57).

70. *PS*, 2:444–46.

71. 1 Corinthians 13:12.

72. Revelation 21:1.

73. John 16:13.

74. *ST* Ia IIae, q. 106, a. 4, ad 2.

75. Georg W. F. Hegel, *Encyclopedia of the Philosophical Sciences in Basic Outline*, Part I, *Science of Logic* (Cambridge: Cambridge University Press, 2010), 24; see *PS*, 1:370–71.

76. See *ME*, 1:94–95; *ME*, 3:327.

77. *C*, 145.

78. Ibid., 165.

79. *ME*, 1:227.

80. See *C*, 143; *ME*, 2:186.

81. *ME*, 1:236.
82. *SC*, 207.
83. *PS*, 1:30.
84. *SC*, 68.
85. See Löwith, *Meaning in History*, 1.
86. *ME*, 2:71.
87. *DG*, 65.
88. *ME*, 2:71–72.
89. Ibid., 1:261.
90. Ibid., 2:101.
91. Ibid., 1:261.
92. *C*, 58.
93. Ibid., 60.
94. Among those texts indicating the extermination of Israel's enemies, de Lubac mentions Isaiah 30:27–33 and the Rabbot Midrash on Song of Songs 7:4: "Often it is said that the pagan nations would be entirely destroyed once the Messianic Kingdom opened. The world was created for Israel, in such a way that, at the end, the other people will be burned and annihilated." Among the texts indicating the subjection of the pagan nations to Israel, de Lubac mentions Isaiah 40:5, 60:1–18, 61:6; Psalm 46:11 ("The Theological Foundation of Mission," *TH*, 372–73).
95. Isaiah 60:11–12.
96. Isaiah 49:6; cited in "The Theological Foundation of Mission," *TH*, 374.
97. Ibid., 378.
98. *ME*, 1:234.
99. As de Lubac notes, this new covenant was already announced by the prophet Jeremiah: "See, the days are coming, declares Yahweh, when I will make with the House of Israel and the House of Judah a new covenant. Not like the covenant I made with their fathers on the day when I took them by the hand to lead them out of the land of Egypt. . . . I will place my Law within them, and in their hearts will I write it, and I will be their God, and they will be my people!" (Jer. 31:31–33; cited in "The Theological Foundation of Mission," *TH*, 378).
100. *ME*, 1:235.
101. "The Light of Christ," *TH*, 207.
102. *ME*, 1:233.
103. According to Origen, for instance, scripture contains three senses (historical, moral, and allegorical) corresponding to the tripartite division of man (body, soul, and spirit). A more widespread tradition—one that de Lubac believes to be theologically superior to Origen's tripartite division—posits a fourfold meaning in scripture. This fourfold rendering is summarized in a popular distich: *Littera gesta docet, quid credas allegoria, / moralis quid agas, quo tendas anagogia*

("The letter teaches what took place, the allegory what to believe, the moral what to do, the anagogy what goal to strive for") ("On an Old Distich: The Doctrine of the 'Fourfold Sense' in Scripture," *TF*, 109). We will return in chapter 5 to treat the significance of this fourfold exegesis for de Lubac's mystical theology.

104. *ME*, 1:225 (emphasis original).

105. As Susan Wood notes, the literal meaning "can refer to a figurative text as well as to an empirical historical event. The literal sense of Scripture does not require that every passage recount a literal historical event"; Wood, *Spiritual Exegesis and the Church in the Theology of Henri de Lubac* (Grand Rapids, MI: William B. Eerdmans, 1998), 32.

106. *ME*, 2:44.

107. Ibid., 1:xix (emphasis added).

108. See George Lindbeck, *The Nature of Doctrine* (London: SPCK, 1984), 117.

109. *C*, 35.

110. Ibid., 29.

111. Gregory of Nyssa, *De hominis opificio*, chap. 16, cited in *C*, 29–30. Similarly, according to Athanasius, "The Creator of the universe fashioned the human race according to his image" (Athanasius, *Discourse against the Greeks*, chap. 2; cited in *C*, 29n14).

112. *C*, 26.

113. Ibid., 29.

114. Thomas follows closely Aristotle's reading of Plato in the *Metaphysics* (1.6) when he insists that, according to Plato, "the Form or Idea [of man] is the specific nature itself by which there exists *man* essentially. But an individual is man by participation inasmuch as the specific nature [man] is participated in by this designated matter." According to Thomas, Plato errs in assuming that the mode of being that a thing has *in reality* is the same as the mode of being that that thing has *in the act of being known*. Thus, though the common nature of a thing may exist in the intellect (through a process of abstraction) as something necessary and universal, it exists in reality only in singular and contingent things. For Thomas, therefore, a common nature does not have any proper being of its own. "Human nature" exists either in the intellect or in particular human beings; see Thomas Aquinas, *Commentary on Aristotle's "Metaphysics"* (Notre Dame, IN: Dumb Ox Books, 1995), bk. I, lect. 10, 153–58; see Joseph Owens, "Common Nature: A Point of Comparison between Thomistic and Scotist Metaphysics," *Medieval Studies* 19 (1957): 1–14; Owens, "Thomistic Common Nature and Platonic Idea," *Medieval Studies* 21 (1959): 211–23.

115. *C*, 31.

116. Ibid., 29.

117. Ibid., 332.

118. Ibid., 335.

119. Ibid., 33.

120. Ibid., 33–34.

121. See ibid., 41.

122. Ibid., 342.

123. See "Internal Causes of the Weakening and Disappearance of the Sense of the Sacred," *TH*, 230; *SC*, 237.

124. See John 17:21–23.

125. *C*, 37–39 (emphasis original).

126. *ST* IIIa, q. 2, a. 2, ad 3.

127. John 11:52.

128. Galatians 3:28.

129. Ephesians 2:13–14.

130. Fulgentius, *Ad Monimum* 2.10; cited in *C*, 37.

131. *C*, 368.

132. See *ME*, 2:183; *SC*, 167.

133. *C*, 157 (emphasis added).

134. See, for example, Paul McPartlan, "Eucharistic Ecclesiology," *One in Christ* 22 no. 4 (1986): 314–31; McPartlan, *The Eucharist Makes the Church* (Fairfax, VA: Eastern Christian Publications, 2006); Wood, *Spiritual Exegesis and the Church in the Theology of Henri de Lubac*; Dennis M. Doyle, "Henri de Lubac and the Roots of Communion Ecclesiology," *Theological Studies* 60, no. 2 (1999): 209–27; Doyle, *Communion Ecclesiology: Vision and Versions* (Maryknoll, NY: Orbis Books, 2000), chap. 4; Lisa Wang, "Sacramentum Unitatis Ecclesiasticae: The Eucharistic Ecclesiology of Henri de Lubac," *Anglican Theological Review* 85, no. 1 (2003): 143–58; Aaron Riches, "Church, Eucharist, and Predestination in Barth and de Lubac: Convergence and Divergence in *Communio*," *Communio* 35 (2008): 565–98; Francesca Murphy, "De Lubac, Ratzinger and von Balthasar: A Communal Adventure in Ecclesiology," in *Ecumenism Today: The Universal Church in the 21st Century*, ed. Francesca A. Murphy and Christopher Asprey (Aldershot: Ashgate, 2008), 45–80; Hans Boersma, "The Eucharist Makes the Church," *Crux* 44, no. 4 (2008): 2–11; Bryan C. Hollon, "Sacramental Realism and the Powers: A Reconsideration of de Lubac's Eucharistic Ecclesiology," *Ashland Theological Journal* 43 (2011): 21–33; Eugene R. Schlesinger, "The Threefold Body in Eschatological Perspective: With and beyond Henri de Lubac on the Church," *Ecclesiology* 10, no. 2 (2014): 186–204.

135. See *CM*; *SC*; *MC*; *CPM*.

136. *C*, 76.

137. Ibid., 68.

138. Ibid., 48.

139. 2 Corinthians 5:18–19.

140. Rowan Williams, "Incarnation and the Renewal of Community," in *On Christian Theology* (Oxford: Blackwell, 2000), 231.

141. "The Church is a mystery; that is to say that she is also a sacrament. She is 'the total *locus* of the Christian sacraments,' and she is herself the great sacrament that contains and vitalizes all the others" (*SC*, 202).

142. *C*, 82.

143. See *CM*; *SC*, 126–60.

144. See, for example, Otto Semmelroth, *Church and Sacrament* (Notre Dame, IN: Fides Publishers, 1965); Edward Schillebeeckx, *Christ the Sacrament of the Encounter with God* (New York: Sheed and Ward, 1963); Karl Rahner, "The Church and the Sacraments," in *Inquiries* (New York: Herder and Herder, 1964), 191–299; Austin Flannery, ed., *Vatican Council II: The Basic Sixteen Documents* (New York: Costello, 2007): *Lumen gentium*, 1, 9, 15, 48; *Gaudium et spes*, 42, 43, 45; *Sacrosanctum concilium*, 2, 5; *Ad gentes divinitus*, 1, 5.

145. See Avery Dulles, *Models of the Church* (New York: Doubleday, 2000), 55–67.

146. Karl Barth, *Church Dogmatics*, IV.3.2 (Peabody, MA: Hendrickson, 2010), 729.

147. John Webster, "On Evangelical Ecclesiology," in *Confessing God: Essays in Christian Dogmatics II* (London: T&T Clark, 2005), 163. A growing number of Roman Catholics have voiced similar concerns about the tendency to what is often referred to as "ecclesiological Monophysitism" (the absorption of the church's humanity into Christ's divinity) in much twentieth-century ecclesiology. See Nicholas M. Healy, "Practices and the New Ecclesiology: Misplaced Concreteness?," *International Journal of Systematic Theology* 5, no. 3 (2003): 287–308; William T. Cavanaugh, "The Sinfulness and Visibility of the Church: A Christological Exploration," in *Migrations of the Holy: God, State, and the Political Meaning of the Church* (Grand Rapids, MI: William B. Eerdmans, 2011), 141–69. De Lubac himself declared a certain form of ecclesiological Monophysitism to be no less dangerous than Christological Monophysitism (*C*, 75; *CPM*, 24).

148. John 19:30.

149. Eberhard Jüngel, "The Church as Sacrament?," in *Theological Essays*, ed. J. B. Webster (Edinburgh: T&T Clark, 1989), 201–2.

150. See *C*, 72–73, 196.

151. *SC*, 121.

152. See ibid., 122; *CPM*, 24.

153. *CPM*, 16, 25.

154. *SC*, 74.

155. Ibid., 68.

156. Ibid., 77. Similarly, "When God will be whole in everyone, in the Church Triumphant, the City of the Elect, there will no longer be any other hierarchy than that of charity" (*PF*, 26).

157. Augustine, *In Psalm 26*, s. 2, n. 23; cited in *C*, 119.

158. *C*, 72.

159. Joseph Flipper, *Between Apocalypse and Eschaton* (Minneapolis: Fortress Press, 2015), 245; see also Schlesinger, "The Threefold Body in Eschatological Perspective," 193.

160. *SC*, 67, 168.

161. The "Church of time," de Lubac insists, "is no other than that of eternity, though it be in quite a different state: 'not yet in fact but nevertheless in hope'" (*ME*, 2:203).

162. *C*, 236.

163. Ibid., 218.

164. In fact, Balthasar appeals directly to the authority of de Lubac in his defense of this position: see Hans Urs von Balthasar, *Dare We Hope: "That All Men Be Saved?," with "A Short Discourse on Hell"* (San Francisco: Ignatius, 1988), 168.

165. *C*, 234; citing Ambrose, *In Psalm 39*, n. 1.

166. *C*, 233.

167. Ibid., 233n43.

168. Ibid., 219.

169. Ibid., 218.

170. Ibid., 219–20.

171. *CPM*, 72–73.

172. Henri Bouillard, "L'Idée de surnaturel et le mystère chrétien," in *L'Homme devant Dieu: Mélanges offerts au Père Henri de Lubac*, Tome 3, *Perspectives d'aujourd'hui* (Paris: Aubier-Montaigne, 1964), 153–66.

173. *ASC*, 198–99.

174. Aquinas, *Summa contra Gentiles* 4.50; cited in *C*, 130.

175. See *C*, 147; *PF*, 93.

176. "The Search for a New Man," *DAH*, 465.

FIVE. Being in Mystery

1. *MS*, 85.

2. *BC*, 13.

3. Ibid., 20.

4. See "The Mystery of the Supernatural," *TH*, 302; *MS*, 83; *BC*, 32.

5. For what follows, see *ST* Ia, q. 93, a. 4.

6. Jean-Pierre Torrell, *Christ and Spirituality in St. Thomas Aquinas* (Washington, DC: The Catholic University of America Press, 2011), 117.

7. *ASC*, 113.

8. André Ravier, ed., *La mystique et les mystiques* (Paris: Desclée de Brouwer, 1965).

9. Noel O'Sullivan, *Christ and Creation: Christology as the Key to Interpreting the Theology of Creation in the Works of Henri de Lubac* (Oxford: Peter Lang, 2009), 349.

10. "Mysticism and Mystery," *TF*, 53.

11. Karl Barth, *Church Dogmatics*, I.2 (Edinburgh: T&T Clark, 1956); de Lubac refers to Barth's critique of mysticism in "Mysticism and Mystery," *TF*, 47.

12. See Emil Brunner, *Die Mystik und das Wort* (Tübingen: J. C. B. Mohr, 1924).

13. See Dionysius the Areopagite, "The Mystical Theology," in *Dionysius the Areopagite on "The Divine Names" and "The Mystical Theology,"* ed. Clarence E. Rolt (New York: Cosimo, 2007), 194.

14. 1 John 1:5.

15. "Collect for Peace," in *The 1979 Book of Common Prayer* (Oxford: Oxford University Press, 2005), 57.

16. "Mysticism and Mystery," *TF*, 44.

17. See "Nietzsche as Mystic," *DAH*, 469–509.

18. "Mysticism and Mystery," *TF*, 39.

19. Ibid., 50.

20. Ibid., 50n51.

21. Ibid., 44.

22. Ibid., 45.

23. Ibid., 46–47.

24. Ibid., 47.

25. Ibid., 64–65.

26. Ibid., 67.

27. Ibid., 68.

28. Ibid., 53.

29. Ibid., 55, 56.

30. Ibid., 54 (emphasis original).

31. See *SC*, 126–60.

32. See *C*, 47.

33. See *CPM*, 13–29.

34. See "The Mystery of the Supernatural," *TH*; *MS*.

35. See *ME*, 2:19–27.

36. According to de Lubac, mystery "conveys dynamism and synthesis. It focuses less on the apparent sign, or rather the hidden reality, than on both at the same time: on their mutual relationship, union and implications, on the way in which one passes into the other, or is penetrated by the other. It focuses on the appeal which the first term makes to the second, or better, on the hidden presence of the second term within the first, already at work secretly but effectively" (*CM*, 51–52).

37. Ibid., 46–49.

38. *ME*, 2:21.

39. Ferdinand de Saussure, *Course in General Linguistics* (New York: Columbia University Press, 2011), 67.

40. Paul VI, "Speech at the Opening of the Second Session of the Second Vatican Council"; quoted in *CPM*, 13.

41. *CPM*, 14 (emphasis original).

42. 1 Timothy 3:16; Colossians 2:3. See also Colossians 1:27; Ephesians 1:7–10, 3:4–6.

43. Augustine, *Letter 187* (to Dardanus), chap. 11, n. 34; quoted by de Lubac in *CPM*, 15; and "The Light of Christ," *TH*, 218.

44. Divo Barsotti, *Vie mystique et mystére liturgique*, quoted in "Mysticism and Mystery," *TF*, 53 (emphasis added).

45. "Mysticism and Mystery," *TF*, 68–69.

46. Ibid., 62. See also *MC*, 113, 117.

47. "Mysticism and Mystery," *TF*, 52.

48. Ibid., 53.

49. Ibid., 55.

50. Ibid., 56.

51. See *CF*, 306–7.

52. Ibid., 150.

53. Ibid., 145–46.

54. Ibid., 293–94.

55. Ibid., 300.

56. "Mysticism and Mystery," *TF*, 56.

57. Ibid., 63.

58. Ibid., 57.

59. For example, according to Irenaeus, "If the Holy Spirit be wanting in the soul, he who is such is indeed of an animal nature, and being left carnal, shall be an imperfect being, possessing indeed the image [of God] in his formation [*in plasmate*], but not receiving the similitude through the Spirit; and thus is this being imperfect" (*Against Heresies* 5.6.1).

60. See Irenaeus, *Against Heresies* 3.18.1, 3.23.1, 3.23.2, 4.38.3, and 4.38.4. According to David Cairns, it is doubtful that Irenaeus is actually using "image" and "likeness" as synonyms, "since of the six passages where the use of the two terms seems to be synonymous, five refer either to unfallen man, or to man regenerate, and therefore do not contradict the generally held view, since, even if the likeness was lost at the Fall, the humanity here described would be in possession of it"; see Cairns, *The Image of God in Man* (London: SCM Press, 1953), 75.

61. Origen, *De principiis* 3.6.1.

62. Irenaeus, *Against Heresies* 5.16.2.

63. Origen, "On Prayer," in *Origen*, trans. Rowan A. Greer (New York, Paulist Press, 1979), 27.2.

64. "Mysticism and Mystery," *TF*, 52.

65. Augustine, *The Trinity* (New York: New City Press, 2012), 14.23–24, emphasis added. This text is quoted by de Lubac in *MS*, 97n103.

66. "Mysticism and Mystery," *TF*, 57.

67. Ibid.

68. Ibid., 62; citing St. John of the Cross, *The Ascent of Mount Carmel*, bk. 2, chap. 4.

69. Ibid., 52 (emphasis added).

70. See *MS*, 85.

71. See "The Mystery of the Supernatural," *TH*, 292; *MS*, 57.

72. "Mysticism and Mystery," *TF*, 53.

73. Ibid., 58.

74. *RD*, 51–58.

75. Ibid., 52.

76. Ibid.

77. Ibid., 55.

78. Ibid., 59.

79. Ibid., 60 (emphasis added).

80. See "On an Old Distich: The Doctrine of the 'Fourfold Sense' in Scripture," *TF*, 109.

81. Ibid., 114.

82. *ME*, 1:237.

83. Ibid., 2:140 (emphasis original).

84. Ibid., 2:182.

85. "Mysticism and Mystery," *TF*, 58.

86. *ME*, 1:237–40.

87. Ibid., 1:261.

88. Ibid., 2:125.

89. *HS*, 446–47; see also *ME*, 2:124.

90. *HS*, 443.

91. "Mysticism and Mystery," *TF*, 60.

92. Kerr, *Twentieth-Century Catholic Theologians*, 80–81. For de Lubac's treatment of the nuptial motif in Origen, see *HS*, 220–22.

93. According to Balthasar, for instance, "A fundamental bridal and covenantal relationship exists between God and the world as such . . . which from all time has arisen from the Logos' mediation at the creation and from the Spirit's hovering over the abyss. This fundamental relationship makes man, in the reciprocity of husband and wife, an image and a likeness of God: of the God who, in his eternal trinitarian mystery, already possesses within himself a nuptial form";

Hans Urs von Balthasar, *The Glory of the Lord*, vol. 1, *Seeing the Form*, 2nd ed. (San Francisco: Ignatius Press, 2009), 577. On the nuptial theme in John Paul II's theological anthropology, see John Paul II, *The Theology of the Body: Human Love in the Divine Plan* (Boston, MA: Pauline Books, 1997).

94. Hosea 3:1.

95. For one of de Lubac's most sustained treatments of this exegetical tradition, see *SC*, 354–70.

96. Isaiah 62:5.

97. Cf. Ephesians 5:22–33; 2 Corinthians 11:2; Revelation 18:7; 21:9–10.

98. See Martin Heidegger, "Letter on 'Humanism,'" in *Pathmarks*, ed. William McNeill (Cambridge: Cambridge University Press, 1999), 249–65.

99. "Mysticism and Mystery," *TF*, 60.

100. *CF*, 148; citing Paul-Marie de la Croix, *L'Évangile de Jean et son témoignage spirituel* (Bruges: Desclee de Brouwer, 1959), 299.

101. "Mysticism and Mystery," *TF*, 60.

102. See C. C. Pecknold and Jacob Wood, "Augustine and Henri de Lubac," in *T&T Clark Companion to Augustine and Modern Theology*, ed. C. C. Pecknold and Tarmo Toom (London: Bloomsbury, 2013), 213–15; Adam G. Cooper, *Naturally Human, Supernaturally God: Deification in Pre-Conciliar Catholicism* (Minneapolis: Fortress Press, 2014), 151–55.

103. Milbank, *The Suspended Middle*, 51–52 (emphasis original).

104. Pecknold and Wood, "Augustine and Henri de Lubac," 214.

105. See *S*, 486–87.

106. Cooper, *Naturally Human, Supernaturally God*, 153.

107. Milbank elsewhere tempers (however vaguely) this Plotinian radicalism by insisting that for de Lubac deification consists in an "ontological transformation into as close a likeness with God *as is consistent with a persisting created status*" (Milbank, *The Suspended Middle*, 17, emphasis added).

108. *ASC*, 186; citing a letter from Blondel to de Lubac on April 5, 1932.

109. "Mysticism and Mystery," *TF*, 62.

110. Ibid. (emphasis added); citing St. John of the Cross, *The Ascent of Mount Carmel*, bk. 2, chap. 4.

111. *C*, 348; citing Maréchal, *Etudes sur la psychologie des mystiques* (Bruges: Beyaert, 1937), 2:15, 253–54.

112. "Mysticism and Mystery," *TF*, 43; citing Anselm Stolz, *Théologie de la mystique* (Chêvetogne: Éditions des Bénédictins d'Amay, 1937), 69, 255.

113. "Mysticism and Mystery," *TF*, 62.

114. See *MC*, 165n19.

115. See *HS*, 420.

116. *MC*, 7–8.

117. *HS*, 422.

118. In addition to the argument advanced in *CM*, see *SC*, 126–60; "Sanctorum Communio" and "Christian Community and Sacramental Communion," *TF*, 11–34, 71–76.

119. *SC*, 133. This tradition is present already in the writings of the first-/second-century bishop and martyr St. Ignatius of Antioch, who, in a letter to the church in Smyrna, declares: "Only that Eucharist which is under the authority of the bishop (or whomever he himself designates) is to be considered valid" ("The Epistle of Ignatius to the Smyrnaeans," chap. 8 in *The Apostolic Fathers in English*, ed. Michael W. Holmes (Grand Rapids, MI: Baker Academic, 2006), 123.

120. 1 Corinthians 10:16–17 (emphasis added).

121. "Sanctorum Communio," *TF*, 24.

122. Exploiting the semantic ambiguity of the Latin *sanctorum communio*, de Lubac argues that the reference to the "communion of saints" in the Apostles' Creed refers principally to the Eucharist. That is, *sanctorum communio* refers at once to the communication of "holy things" and to the community of persons brought about by this communication (see ibid., 13–15).

123. "Christian Community and Sacramental Communion," *TF*, 72.

124. "Mysticism and Mystery," *TF*, 62.

125. See the foreword to *CF*, 9–15.

126. "Mysticism and Mystery," *TF*, 62. De Lubac is likely alluding to the German Lutheran mystic Jacob Böhme [Boehme] (1575–1674), for whom, as Cyril O'Regan has demonstrated, the *Ungrund* refers to "the divine that is beyond being, or better, the divine that transcends God considered as personal, creative, and redemptive ground of reality"; see O'Regan, *Gnostic Apocalypse: Jacob Boehme's Haunted Narrative* (Albany: State University of New York Press, 2002), 69. On the place of Böhme in de Lubac's Joachite genealogy, see *PS*, 1:205–33.

127. *CF*, 112. In a chapter of *CF* devoted to "The Economic Trinity" (containing perhaps de Lubac's most sustained treatment of the doctrine of God), de Lubac contests those theologians who restrict knowledge of God to the divine works *ad extra*. Although de Lubac readily grants "that it is through the 'economy,' and only through it, that we have access to 'theology,'" he is nevertheless emphatic that the divine "missions" truly reveal the intra-Trinitarian "processions." The necessary distinction between God's activity *ad extra* and God's activity *ad intra* does not mean "that nothing concerning the internal 'processions,' nothing concerning 'theology,' properly speaking, is accessible to us. In no way does it mean that the doctrine about God must be reduced to the doctrine about salvation, for in that case the latter would risk being purely illusory doctrine" (ibid., 90–91).

128. *SC*, 237.

129. See *MC*, 118.

130. As Noel O'Sullivan notes, for de Lubac, "'likeness' is not an individualistic condition but is communitarian in essence. The basis for this lies in de Lubac's understanding of 'person' . . . and, more fundamentally, the Trinitarian nature of 'likeness'" (O'Sullivan, *Christ and Creation*, 362).

131. *C*, 334–35.

132. Ibid., 11.

133. "The whole of dogma," remarks de Lubac, is "but a series of paradoxes, disconcerting to natural reason and requiring not an impossible proof but reflective justification" (ibid., 327). By paradox, de Lubac means the revelation and corresponding articulation of two apparently contradictory assertions. As de Lubac argues elsewhere, paradox is not simply epistemic. It does not merely denote the mind's inability to arrive at some final synthesis. "For paradox exists everywhere in reality, before existing in thought. . . . Paradox, in the best sense, is objectivity" (*PF*, 10).

134. See Jürgen Moltmann, *The Trinity and the Kingdom of God: The Doctrine of God* (San Francisco: Harper & Row, 1981); John Zizioulas, *Being as Communion: Studies in Personhood and the Church* (Crestwood, NY: St. Vladimir's Seminary Press, 1985); Miroslav Volf, "'The Trinity's Our Social Program': The Doctrine of the Trinity and the Shape of Social Engagement," *Modern Theology* 14 (1998): 403–23.

135. *C*, 342.

136. "Internal Causes of the Weakening and Disappearance of the Sense of the Sacred," *TH*, 342.

137. *C*, 332.

138. "Mysticism and Mystery," *TF*, 63.

139. Rowan Williams, "*Sapientia* and the Trinity: Reflections on the *De Trinitate*," in *Collectanea Augustinia: Mélanges T. J. van Bavel*, ed. B. Bruning, M. Lamberigits, and J. van Houtem (Leuven: Leuven University Press, 1990), 321.

140. Michel Sales, *L'etre humain et la connaissance naturelle qu'il a de Dieu: Essai sur la structure anthropo-theologique fondamentale de la revelation chretienne dans la pensee du p. Henri de Lubac* (Paris: Parole et Silence, 2003), 87 (emphasis original).

141. According to Rousselot, "our faith is not only the power of believing in certain truths of the supernatural order: it is also, *and at the same time*, a new power of interpreting the visible world and natural being; a renaissance of reason" (cited in de Lubac, "On Christian Philosophy," 498 [emphasis original]).

142. "Mysticism and Mystery," *TF*, 56.

143. Ibid., 52.

144. *MC*, 154.

Conclusion

1. *C*, 309 (emphasis added).
2. See ibid., 327.
3. Jude 3.

4. *C*, 313.

5. See *CM*, 251.

6. *S*, 483 (emphasis added).

7. Thomas Joseph White, "Good Extrinsicism: Matthias Scheeben and the Ideal Paradigm of Nature-Grace Orthodoxy," *Nova et Vetera* (English ed.), 11, no. 2 (2013): 555.

8. *De Lubac: A Theologian Speaks* (Los Angeles: Twin Circles, 1985), 12.

9. Long, *Natura Pura*, 98.

10. Ibid., 99.

11. Ibid., 100.

12. Oliver O'Donovan, *Resurrection and Moral Order: An Outline for Evangelical Ethics* (Leicester: Inter-Varsity Press, 1986), 19.

13. Ibid., 20.

14. "Mystery of the Supernatural," *TH*, 302.

15. *MS*, 84.

16. "The Search for a New Man," *DAH*, 465.

17. See de Lubac's letter to Karl Rahner of May 24, 1965, in *VCN*, 2:354–55.

18. See *MP*, 44.

19. Ibid., 45.

20. *VCN*, 2:304.

21. Tracey Rowland, *Catholic Theology* (London: T&T Clark, 2017), 91.

22. *BC*, 236.

23. See Karl Rahner, "Concerning the Relationship between Nature and Grace," in *Theological Investigations 1* (London: Darton, Longman and Todd, 1961), 298, 300; Edward Schillebeeckx, "The Church and Mankind," in *The Language of Faith: Essays on Jesus, Theology, and the Church* (New York: Orbis Books, 1995), 1.

24. Gustavo Gutierrez, *A Theology of Liberation* (New York: Orbis Books, 1973), 70. According to Gutierrez, "This point of view was first supported by Yves de Montcheuil and Henri de Lubac."

25. Rahner, "Concerning the Relationship between Nature and Grace," 311.

26. Karl Rahner, *Foundations of Christian Faith* (New York: Crossroad, 1996), 127.

27. See Karen Kilby, *Karl Rahner: Theology and Philosophy* (London: Routledge, 2004), 56.

28. Rahner, *Foundations of Christian Faith*, 154.

29. *ASC*, 62n5.

30. *MS*, 101–2n2.

31. For what follows, see *CPM*, 85–93.

32. Ibid., 85.

33. Ibid., 90.

34. Rahner, *Foundations of Christian Faith*, 126.

35. Joseph Ratzinger, *Principles of Catholic Theology: Building Stones for a Fundamental Theology* (San Francisco: Ignatius, 1987), 167.

36. *CPM*, 91, 93.

37. Gemma Simmonds, "The Mystical Body: Ecclesiology and Sacramental Theology," in Hillebert, ed., *T&T Clark Companion to Henri de Lubac*, 171–72.

38. Joseph Flipper, *Between Apocalypse and Eschaton: History and Eternity in Henri de Lubac* (Minneapolis: Fortress Press, 2015), 253. For an earlier sketch of the argument that follows, see Jordan Hillebert, "Review of Joseph Flipper, *Between Apocalypse and Eschaton*," *Modern Theology* 33, no. 3 (2017): 497.

39. Hans Urs von Balthasar, "Current Trends in Catholic Theology and the Responsibility of the Christian," *Communio* 5, no. 1 (1978): 83–84.

40. See Gutierrez, *A Theology of Liberation*, 69–72. Gutierrez often follows suit in designating this end "supernatural," but he prefers to speak of this reality as "the fullness of all that is human in the free gift of the self-communication of God" (172).

41. Ibid., 152, 175.

42. Ibid., 151.

43. See *BC*, 157–66.

44. Ibid., 159.

45. Gutierrez, *A Theology of Liberation*, x.

46. Ibid., 35 (emphasis added).

47. Henri de Lubac, "The Total Meaning of Man and the World," *Communio* 35 (Winter 2008): 637–38.

48. *BC*, 160 (emphasis original).

49. See Edward Schillebeeckx, "Church and World," in *World and Church* (London: Bloomsbury, 2014), 74–75.

50. Edward Schillebeeckx, *Approches théologiques* (Brussels: Editions du Cep, 1967), vol. 3, chap. 2, sec. 1; cited in *BC*, 191.

51. See Schillebeeckx, "The Church and Mankind," 4–5.

52. Schillebeeckx, "Church and World," 75.

53. Ibid., 78.

54. Schillebeeckx, "The Church and Mankind," 19.

55. Ibid., 5.

56. Schillebeeckx, "Church and World," 77.

57. *VCN*, 2:195 (October 16, 1964).

58. De Lubac records his reaction to the initial editorial meeting on November 28, 1963: "The organization seemed sound. The spirit, too dry, too 'scholarly'; the language, of too 'scientific' a pretension; the theologians taking themselves too seriously, etc. yet the two editors [Rahner and Schillebeeckx] proved to be likeable" (ibid.).

59. Schillebeeckx, "L'Église et le monde," in *Approches théologiques*, vol. 3, *Le monde et l'église* (Brussels: Editions du Cep, 1967), 149–67.

60. *VCN*, 2:198 (October 17, 1964).

61. Ibid., 2:355.

62. *BC*, 222.

63. *C*, 76 (emphasis added).

64. *BC*, 194.

65. Ibid., 212 (emphasis added).

66. *BC*, 110–11 (emphasis original).

67. For recent contributions in this area, see Christopher J. Walsh, "De Lubac's Critique of the Postconciliar Church," *Communio* (Fall 1992): 404–32; Matthew Levering, *An Introduction to Vatican II as an Ongoing Theological Event* (Washington, DC: Catholic University of America Press, 2017); Riches, "Henri de Lubac and the Second Vatican Council."

BIBLIOGRAPHY

Anselm of Canterbury. *Proslogion*. In *Anselm of Canterbury: The Major Works*, edited by Brian Davies and G. R. Evans, 82–104. Oxford: Oxford University Press, 2008.

Aquinas, Thomas. *Commentary on Aristotle's "Metaphysics."* Notre Dame, IN: Dumb Ox Books, 1995.

———. *Compendium of Theology*. Translated by Richard J. Regan. Oxford: Oxford University Press, 2009.

———. *On Creation [Quaestiones Disputatae de Potentia Dei, Q. 3]*. Translated by S. C. Selner-Wright. Washington, DC: Catholic University of America Press, 2011.

———. *Summa Theologica*. 11 vols. Translated by the Fathers of the English Dominican Province. London: Burns, Oates & Washbourne, 1921.

Atkin, Nicholas. "The Politics of Legality: The Religious Orders in France, 1901–45." In *Religion, Society and Politics in France since 1789*, edited by Frank Tallett and Nicholas Atkin, 149–65. London: The Hambledon Press, 1991.

Augustine. *The Trinity*. Translated by Edmund Hill. New York: New City Press, 2012.

Balthasar, Hans Urs von. *Apokalypse der deutschen Seele: Studien zu einer Lehre letzten Haltungen*. 3 vols. Salzburg: Anton Pustet, 1937–1939.

———. "Current Trends in Catholic Theology and the Responsibility of the Christian." *Communio* 5, no. 1 (1978): 77–85.

———. *Dare We Hope: "That All Men Be Saved?," with "A Short Discourse on Hell."* San Francisco: Ignatius, 1988.

———. *The Glory of the Lord*. 7 vols. San Francisco: Ignatius, 1983–1991.

———. *Theo-Drama: Theological Dramatic Theory*. 5 vols. San Francisco: Ignatius, 1988–1998.

———. *The Theology of Henri de Lubac: An Overview*. San Francisco: Ignatius, 1991.

———. *A Theology of History*. London: Sheed & Ward, 1964.

Balthasar, Hans Urs von, and Angelo Scola. *Test Everything, Hold Fast to What Is Good*. Translated by Maria Shrady. San Francisco: Ignatius Press, 1989.

Baring, Edward. "Humanist Pretensions: Catholics, Communists, and Sartre's Struggle for Existentialism in Postwar France." *Modern Intellectual History* 7, no. 3 (2010): 581–609.

———. *The Young Derrida and French Philosophy, 1945–1968.* Cambridge: Cambridge University Press, 2011.

Barth, Karl. *Church Dogmatics.* 14 vols. Peabody, MA: Hendrickson, 2010.

Berdyaev, Nicholas. *The Fate of Man in the Modern World.* Translated by Donald A. Lowrie. London: Student Christian Movement Press, 1935.

Blanchette, Oliva. *Maurice Blondel: A Philosophical Life.* Grand Rapids, MI: William B. Eerdmans, 2010.

Blanchot, Maurice. "On Nietzsche's Side." In *The Work of Fire*, translated by Charlotte Mandell, 287–99. Stanford, CA: Stanford University Press, 1995.

Bloch, Ernst. *The Principle of Hope.* Vol. 2. Cambridge, MA: MIT Press, 1995.

Blondel, Maurice. *Action (1893): Essay on a Critique of Life and a Science of Practice.* Translated by Oliva Blanchette. Notre Dame, IN: University of Notre Dame Press, 2007.

———. "Does Christian Philosophy Exist as Philosophy?" In *Reason Fulfilled by Revelation: The 1930s Christian Philosophy Debates in France*, edited by Gregory B. Sadler, 141–49. Washington, DC: Catholic University of America Press, 2010.

———. "Is There a Christian Philosophy?" In *Reason Fulfilled by Revelation: The 1930s Christian Philosophy Debates in France*, edited by Gregory B. Sadler, 150–59. Washington, DC: Catholic University of America Press, 2010.

———. *L'Etre et les êtres: Essai d'ontologie concrete et intégrale.* Paris: Alcan, 1935.

———. *The Letter on Apologetics and History and Dogma.* Translation by Alexander Dru and Illtyd Trethowan. Grand Rapids, MI: William B. Eerdmans, 1964.

———. *Le Problème de la philosophie catholique.* Paris: Bloud et Gay, 1932.

Bloomfield, Morton W. "Joachim of Flora: A Critical Survey of His Canon, Teachings, Sources, Biography and Influence." *Traditio* 13 (1957): 249–311.

Boersma, Hans. "The Eucharist Makes the Church," *Crux* 44, no. 4 (2008): 2–11.

———. "Sacramental Ontology: Nature and the Supernatural in the Ecclesiology of Henri de Lubac." *New Blackfriars* 88, no. 1015 (2007): 242–73.

Bonino, Serge-Thomas. "The Theory of Limbo and the Mystery of the Supernatural in St. Thomas Aquinas." In "*Surnaturel*": *A Controversy at the Heart of Twentieth-Century Thomistic Thought*, edited by Serge-Thomas Bonino, 117–54. Ave Maria, FL: Sapientia Press, 2009.

Bouillard, Henri. *Blondel and Christianity.* Washington, DC: Corpus Books, 1970.

———. "Croire et comprendre." In *Mythe et foi*, edited by Enrico Castelli, 294–300. Paris: Aubier, 1966.

———. "L'Idée de surnaturel et le mystère chrétien." In Henri de Lubac, *L'Homme devant Dieu: Mélanges offerts au Père Henri de Lubac*, Tome 3, *Perspectives d'aujourd'hui*, 153–66. Paris: Aubier-Montaigne, 1964.

Bouyer, Louis. *Le sens de la vie monastique*. Turnhout: Éditions Brepols 1950.

Bradley, Dennis J. M. *Aquinas on the Twofold Human Good*. Washington, DC: Catholic University of America Press, 1997.

Braine, David. "The Debate between Henri de Lubac and His Critics." *Nova et Vetera* (2008): 543–90.

Bréhier, Emile. "Is There a Christian Philosophy?" In Sadler, ed., *Reason Fulfilled by Revelation*, 99–127.

Brown, David. "Sacramentality." In *The Oxford Handbook of Theology and Modern European Thought*, edited by Nicholas Adams, George Pattison, and Graham Ward, 615–32. Oxford: Oxford University Press, 2013.

Brunner, Emil. *Die Mystik und das Wort*. Tübingen: J. C. B. Mohr, 1929.

Bultmann, Rudolf. *The Presence of Eternity: History and Eschatology*. New York: Harper, 1957.

Cairns, David. *The Image of God in Man*. London: SCM Press, 1953.

Cavanaugh, William T. "The Sinfulness and Visibility of the Church: A Christological Exploration." In *Migrations of the Holy: God, State, and the Political Meaning of the Church*, 141–69. Grand Rapids, MI: William B. Eerdmans, 2011.

Chantraine, Georges. *Henri de Lubac. Tome 1, De la naissance à la démobilisation (1896–1919)*. Paris: Cerf, 2007.

———. "La théologie du Surnaturel selon Henri de Lubac." *Nouvelle revue théologique* 119, no. 2 (1997): 218–35.

Cleary, D. "Ontologism." In *New Catholic Encyclopedia*, 2nd ed., 10:603–5. Washington, DC: Catholic University of America Press, 2003.

Coffey, David. "Some Resources for Students of *La nouvelle théologie*." *Philosophy and Theology* 11, no. 2 (1999): 367–402.

Comte, Auguste. *The Catechism of Positive Religion*. London: John Chapman, 1858.

Cooper, Adam G. *Naturally Human, Supernaturally God: Deification in Pre-Conciliar Catholicism*. Minneapolis: Fortress Press, 2014.

Daniélou, Jean. *The Lord of History: Reflections on the Inner Meaning of History*. London: Longmans, 1958.

Dansette, Adrien. *Religious History of Modern France*. 2 vols. Edinburgh: Nelson, 1961.

Davis, Joshua B. *Waiting and Being: Creation, Freedom, and Grace in Western Theology*. Minneapolis: Fortress Press, 2013.

DeHart, Paul J. *The Trial of the Witnesses: The Rise and Decline of Postliberal Theology*. Malden, MA: Blackwell, 2006.

de Lubac, Henri. *Affrontements mystiques*. Paris: Éditions du Témoignage chrétien, 1950.

———. "Apologetics and Theology." In *Theological Fragments*, 91–104. San Francisco: Ignatius, 1989.

———. "Apologétique et Théologie." *Nouvelle revue théologique* 57 (1930): 361–78.

———. "À propos de la conception medieval de l'ordre surnaturel (Échange de vues avec J. De Blic)." *Melanges de science religieuse* 4 (1947): 365–73.

———. *Athéisme et sens de l'homme: Une double requite de "Gaudium et Spes."* Paris: Éditions du Cerf, 1968.

———. *At the Service of the Church: Henri De Lubac Reflects on the Circumstances that Occasioned His Writings.* Translated by Anne Elizabeth Englund. San Francisco: Communio, 1993.

———. *Augustinianism and Modern Theology.* Translated by Lancelot Sheppard. Introduction by Louis Dupré. New York: Crossroad, 2000.

———. *Augustinisme et théologie moderne.* Paris: Aubier, 1965.

———. *A Brief Catechesis on Nature and Grace.* Translated by Richard Arnandez. San Francisco: Ignatius, 1984.

———. *Catholicism: Christ and the Common Destiny of Man.* Translated by Lancelot C. Sheppard and Elizabeth Englund. San Francisco: Ignatius, 1988.

———. "Christian Community and Sacramental Communion." In *Theological Fragments*, translated by Rebecca Howell Balinski, 71–76.

———. "Christian Explanation of Our Times." In *Theology in History*, translated by Anne Englund Nash, 440–56. San Francisco: Ignatius, 1996.

———. *The Christian Faith: An Essay on the Structure of the Apostles' Creed.* Translated by Richard Arnandez. San Francisco: Ignatius, 1986.

———. *Christian Resistance to Anti-Semitism: Memories from 1940–1944.* Translated by Elizabeth Englund. San Francisco: Ignatius, 1990.

———. *The Church: Paradox and Mystery.* Translated by James R. Dunne. Staten Island, NY: Alba House, 1969.

———. "Le combat spiritual." *Cité nouvelle* (1943): 769–83.

———. "The Conditions of Ontological Affirmation as Set Forth in *L'Action* by Maurice Blondel (1899)." In *Theological Fragments*, translated by Rebecca Howell Balinski, 377–92.

———. *Corpus Mysticum: The Eucharist and the Church in the Middle Ages.* Translated by Gemma Simmonds, Richard Price, and Christopher Stephens. Edited by Laurence Paul Hemming and Susan Frank Parsons. Notre Dame, IN: University of Notre Dame Press, 2007.

———. *De la connaissance de Dieu.* Paris: Editions du Témoignage Chrétien, 1945.

———. "Deux augustiniens fourvoyés." *Recherches de science religieuse* 21 (1931): 422–43, 513–40.

———. *The Discovery of God.* Translated by Alexander Dru. Footnotes translated by Mark Sebanc and Cassian Fulsom. Edinburgh: T&T Clark, 1996.

———. *The Drama of Atheist Humanism.* Translated by Edith M. Riley, Anne Englund Nash, and Mark Sebanc. San Francisco: Ignatius, 1995.

———. "Duplex Hominis Beatitudo." *Communio* 25 (Winter 2008): 599–612.

———. "Duplex hominis beatitudo." *Recherches de science religieuse* 35 (1948): 290–99.

———. "Esprit et liberté dans la tradition théologique." *Bulletin de literature ecclésiastique* 40 (1939): 121–50, 189–207.

———. *History and Spirit: The Understanding of Scripture according to Origen.* Translation from French by Anne Englund Nash. Greek and Latin translation by Juvenal Merriell. San Francisco: Ignatius, 2007.

———. "L'idée chrétien de l'homme et la recherche d'un homme nouveau." *Etudes* (October 1947): 1–25, and (November 1947): 145–69.

———. "Internal Causes of the Weakening and Disappearance of the Sense of the Sacred." In *Theology in History*, 223–40.

———. *Letters of Étienne Gilson to Henri de Lubac.* Translated by Mary Emily Hamilton. San Francisco: Ignatius, 1988.

———. "Letter to My Superiors." In *Theology in History*, 428–39.

———. *Lettres de M. Étienne Gilson adressées au P. Henri de Lubac et commentées par celui-ci.* Paris: Cerf, 1986.

———. "The Light of Christ." In *Theology in History*, 201–20.

———. *Medieval Exegesis.* 3 vols. Grand Rapids, MI: William B. Eerdmans, 1998, 2000, 2009.

———. *Mémoire sur l'occasion de mes écrits.* Paris: Cerf, 2006.

———. *The Motherhood of the Church: Followed by Particular Churches in the Universal Church and an Interview Conducted by Gwendoline Jarczyk.* San Francisco: Ignatius, 1982.

———. "Le mystère du surnaturel." *Recherches de Science Religieuse* 36 (1949): 80–121.

———. *Le Mystère du Surnaturel.* Paris: Aubier, 1965.

———. "The Mystery of the Supernatural." In *Theology in History*, 281–316.

———. *The Mystery of the Supernatural.* Translated by Rosemary Sheed. Introduction by David L. Schindler. New York: Crossroad, 1998.

———. "Mysticism and Mystery." In *Theological Fragments*, 35–69.

———. "Nature and Grace." In *The Word in History*, edited by T. Patrick Burke, 24–40. New York: Sheed and Ward, 1966.

———. "The New Man: The Marxist and the Christian View." *Dublin Review* 442 (1948): 5–35.

———. "On an Old Distich: The Doctrine of the 'Fourfold Sense' in Scripture." In *Theological Fragments*, 109–38.

———. "On Christian Philosophy." *Communio* 19, no. 3 (1992): 478–506.

———. "The Origin of Religion." In *Theological Fragments*, 309–32.

———. *Paradoxes of Faith.* San Francisco: Ignatius, 1987.

———. "Petite catéchèse sur la 'nature' et la 'grâce.'" *Revue international Communio* 2, no. 4 (1977): 11–23.

———. *Petite catéchèse sur nature et grâce.* Paris: Fayard, 1980.

———. *Pic de La Mirandole: Études et discussions.* Paris: Aubier Montaigne, 1974.

———. *La Postérité spirituelle de Joachim de Flore.* 2 vols. Paris: Lethielleux, 1978, 1981.

———. *Proudhon et le christianisme.* Paris: Éditions de Seuil, 1945.

———. "La recontre de 'superadditum' et de 'supernaturale' dans la théologie medieval." *Revue du Moyen Âge Latin* 1 (1945): 27–34.

———. "Remarques sur l'histoire du mot 'surnaturel.'" *Nouvelle revue théologique* 61 (1934): 225–49, 350–70.

———. *La Révélation divine.* In *Révélation divine; Affrontements mystiques; Athéisme et sens de l'homme*, 36–230. Paris: Cerf, 2006.

———. "Saint Thomas: *Compendium theologiae*, c. 104." *Recherches de science religieuse* 36 (1949): 300–305.

———. "Sanctorum Communio." In *Theological Fragments*, 11–34.

———. "The Search for a New Man." In *The Drama of Atheist Humanism*, translated by Edith M. Riley, Anne Englund Nash, and Mark Sebanc, 399–468. San Francisco: Ignatius, 1995.

———. "Spiritual Warfare." In *Theology in History*, 488–501.

———. *The Splendor of the Church.* Translated by Michael Mason. San Francisco: Ignatius, 1986.

———. "The 'Supernatural' at Vatican II." In *A Brief Catechesis on Nature and Grace*, translated by Richard Arnandez, 177–90. San Francisco: Ignatius, 1984.

———. "Sur la philosophie chrétienne." In *Recherche dans la foi: Trois etudes sur Origène, saint Anselme et la philosophie chrétienne*, 81–124. Paris: Beauchesne, 1979.

———. *Sur les chemins de Dieu.* Paris: Aubier, 1956.

———. *Surnaturel: Études historiques.* Paris: Éditions Desclée de Brouwer, 1991.

———. "The Theological Foundation of the Missions." In *Theology in History*, 367–427.

———. *Theological Fragments.* Translated by Rebecca Howell Balinski. San Francisco: Ignatius, 1989.

———. *Theology in History.* Translated by Anne Englund Nash. San Francisco: Ignatius, 1996.

———. "The Total Meaning of Man and the World." *Communio* 35 (Winter 2008): 613–41.

———. *Vatican Council Notebooks.* 2 vols. Translated by Andrew Stefanelli and Anne Englund Nash. San Francisco: Ignatius, 2015, 2016.

de Lubac, Henri, and Scola, Angelo. *De Lubac: A Theologian Speaks.* Los Angeles: Twin Circles, 1985.

Derrida, Jacques. "The Ends of Man." In *Margins of Philosophy*, translated by Alan Bass, 109–36. Brighton: Harvester Press, 1982.

De Saussure, Ferdinand. *Course in General Linguistics.* New York: Columbia University Press, 2011.

Dockx, S. "Du désir naturel de voir l'essence divine d'après saint Thomas." *Archives de philosophie* 27 (1964): 49–96.

Donnelly, Philip J. "Discussions on the Supernatural Order." *Theological Studies* 9, no. 2 (1948): 213–49.

———. "The Gratuity of the Beatific Vision and the Possibility of a Natural Destiny." *Theological Studies* 11 (1950): 372–404.

Doyle, Dennis M. *Communion Ecclesiology: Vision and Versions.* Maryknoll, NY: Orbis Books, 2000.

———. "Henri de Lubac and the Roots of Communion Ecclesiology." *Theological Studies* 60, no. 2 (1999): 209–27.

Dulles, Avery. "Faith and Reason: From Vatican I to John Paul II." In *The Two Wings of Catholic Thought: Essays on "Fides et ratio,"* edited by David Ruel Foster and Joseph W. Koterski, 193–208. Washington, DC: Catholic University of America Press, 2003.

———. *A History of Apologetics.* San Francisco: Ignatius, 1999.

———. *Models of the Church.* New York: Doubleday, 2000.

Feingold, Lawrence. *The Natural Desire to See God according to St. Thomas Aquinas and His Interpreters.* 2nd ed. Ave Maria, FL: Sapientia Press, 2010.

Feuerbach, Ludwig. *The Essence of Christianity.* Translated and introduction by George Eliot. New York: Prometheus Books, 1989.

Flannery, Austin. *Vatican Council II: The Basic Sixteen Documents.* New York: Costello, 2007.

Flipper, Joseph. *Between Apocalypse and Eschaton.* Minneapolis: Fortress Press, 2015.

Foucault, Michel. *The Order of Things: An Archeology of the Human Sciences.* New York: Pantheon, 1970.

Garrigou-Lagrange, Reginald. *God, His Existence and His Nature.* Vol. 1, *A Thomistic Solution of Certain Agnostic Antinomies.* St. Louis, MO: B. Herder Book Co., 1939.

Geroulanos, Stefanos. *An Atheism That Is Not Humanist Emerges in French Thought.* Palo Alto, CA: Stanford University Press, 2010.

Gilbert, Paul. "Ontologism." In *Encyclopedia of Christian Theology,* edited by Jean-Yves Lacoste, 2:1155–57. New York: Routledge, 2005.

Gilson, Étienne. "The Notion of Christian Philosophy." In Sadler, ed., *Reason Fulfilled by Revelation,* 128–40.

———. *The Spirit of Mediaeval Philosophy.* London: Sheed and Ward, 1936.

———. *Thomism.* 6th ed. Toronto: Pontifical Institute of Mediaeval Studies, 2002.

Grumett, David. *De Lubac: A Guide for the Perplexed.* London: T&T Clark, 2007.

———. "De Lubac, Grace, and the Pure Nature Debate." *Modern Theology* 31, no. 1 (2015): 123–46.

Gutierrez, Gustavo. *A Theology of Liberation.* New York: Orbis Books, 1973.

Healy, Nicholas J. "Henri de Lubac on Nature and Grace: A Note on Some Recent Contributions to the Debate." *Communio* 35 (Winter 2008): 535–64.

Healy, Nicholas M. "Practices and the New Ecclesiology: Misplaced Concreteness?" *International Journal of Systematic Theology* 5, no. 3 (2003): 287–308.

Hegel, Georg Wilhelm Friedrich. *Encyclopedia of the Philosophical Sciences in Basic Outline*. Part I, *Science of Logic*. Cambridge: Cambridge University Press, 2010.

———. *Lectures on the Philosophy of Religion*. 3 vols. Edited by Peter C. Hodgson. Translated by R. F. Brown, P. C. Hodgson, and J. M. Steward. Berkeley: University of California Press, 1984, 1985, 1987.

Heidegger, Martin. "Letter on 'Humanism.'" In *Pathmarks*, edited by William McNeill, 239–76. Cambridge: Cambridge University Press, 1999.

Hillebert, Jordan. "The Death of God and the Dissolution of Humanity." *New Blackfriars* 95, no. 1060 (2014): 674–88.

———. "Introducing Henri de Lubac." In *T&T Clark Companion to Henri de Lubac*, edited by Jordan Hillebert, 3–27. London: T&T Clark, 2017.

———, ed. *T&T Clark Companion to Henri de Lubac*. London: T&T Clark, 2017.

Hodgson, Peter C. *Hegel and Christian Theology: A Reading of the Lectures on the Philosophy of Religion*. Oxford: Oxford University Press, 2005.

Hollon, Bryan C. "Sacramental Realism and the Powers: A Reconsideration of de Lubac's Eucharistic Ecclesiology." *Ashland Theological Journal* 43 (2011): 21–33.

Hommes, Jakob. *Der technische Eros*. Freiburg: Herder, 1955.

Hütter, Reinhard. *Dust Bound for Heaven: Explorations in the Theology of Thomas Aquinas*. Grand Rapids, MI: William B. Eerdmans, 2012.

Ignatius of Antioch. "The Epistle of Ignatius to the Smyrnaeans." In *The Apostolic Fathers in English*, edited by Michael W. Holmes, 121–25. Grand Rapids, MI: Baker Academic, 2006.

Irenaeus. *Against Heresies*. In Roberts and Donaldson, eds., *Ante-Nicene Fathers*, vol. 1, *The Apostolic Fathers, Justin Martyr, Irenaeus*, 315–602.

Jackson, Julian. *France: The Dark Years, 1940–1944*. Oxford: Oxford University Press, 2001.

John Paul II. *The Theology of the Body: Human Love in the Divine Plan*. Boston, MA: Pauline Books, 1997.

Jüngel, Eberhard. "The Church as Sacrament?" In *Theological Essays*, translated and edited by J. B. Webster, 1:189–213. Edinburgh: T&T Clark, 1989.

———. *God as the Mystery of the World*. Translation by Darrell L. Guder. Edinburgh: T&T Clark, 1983.

Kant, Immanuel. *Critique of Pure Reason*. Translated and edited by Paul Guyer and Allen W. Wood. Cambridge: Cambridge University Press, 1998.

Kelly, Michael. "Catholics and Communism in Liberation France." In *Religion, Society, and Politics in France since 1789*, edited by Frank Tallett and Nicholas Atkin, 187–202. London: The Hambledon Press, 1991.

———. *The Cultural and Intellectual Rebuilding of France after the Second World War.* New York: Palgrave Macmillan, 2004.

———. "Humanism and National Unity: The Ideological Reconstruction of France." In *The Culture of Reconstruction: European Literature, Thought and Film, 1945–50*, edited by Nicholas Hewitt, 103–19. Hampshire: Macmillan, 1989.

Kerr, Fergus. "A Catholic Response to the Programme of Radical Orthodoxy." In *Radical Orthodoxy?—A Catholic Enquiry*, edited by Laurence Paul Hemming, 46–59. Aldershot: Ashgate, 2000.

———. "French Theology: Yves Congar and Henri de Lubac." In *The Modern Theologians*, 2nd ed., edited by David Ford, 105–17. Malden, MA: Blackwell, 1997.

———. *Twentieth-Century Catholic Theologians: From Neoscholasticism to Nuptial Mysticism.* Malden, MA: Blackwell, 2007.

Kilby, Karen. *Karl Rahner: Theology and Philosophy.* London: Routledge, 2004.

Kirwan, Jon. *An Avant-garde Theological Generation: The "Nouvelle Théologie" and the French Crisis of Modernity.* Oxford: Oxford University Press, 2018.

Komonchak, Joseph. "Theology and Culture at Mid-Century: The Example of Henri de Lubac." *Theological Studies* 51 (1990): 579–602.

Körner, Bernard. "Henri de Lubac and Fundamental Theology." *Communio* 23 (Winter 1996): 710–24.

Körner, Stephan. "The Impossibility of Transcendental Deductions." *The Monist* 51, no. 3 (1967): 317–31.

Laberthonnière, Lucien. *Le réalisme chrétien et l'idealisme grec.* Paris: Seuil, 1966.

Lackerstein, Debbie. *National Regeneration in Vichy France: Ideas and Policies, 1930–1944.* Farnham: Ashgate, 2011.

Laporta, Jorge. *La Destinée de la nature humaine selon Thomas d'Aquin.* Paris: J. Vrin, 1965.

Lefebvre, Henri. *Le matérialisme dialectique.* Paris: Presses universitaires de France, 1947.

Leo XIII. "*Aeterni Patris*: Encyclical Letter on the Restoration of Christian Philosophy." *Acta Sanctae Sedis* 12 (1879): 97–115.

Levering, Matthew. *An Introduction to Vatican II as an Ongoing Theological Event.* Washington, DC: Catholic University of America Press, 2017.

Levinas, Emmanuel. *Humanism of the Other.* Translation by Nidra Poller. Introduction by Richard A. Cohen. Chicago: University of Illinois Press, 2006.

———. "On Maurice Blanchot." In *Proper Names*, translated by Michael B. Smith, 127–70. London: The Athlone Press, 1996.

Lindbeck, George. *The Nature of Doctrine: Religion and Theology in a Postliberal Age.* London: SPCK, 1984.

Long, D. Stephen. *Speaking of God.* Grand Rapids, MI: William B. Eerdmans, 2009.

Long, Steven A. *Natura Pura: On the Recovery of Nature in the Doctrine of Grace.* New York: Fordham University Press, 2010.

Longton, Ryan A. "A Reconsideration of Maurice Blondel and the 'Natural' Desire." *Heythrop Journal* (2015): 919–30.

Löwith, Karl. *Meaning in History.* Chicago: Chicago University Press, 1949.

Malloy, Christopher J. "De Lubac on Natural Desire: Difficulties and Antitheses." *Nova et Vetera* (2011): 567–624.

Mansini, Guy. "The Abiding Theological Significance of Henri de Lubac's *Surnaturel*." *The Thomist* 73 (2009): 593–619.

Maréchal, Joseph. *A Maréchal Reader.* Edited by Joseph Donceel. New York: Herder and Herder, 1970.

Maritain, Jacques. *An Essay on Christian Philosophy.* New York: Philosophical Library, 1955.

———. *Integral Humanism: Temporal and Spiritual Problems of a New Christendom.* Translated by Joseph W. Evans. Notre Dame, IN: University of Notre Dame Press, 1973.

———. *The Range of Reason.* London: Geoffrey Bles, 1953.

Marx, Karl. "Contribution to the Critique of Hegel's *Philosophy of Right*." In *The Marx–Engels Reader*, edited by Robert C. Tucker, 16–25. New York: W. W. Norton, 1978.

———. *A Contribution to the Critique of Political Economy.* Chicago: Charles H. Kerr & Company, 1904.

———. "Foreword to Thesis: The Difference between the Natural Philosophy of Democritus and the Natural Philosophy of Epicurus." In *On Religion*, 13–15. New York: Schocken, 1964.

———. "Theses on Feuerbach." In *Writings of the Young Marx*, edited by Loyd D. Easton and Kurt H. Guddat, 400–402. New York: Doubleday, 1967.

Marx, Karl, and Frederick Engels. *The Communist Manifesto.* London: Verso, 1988.

Matteo, Anthony M. *Quest for the Absolute: The Philosophical Vision of Joseph Maréchal.* DeKalb: Northern Illinois University Press, 1992.

McCool, Gerald A. *Catholic Theology in the Nineteenth Century: The Quest for a Unitary Method.* New York: Seabury Press, 1977.

McGinn, Bernard. "The Abbot and the Doctors: Scholastic Reactions to the Radical Eschatology of Joachim of Fiore." In *Apocalypticism in the Western Tradition*, ix.30–47. Aldershot: Variorum, 1994.

———. "*Teste David cum Sibylla*: The Significance of the Sibylline Tradition in the Middle Ages." In *Apocalypticism in the Western Tradition*, iv.7–35. Aldershot: Variorum, 1994.

———. *Visions of the End: Apocalyptic Traditions in the Middle Ages.* New York: Columbia University Press, 1979.

McInerny, Ralph. *Praeambula fidei: Thomism and the God of the Philosophers.* Washington, DC: Catholic University of America Press, 2006.

McPartlan, Paul. "Eucharistic Ecclesiology." *One in Christ* 22, no. 4 (1986): 314–31.

———. *The Eucharist Makes the Church.* Fairfax, VA: Eastern Christian Publications, 2006.

Milbank, John. "The Programme of Radical Orthodoxy." In *Radical Orthodoxy?—A Catholic Enquiry*, edited by Laurence Paul Hemming, 33–45. Aldershot: Ashgate, 2000.

———. *The Suspended Middle: Henri de Lubac and the Debate concerning the Supernatural.* 1st ed. Grand Rapids, MI: William B. Eerdmans, 2005.

———. *The Suspended Middle: Henri de Lubac and the Renewed Split in Modern Catholic Theology.* 2nd ed. Grand Rapids, MI: William B. Eerdmans, 2014.

———. *Theology and Social Theory: Beyond Secular Reason.* Oxford: Blackwell, 2006.

Milbank, John, and Catherine Pickstock. *Truth in Aquinas.* London: Routledge, 2001.

Milbank, John, et al., eds. *Radical Orthodoxy: A New Theology.* London: Routledge, 1999.

Moltmann, Jürgen. *The Trinity and the Kingdom of God: The Doctrine of God.* San Francisco: Harper & Row, 1981.

Moulins-Beaufort, Eric. *Anthropologie et mystique selon Henri de Lubac: "L'esprit de l'homme," ou la présence de Dieu en l'homme.* Paris: Cerf, 2003.

Mounier, Emmanuel. "Refaire la Renaissance." In *Oeuvres, Tome 1, 1931–1939.* Paris: Editions du Seuil, 1961.

Mulcahy, Bernard. *Aquinas's Notion of Pure Nature and the Christian Integralism of Henri de Lubac: Not Everything Is Grace.* New York: Peter Lang, 2011.

Murphy, Francesca. *Art and Intellect in the Philosophy of Étienne Gilson.* Columbia: University of Missouri Press, 2004.

———. "De Lubac, Ratzinger and von Balthasar: A Communal Adventure in Ecclesiology." *Ecumenism Today: The Universal Church in the 21st Century*, edited by Francesca A. Murphy and Christopher Asprey, 45–80. Aldershot: Ashgate, 2008.

———. "The Influence of Maurice Blondel." In Hillebert, ed., *T&T Clark Companion to Henri de Lubac*, 57–91.

Nichols, Aidan. "Henri de Lubac: Panorama and Proposal." *New Blackfriars* 93, no. 1043 (2012): 3–33.

Nietzsche, Friedrich. *Ecce Homo.* Translated, introduction, and notes by Duncan Large. Oxford: Oxford University Press, 2007.

———. *Thus Spoke Zarathustra.* Edited by Adrian Del Caro and Robert B. Pippin. Translated by Adrian Del Caro. New York: Cambridge University Press, 2006.

———. *The Will to Power.* New York: Vintage, 1968.

Nicolas, Jean-Hervé. "Les Rapports entre la Nature et le surnaturel dans le Débats Contemporaines." *Revue Thomiste* 95, no. 3 (1995): 399–418.

Oakes, Edward T. "The Paradox of Nature and Grace: On John Milbank's *The Suspended Middle: Henri de Lubac and the Debate concerning the Supernatural.*" *Nova et Vetera* 4, no. 3 (2006): 667–96.

———. "The *Surnaturel* Controversy: A Survey and a Response." *Nova et Vetera* 9, no. 3 (2011): 625–56.

O'Collins, Gerald. *The Second Vatican Council: Message and Meaning.* Collegeville, MN: Liturgical Press, 2014.

O'Donovan, Oliver. *Resurrection and Moral Order: An Outline for Evangelical Ethics.* Leicester: Inter-Varsity Press, 1986.

O'Regan, Cyril. *Gnostic Apocalypse: Jacob Boehme's Haunted Narrative.* Albany: State University of New York Press, 2002.

———. *Gnostic Return in Modernity.* Albany: State University of New York Press, 2001.

———. *The Heterodox Hegel.* Albany: State University of New York Press, 1994.

———. *Theology and the Spaces of Apocalyptic.* Milwaukee, WI: Marquette University Press, 2009.

Origen. "On Prayer." In *Origen*, translated by Rowan A. Greer, 81–170. New York: Paulist Press, 1979.

O'Sullivan, Noel. *Christ and Creation: Christology as the Key to Interpreting the Theology of Creation in the Works of Henri de Lubac.* Oxford: Peter Lang, 2009.

Owens, Joseph. "Common Nature: A Point of Comparison between Thomistic and Scotist Metaphysics." *Medieval Studies* 19 (1957): 1–14.

———. "Thomistic Common Nature and Platonic Idea." *Medieval Studies* 21 (1959): 211–23.

Oxford University Press. *The 1979 Book of Common Prayer.* Oxford: Oxford University Press, 2005.

Paxton, Robert O. *Vichy France: Old Guard and New Order, 1940–1944.* London: Barrie & Jenkins, 1972.

Pecknold, C. C., and Jacob Wood. "Augustine and Henri de Lubac." In *T&T Clark Companion to Augustine and Modern Theology*, edited by C. C. Pecknold and Tarmo Toom, 196–222. London: Bloomsbury, 2013.

Pius X. "The Oath against the Errors of Modernism." In *The Sources of Catholic Dogma*, edited by Heinrich Denzinger, 549–51. St. Louis, MO: Herder Book Co., 1957.

Pius XII. "*Humani Generis*: Encyclical Letter concerning Some False Opinions Threatening to Undermine the Foundations of Catholic Dogma." *Acta Apostolicae Sedis* 42 (August 12, 1950): 561–78.

Quash, Ben. *Theology and the Drama of History.* Cambridge: Cambridge University Press, 2005.

Rahner, Karl. "The Church and the Sacraments." In *Inquiries*, 191–299. New York: Herder and Herder, 1964.

———. "Concerning the Relationship between Nature and Grace." In *Theological Investigations*, 1:297–317. London: Darton, Longman and Todd, 1961.

———. *Foundations of Christian Faith: An Introduction to the Idea of Christianity.* London: Darton, Longman and Todd, 1978.

———. "Nature and Grace." In *Theological Investigations*, 4:165–88. Baltimore: Helicon Press, 1966.

———. "Questions of Controversial Theology on Justification." In *Theological Investigations*, 4:189–218. Baltimore: Helicon Press, 1966.

Ratzinger, Joseph. *Principles of Catholic Theology: Building Stones for a Fundamental Theology.* San Francisco: Ignatius, 1989.

Ravier, André, ed. *La mystique et les mystiques.* Paris: Desclée de Brouwer, 1965.

Reeves, Marjorie. Review of *La Postérité spirituelle de Joachim de Flore, T 1: De Joachim à Schelling. Journal of Theological Studies* 32, no. 1 (1981): 191–94.

Reeves, Marjorie, and Beatrice Hirsch-Reich. *The "Figurae" of Joachim of Fiore.* Oxford: Clarendon, 1972.

Riches, Aaron. "Church, Eucharist, and Predestination in Barth and de Lubac: Convergence and Divergence in *Communio*." *Communio* 35 (2008): 565–98.

_____. "Henri de Lubac and the Second Vatican Council." In Hillebert, ed., *T&T Clark Companion to Henri de Lubac*, 121–56.

Rousselot, Pierre. *The Eyes of Faith.* Translated by Joseph Donceel. Introduction by John M. McDermott. New York: Fordham University Press, 1990.

Rowland, Tracey. *Catholic Theology.* London: T&T Clark, 2017.

Sadler, Gregory B., ed., *Reason Fulfilled by Revelation: The 1930s Christian Philosophy Debates in France.* Washington, DC: Catholic University of America Press, 2010.

Sánchez, Santiago Sanz, and John Watson. "The Revival of the Notion of Pure Nature in Recent Debates in English Speaking Theology." *Annales Theologici* 31 (2017): 171–250

Sartre, Jean-Paul. *Existentialism and Humanism.* Translation and introduction by Philip Mairet. London: Methuen & Co., 1968.

Schillebeeckx, Edward. *Christ the Sacrament of the Encounter with God.* New York: Sheed and Ward, 1963.

———. "The Church and Mankind." In *The Language of Faith: Essays on Jesus, Theology, and the Church*, 1–24. New York: Orbis Books, 1995.

———. "Church and World." In *World and Church*, 73–87. London: T&T Clark, 2014.

———. "L'Église et le monde." In *Approches théologiques*, vol. 3, *Le monde et l'église*, 149–67. Brussels: Editions du Cep, 1967.

Schlesinger, Eugene R. "The Threefold Body in Eschatological Perspective: With and beyond Henri de Lubac on the Church." *Ecclesiology* 10, no. 2 (2014): 186–204.

Semmelroth, Otto. *Church and Sacrament.* Notre Dame, IN: Fides Publishers, 1965.

Simmonds, Gemma. "The Mystical Body." In Hillebert, ed., *T&T Clark Companion to Henri de Lubac,* 159–79.

Soltau, Roger. *French Political Thought in the Nineteenth Century.* London: Ernest Benn, 1931.

Stewart, David. "Existential Humanism." In *Studies in the Philosophy of Paul Ricoeur,* edited by Charles E. Reagan, 21–32. Athens: Ohio University Press, 1979.

Swafford, Andrew Dean. *Nature and Grace: A New Approach to Thomistic Ressourcement.* Eugene, OR: Pickwick, 2014.

Tanner, Norman P. *Decrees of the Ecumenical Councils.* Vol. 2, *Trent to Vatican II.* London: Sheed and Sheed, 1990.

Taylor, Charles. *A Secular Age.* Cambridge, MA: Harvard University Press, 2007.

Torrell, Jean-Pierre. *Christ and Spirituality in St. Thomas Aquinas.* Translated by Bernhard Blankenhorn. Washington, DC: Catholic University of America Press, 2011.

———. "Chronique de theologie fondamentale." *Revue Thomiste* 66 (1966): 93–107.

———. *Saint Thomas Aquinas.* Vol. 2, *Spiritual Master.* Washington, DC: Catholic University of America Press, 2003.

Voderholzer, Rudolf. *Meet Henri de Lubac: His Life and Work.* Translated by Michael J. Miller. San Francisco: Ignatius, 2008.

Voegelin, Eric. *The New Science of Politics: An Introduction.* Chicago: University of Chicago Press, 1987.

Volf, Miroslav. "'The Trinity Is Our Social Program': The Doctrine of the Trinity and the Shape of Social Engagement." *Modern Theology* 14 (1998): 403–23.

Wagner, Jean-Pierre. *La Théologie fondamentale selon Henri de Lubac.* Paris: Cerf, 1997.

Walsh, Christopher J. "De Lubac's Critique of the Postconciliar Church." *Communio* (Fall 1992): 404–32.

Wang, Lisa. "Sacramentum Unitatis Ecclesiasticae: The Eucharistic Ecclesiology of Henri de Lubac." *Anglican Theological Review* 85, no. 1 (2003): 143–58.

Webster, John. "The Human Person." In *The Cambridge Companion to Postmodern Theology,* edited by Kevin J. Vanhoozer, 219–34. Cambridge: Cambridge University Press, 2003.

———. "'Love Is Also a Lover of Life': *Creatio ex Nihilo* and Creaturely Goodness." *Modern Theology* 29, no. 2 (2013): 156–71.

———. "On Evangelical Ecclesiology." In *Confessing God: Essays in Christian Dogmatics II,* 153–94. London: T&T Clark, 2005.

White, Thomas Joseph. "Good Extrinsicism: Matthias Scheeben and the Ideal Paradigm of Nature-Grace Orthodoxy." *Nova et Vetera* (English ed.), 11, no. 2

(2013): 537–63.

———. "Imperfect Happiness and the Final End of Man: Thomas Aquinas and the Paradigm of Nature-Grace Orthodoxy." *The Thomist* 78 (2014): 247–89.

Williams, Rowan. "Incarnation and the Renewal of Community." In *On Christian Theology*, 225–38. Oxford: Blackwell, 2000.

———. "*Sapientia* and the Trinity: Reflections on the *De Trinitate*." In *Collectanea Augustinia: Mélanges T. J. van Bavel*, edited by B. Bruning, M. Lamberigitis, and J. van Houtem, 317–32. Leuven: Leuven University Press, 1990.

Wood, Susan K. *Spiritual Exegesis and the Church in the Theology of Henri de Lubac.* Grand Rapids, MI: William B. Eerdmans, 1998.

Wright, John. *Postliberal Theology and the Church Catholic.* Grand Rapids, MI: Baker Academic, 2012.

Zizioulas, John. *Being as Communion: Studies in Personhood and the Church.* Crestwood, NY: St. Vladimir's Seminary Press, 1985.

INDEX

JORDAN HILLEBERT
is director of formation at St. Padarn's Institute
and an honorary lecturer in theology at Cardiff University.
He is the editor of *T&T Clark Companion to Henri de Lubac.*

Lightning Source UK Ltd.
Milton Keynes UK
UKHW022147030221
378191UK00003B/187

9 780268 108571